As It Is in Heaven

VERITAS
Series Introduction

"... the truth will set you free" (John 8:32)

In much contemporary discourse, Pilate's question has been taken to mark the absolute boundary of human thought. Beyond this boundary, it is often suggested, is an intellectual hinterland into which we must not venture. This terrain is an agnosticism of thought: because truth cannot be possessed, it must not be spoken. Thus, it is argued that the defenders of "truth" in our day are often traffickers in ideology, merchants of counterfeits, or anti-liberal. They are, because it is somewhat taken for granted that Nietzsche's word is final: truth is the domain of tyranny.

Is this indeed the case, or might another vision of truth offer itself? The ancient Greeks named the love of wisdom as *philia*, or friendship. The one who would become wise, they argued, would be a "friend of truth." For both philosophy and theology might be conceived as schools in the friendship of truth, as a kind of relation. For like friendship, truth is as much discovered as it is made. If truth is then so elusive, if its domain is *terra incognita*, perhaps this is because it arrives to us—unannounced—as gift, as a person, and not some thing.

The aim of the Veritas book series is to publish incisive and original current scholarly work that inhabits "the between" and "the beyond" of theology and philosophy. These volumes will all share a common aspiration to transcend the institutional divorce in which these two disciplines often find themselves, and to engage questions of pressing concern to both philosophers and theologians in such a way as to reinvigorate both disciplines with a kind of interdisciplinary desire, often so absent in contemporary academe. In a word, these volumes represent collective efforts in the befriending of truth, doing so beyond the simulacra of pretend tolerance, the violent, yet insipid reasoning of liberalism that asks with Pilate, "What is truth?"—expecting a consensus of non-commitment; one that encourages the commodification of the mind, now sedated by the civil service of career, ministered by the frightened patrons of position.

The series will therefore consist of two "wings": (1) original monographs; and (2) essay collections on a range of topics in theology and philosophy. The latter will principally be the products of the annual conferences of the Centre of Theology and Philosophy (www.theologyphilosophycentre .co.uk).

Conor Cunningham and Eric Austin Lee, *Series editors*

Not available from Cascade

Deane-Peter Baker	*Tayloring Reformed Epistemology: The Challenge to Christian Belief.*
P. Candler & C. Cunningham (eds.)	*Belief and Metaphysics.*
Marcus Pound	*Theology, Psychoanalysis, and Trauma.*
Espen Dahl	*Phenomenology and the Holy.*
C. Cunningham et al. (eds.)	*Grandeur of Reason: Religion, Tradition, and Universalism.*
A. Pabst & A. Paddison (eds.)	*The Pope and Jesus of Nazareth: Christ, Scripture, and the Church.*
J. P. Moreland	*Recalcitrant Imago Dei: Human Persons and the Failure of Naturalism.*

Available from Cascade Books

[Nathan Kerr	*Christ, History, and Apocalyptic: The Politics of Christian Mission.*]1
Anthony D. Baker	*Diagonal Advance: Perfection in Christian Theology.*
D. C. Schindler	*The Perfection of Freedom: Schiller, Schelling, and Hegel between the Ancients and the Moderns.*
Rustin Brian	*Covering Up Luther: How Barth's Christology Challenged the* Deus Absconditus *that Haunts Modernity.*
Timothy Stanley	*Protestant Metaphysics After Karl Barth and Martin Heidegger.*
Christopher Ben Simpson	*The Truth Is the Way: Kierkegaard's* Theologia Viatorum.
Richard H. Bell	*Wagner's Parsifal: An Appreciation in the Light of His Theological Journey.*
Antonio Lopez	*Gift and the Unity of Being.*
Toyohiko Kagawa	*Cosmic Purpose.* Translated and introduced by Thomas John Hastings.
Nigel Zimmerman	*Facing the Other: John Paul II, Levinas, and the Body.*
Conor Sweeney	*Sacramental Presence after Heidegger: Onto-theology, Sacraments, and the Mother's Smile.*
John Behr et al. (eds.)	*The Role of Death in Life: A Multidisciplinary Examination of the Relation between Life and Death.*

1... Note: Nathan Kerr, *Christ, History, and Apocalyptic*, although volume 3 of the original SCM Veritas series, is available from Cascade as part of the Theopolitical Visions series.

As It Is in Heaven

Some Christian Questions
on the Nature of Paradise

CAITLIN SMITH GILSON

CASCADE *Books* · Eugene, Oregon

AS IT IS IN HEAVEN
Some Christian Questions on the Nature of Paradise

Veritas Series

Cascade Books
An Imprint of Wipf and Stock Publishers
199 W. 8th Ave., Suite 3
Eugene, OR 97401

www.wipfandstock.com

PAPERBACK ISBN: 978-1-7252-9562-9
HARDCOVER ISBN: 978-1-7252-9561-2
EBOOK ISBN: 978-1-7252-9563-6

Cataloguing-in-Publication data:

Names: Smith Gilson, Caitlin [author].

Title: As it is in heaven : some Christian questions on the nature of paradise / Caitlin Smith Gilson.

Description: Eugene, OR: Cascade Books, 2022 | Series: Veritas Series | Includes bibliographical references and index.

Identifiers: ISBN 978-1-7252-9562-9 (paperback) | ISBN 978-1-7252-9561-2 (hardcover) | ISBN 978-1-7252-9563-6 (ebook)

Subjects: LCSH: Heaven—Christianity | Eschatology | Eschatology—Biblical teaching | Hope—Religious aspects—Christianity | Death—Religious aspects—Christianity

Classification: BT846.3 S55 2022 (print) | BT846.3 (ebook)

For my dear friend Pam, and for her wisdom along the soft passage of grief, too gentle for sleep, too brutal to endure alone, ever the opposite of what it needs to be. For the heart of Our Lady that lives within her, and for our lovely Josh and Daisi who will remain with us into our graves.

For my loves, Fred, Mary, and Lily, you are the eternal, you will always by my eternal.

Special thanks to my dear friend, Ms. Carol Scott, for the use of her artwork, St. Joseph's Day Altar, as cover for the book.

For my Mom and Dad—1 Corinthians 13:4–8.

Table of Contents

Preface

Heaven Misplaced

THE LOSS OF A real and heartfelt belief in God—and by "real" I mean an experience that is both steady and moving, ethereal though down-to-earth, sentimental but never trite—comes from an earlier more foundational *loss*, namely that of an ardent and directed desire for heaven, and more specifically, that paradisal longing for the resurrected life. Have we lost what it means to *desire* the afterlife? The nature of heaven itself may play a part: mystery left unnurtured even degrades into something "out-there" and unknown, degraded further into a vague wish for immortality, and finally into the blank and empty words of consolation. Or even worse, the almost comic-book reduction of heaven to an earthly social(ist) paradise, the immanentization of the Christian eschaton.[1] The "better place," which means well, often means nothing at all, or worse than that becomes the very foil when approaching the mystery of grief, and the possibility of a meaningful and spiritually fruitful conversion through it. The implicit sense of heaven within those words may itself actually be further obscured; the afterlife is only thought of from within the fear and folly of death, and serves only to distance us from the anxiety and homelessness that occurs in the living after the loved one fades from view. Somehow, we simultaneously remember and neglect the words of St. Paul: "For this world is not our permanent home; we are looking forward to a home yet to come."[2] And this neglect is a different type of forgetting than the briefly misplaced book, only to be rediscovered in the armchair, just

1. Cf. Voegelin, "The New Science of Politics," *Collected Works*, Vol. 5, 185.
2. Heb 13–14.

as intact as it was before. The heaven which is our home is not as easily rediscovered, nor are we as easily recovered intact,[3] and death becomes yet another social inconvenience.[4]

At the same time, we must be mindful of the important balance between the unveiled and veiled reflections of the divine realm. Our concern is primarily that the latter should not be confused with thoughtless vagary, because in doing so the very yearnings for heaven come to be repeatedly cut down in the course of a life, perilously closer to their roots, so that one day perhaps nothing, no transcendent longing, will grow again. And such a one would be so painfully far from God, and from the true childlike and profound wisdom that is granted access into the kingdom of heaven. Thus, this work seeks to reside in the most interior form of evangelization, into the region that unites lovers bonded in the clarity of truth and the humility of mercy, which Saint John Henry Newman called the "*cor ad cor loquitur*," heart speaks *unto* heart.[5] Here we are mindful that God gives us moral agency, with all the risks and rewards involved. Through this agency, and in the union of God's grace, is the pearl of great price discovered.[6] We are called *by* God *unto* God in every moment of our lives, but we are free not only to ignore that call of and to Beauty but, once we have ignored it, to put the earthly effects of that divine call out of their proper place. We can and do, therefore, obscure the road back to our permanent home. Even the well-meaning but often unexamined language of the "better place," is such an example of how those effects have been exiled from their proper place. This creates a visibly inescapable netting across all features of human life, entrapping persons for the length it takes them no longer even to recognize what is

---

3. Gilson, *Reason and Revelation*, 70–71: "Now, in everyday life, the problem of putting a thing in its proper place is a comparatively simple one. It seldom amounts to more than putting it away always in the same place and remembering where it is." Not so in "philosophy, where there is but one conceivable proper place for any given thing. Unless you find it, that thing is lost, not in the usual sense that it is not to be found where you expected it to be, but in the much more radical sense that it is no longer to be found anywhere. Out of its proper place, the thing simply cannot exist at all. For indeed, the place of each thing is determined there by its own essence, and unless you know first what the thing is you shall never be able to define its relations to what it is not."

4. Heidegger, *Being and Time*, §46–52.

5. Newman, *The Idea of a University*, 410.

6. Matt 13:45–46.

amiss, and in doing so only further lengthens an already perilous journey to God. If with Newman:

> Christ is calling us. . . . He called us first in Baptism; but afterwards also; whether we obey his voice or not, He graciously calls us still. If we fall from baptismal grace, He calls us to repent; if we are striving to fulfill our calling, He calls us from grace to grace, and from holiness to holiness, while life is given us.[7]

Then, given that this relentlessly loving call has revealed us and our actions to be its effects, we are, indeed, tasked with the responsibility of heeding the call that is our very source and lifeblood. This heeding evokes a twofold reality: we should follow it not only because our actions are the effects of Christ's beckoning to us, but also because the gift of moral agency enables us creatively to participate in this call by working to rediscover the message and mission of salvation. Thus, we have an obligation of moral and spiritual dimensions to emancipate the meaning of heaven from a homeless place, out of place, and out of heart and mind. And to work towards this goal, while being the very effects of Christ's call, means that to rediscover a genuine inkling of the power and primacy of heaven in its proper place is to know ourselves most truly, and perhaps even for the first time. Who we are as persons is tied up with what constitutes our permanent home: if we lose a sense of that home and proceed to impart a dead-end aversion, we are no longer travelers along the way who know ourselves as such, but stranded without a compass or a map either to heaven or to ourselves.

Neither should our expressions of heaven inhabit a rationalism that acts as if all the answers are set before us in a road map with navigation key, ultimately misplacing heaven to be on our level of comprehension through a highway of rationalizations, so often aligned with the promise of immanent creature comforts. Such a reductionism is often the inevitable result of the clumsily conceived spiritual banquet that dispels the essential mystery and beyond-human conception that is at the very core of the gift of paradise. We are thus mindful that any illumination of, and yearning for, heaven must invoke a certain restraint, and seek that edifying humility to encounter the good mystery that shapes our very being.[8]

7. Newman, *Parochial and Plain Sermons,* Vol. VIII, 23.

8. Cf. Pope John Paul II, "General Audience," (07/21/99) §4: "In the context of Revelation, we know that the 'Heaven' or 'happiness' in which we will find ourselves is neither an abstraction nor a physical place in the clouds but a living, personal relationship with the Holy Trinity. It is our meeting with the Father that takes place in the risen

Death and Grief: Unexpiated Tears

The central defining figure, sometimes a figure of release and at other times a foil, is death. And, as such, any meditation on paradise that seeks to renegotiate the expression "a better place," revealing its authentic and inauthentic meaning structures, must face this most elusive yet ever-present specter. The realm of grief, loss, descent, inversion and conversion, mercy and judgment, judgment *as* mercy, which enshrines death as if to be a halo outlining a collision of worlds, must make its presence known within this work and we must hold fast, seeking not to look away, but in and through it and towards, if possible, our true home. This collision of worlds is most supremely manifested in the figure of Christ, who will be our guide in navigating this intermixing of the seemingly impossible, the deadening and the reviving, the painful and the joyous, of loss and gain. For, indeed, it is Christ himself whose descent not only realizes the alienating possibility of hell[9]—the type of death that *has* a sting[10]—but whose very incarnation, whose flesh,[11] even more foundationally realizes and completes the fulfillment of heaven itself, as unique to the intensified unity of human and divine natures. And through Christ we discover something strange about the nature of grief, most particularly as a response to the death of the other, the loved one. This tragic and

---

Christ through the communion of the Holy Spirit. It is always necessary to maintain a certain restraint in describing these 'ultimate realities' since their depiction is always unsatisfactory."

9. Cf. Blondel, *Diary before God* in Balthasar, *Dare We Hope*, 95: "The Passion is not only redemption; it is Christ's very experience of Hell: through this experience, Hell becomes real and man is damned. Christ is the one who makes all things real."

10. Cf. 1 Cor 15:55–56.

11. Cf. Newsome Martin, "The Christian Future of Metaphysics" (unpublished lecture): "The 'carnal' or the 'flesh' as I am deploying the term is not exactly the same as the facticity of embodiment but includes within it also the 'advent' posture of structural openness to futurity and ontological promise. This sort of Christian metaphysics would thereby not exclude but would rather embrace and even centralize the body, history, time, becoming, sensuality, eroticism, aesthetics, language, contingency, precarity, development, growth, organicity as it refuses an essentialist metaphysics given to stasis and concept over movement and mystery. What ultimately will make this metaphysic Christian is its trinitarian and Christological foundation: first that creaturely difference is grounded in the plenitude and freedom of intra-divine relations, and second, that the *skandalon* of the Incarnation of Christ renders Christianity distinctive. Only Christianity, as Balthasar understands it, 'has found in the flesh, in the mortal, eucharistic, mystical, resurrecting flesh, the unsurpassable end of the ways of God.'"

transcendent collision of worlds seen in the figure of Christ in the Gospels, is grafted into each of us, and we each enact its mystery from cradle to grave. We must turn our attention to the coalface, we must look into its dust, impenetrable night, and experience what grief does to the living when severed by death from union with the loved one.

For years prior to writing this work, I had the uneasy sense that the way we looked at heaven short-circuited our faith, or rather that our personal exercise of the faith leads us to this short-sighted view. But such thoughts of heaven, of putting into words a preliminary sketch of paradise that is meaningful (in that it simultaneously does justice to it and to its inability to do so) has always caused a subterranean apprehension that prevented in advance any real and prolonged contemplation. As such, my own sense still participated in this reduction, in the faith short-circuited by a notion of paradise that oscillated among and between a comic-book understanding, a vacant phrasebook expressionism, and a half-terrified desire for something truer and far more merciful and just than I would ever dare to envision. But death obliterates conceptual distinctions and demands that, rather than lead the discourse, it be followed with its own set of universal yet somehow unpredictable rules of grief and engagement. These rules, while generationally experienced, are never predicated on one firmly grasped earthly or finite moment, even and especially if the event that prompts grief and suffering is, as it always is, earthly and finite. The rules that death lays out on the table evoke an unrepeatable experience that communicates through stasis and movement; and wherever you are, death is at the opposite end of the pendulum. Should one in grief enter into the stillness preceding and inhabiting memory, death reminds us of movement—the sun rises, the tides change, life goes on, and if one embarks again on these motions of life, death reaffirms such a stasis that returns us to the coalface and to the unexpiated need for what is lost to be found and to be loved as it was, once again. Nothing is as it seems, and nothing is recovered. In the grief that separates the living from the dead, the living are compelled to live in a realm where worlds—which by logic and good reason—should never collide and inhabit the same person; but they do just that, cultivating a new avenue of experience. And it is never quite so simple to say that this *is*, this finally *is*, the road home. But perhaps in every case we must pose this possibility (particularly since we live in a world that has made suffering the enemy of life to be expiated by abortion or euthanasia or physician-assisted suicide) that grief and suffering are seen to have no contributive value in the formation of the person and of his experiences.

Grief Endured: A Personal Memoir in Brief

Talk to me about the truth of religion and I'll listen gladly. Talk to me about the duty of religion and I'll listen submissively. But don't come talking to me about the consolations of religion or I shall suspect that you don't understand. Unless, of course, you can literally believe all that stuff about family reunions "on the further shore," pictured in entirely earthly terms. But that is all unscriptural, all out of bad hymns and lithographs. There's not a word of it in the Bible. And it rings false. We know it couldn't be like that. Reality never repeats. The exact same thing is never taken away and given back. How well the Spiritualists bait their hook! "Things on this side are not so different after all." There are cigars in Heaven. For that is what we should all like. The happy past restored. . . . If a mother is mourning not for what she has lost but for what her dead child has lost, it is a comfort to believe that the child has not lost the end for which it was created. And it is a comfort to believe that she herself, in losing her chief or only natural happiness, has not lost a greater thing, that she may still hope to "glorify God and enjoy Him forever." A comfort to the God-aimed, eternal spirit within her. But not to her motherhood. The specifically maternal happiness must be written off. Never, in any place or time, will she have her son on her knees, or bathe him, or tell him a story, or plan for his future, or see her grandchild.[12]

The conceptual distance once afforded to me, since I was, and perhaps still am, a novice in grief, has relinquished its relief. And I have found myself inside two experiences of grief in and towards death, which must—but hesitatingly so—be laid out in order to give a more truthful and authentic direction to this work. The first experience involves the recent death of my beloved niece, our family's beautiful little girl. At the end of April 2020 and within the irony of it being springtime, she was struck and killed by a motorist. It was four days after her fifteenth birthday and the language of chance, probabilities, possibilities, *ifs* and *what ifs* populate every recollection as if they aren't dead-ends, but then serve only to remind us that they indeed are such cul-de-sacs of unexpiated pain

12. Cf. Lewis, *A Grief Observed*, 25–27.

and irresolution. In this situation, everything was timing: inopportune timing, bad timing, terrible, terrifying lamentable time; if only a minute later, a day earlier, and so on. Our dear beautiful girl wrapped up in the fatalism of chance. And so, timing has a way of altering memories, of inhabiting past happiness with such an aching chasm of the unfinished, unresolved, and unsaid: the horseback riding, beach bonfires, eccentric number of sneakers, snuggled scary movies under cover become something other altogether. A universal story so strangely intimate and unrepeatable, even and especially as it is repeated in its own way on a daily basis by strangers forever shared and unshared in grief. Months topple on together, pile and eviscerate the many dark nights of the soul until they expel what remains of the living, and the living must go on. The irony is not lost on the living (and perhaps not lost on the dead). We have, like so many others before us, carried the many happy memories now laced with gall, and lanced of their once pure sweetness. The last time I saw her, my daughters and my niece cycled around our little town in the bliss as close to *arcadia*, and went to an antique shop and picked up a curiously painted Madonna statue with red hair. She gave it to me and said, "she has hair like yours!" All our joys have within them, for St. Thomas Aquinas, a "natural pendent of sadness."[13]

We cannot escape evil in this world, there are no utopias to be made, and when they are attempted, it turns too brutal and ugly to encapsulate the devastation of transcendent meaning. In the midst of such spiritual detritus, we barely see how much is lost. Today's "cancel culture" mentality of radical liberalism is itself the result of a pernicious relativism that tries to reduce evil to perception, and attempts to manage human sins as if they can be wiped off the face of the earth by mere human calculation and indoctrination. Such aggressive utopia-making isn't original—it spans all political ideologies—and is merely a more conscious, granted more vicious, immanentizing of the anemic eternal festival that had earlier initiated the protracted relinquishing of genuine transcendent meaning, which alone engages heaven, as central to understanding human nature. Grief, the result of the gaping wound of original sin, cannot be bettered in like manner as other worldly problems.[14] Thus, this unser-

---

13. SCG III, 48, 8.

14. Cf. Maritain, *St, Thomas and the Problem of Evil*, 3: "That which has no being in itself, nor essence nor form, nor order, nor determination, and cannot have—in other words, that evil exists, is real and efficacious—it is in this that appears to us evil's metaphysical monstrosity. The whole spectacle of things is that of a procession of

viceability to manage or "fix" grief in relation to death must enter into our conversations as we encounter a glimpse of paradise; it cannot nor should be quickly passed over as just a stage of weak belief.

The first of two experiences, perhaps to be experienced till I am relieved of it through my own death, is the death of the child, and the subsequent crisis of love. What is occurring in us when we have made ourselves a gift to the other who now has died?[15] This primary Christian vocation of making ourselves a self-gift to the other must confront death, and what becomes of this vocation if that unmanageable confrontation cannot be conceptualized? All the power of grief is impotent. All its majestic and cruel urgency crumbles when confronted with even the most delicate remembrance of the lost child; all power falls instead at the feet of the absent child, and we are unable to wash them with our weeping.

The second experience, a companion to the first, involves the sharing of grief with another who has experienced the yawning chasm that permits stares, tears, and the gnashing of teeth, and even permits moments of peace and a fecundity of transcendent love, but still, it does not permit a clarified bridge to the "other side." Due to the thoughtfulness

---

things good, of a procession of goods, wounded by non-being and producing by their activity an indefinitely increasing accumulation of being and of good, in which that same activity also carries the indefinitely growing wound, as long as the world exists, of non-being and of evil."

15. Cf. Levinas, *Is It Righteous to Be?* 143: "I will say this quite plainly, what truly a human is—and don't be afraid of this word—love. And I mean it even with everything that burdens love or, I could say it better, responsibility is actually love. . . . It is preeminently the access to the singular. I always say: with knowledge in a logical operation, from genus to species to individual, one cannot get to singularity! Love, or responsibility, is instead that which gives meaning to singularity." For Levinas, otherness becomes essential to how we grow and change towards the beautiful as life-giving, or its opposition as deadening. At root in this becoming ourselves as simultaneously always bonded to the other is the realization that any true growth comes from the affection and love for other people, and from them, as what can truly shape those experiences as redemptive. We are wholly responsible for others, for we are made up of others, as they are for us, for they are made of us. Levinas called this a "form of economic life," and here we are reminded of *oikonomia*, that we see in such understandings of the economic Trinity. This is not seeing the Trinity only immanently or in itself, but in its greater operations such as the role of God, redemption, suffering, the Holy Family, Sacraments. Levinas is utilizing that older Greek term to evoke the unified nature of each of ourselves not as "immanent" but as economic, utterly entrenched in the other and the only way to make sense of this entrenchment is not alienation but love. Cf. Pope John Paul II, "The Human Person Becomes a Gift in the Freedom of Love." http://www.vatican.va/content/john-paul-ii/en/audiences/1980/documents/hf_jp-ii_aud_19800116.html

and foresight of a good parish priest, I was put in touch with a mother who lost her child in a car accident, which took the lives of his friends as well. Our correspondence has had the anonymity of letters only, but this anonymity conspires to unite us in ways surprising and gentle, where grace itself is understood to be at the forefront of all truly kind and generous action.[16] These reflections are themselves tears presented in another form, perhaps how the tears of Our Lady find their way to earth and nourish us with her dolor. There is a wisdom carved from holy weakness which I imagine flings open the gates of heaven. A whole lifetime passes through me when I see the photos of her child and read her words; as if my legs and arms become weakened with age, not the passing age, not even the historical age, but of an immemoriality that seeps into these ages to unite them in and to the crucifixion. My limbs are indeed weakened to the point of no return, and then rebuilt to walk anew. And I imagine now a heaven where our families will share such joy, because we have shared that untranslatable region of suffering that breaks hearts so purely, and so finely, that there is no way to pick up the pieces, only to move with that change that is always unchanging, and that unchanging core that enshrouds all change.

I have realized through this mother's letters that there is a *release* that happens in the heart stricken with grief, patterned after the stigmata: the lance to Christ's side makes its way up to our heart muscles rendering them unable to pump as they used to before the curtain fell. This release as lancing keeps recurring because there is no other alternative but to breathe again, to be distracted with *this* or *that*. And yet in the shade of such repeated releases, one responds with anger and resentment for providing such interludes of peace! And then a resulting sadness and a different form of anger or active regret materializes in such weighted hearts for squandering that peace, or for darkening the appreciation of it, for it is

---

16. A passage sent to me by this mother, perfectly reflects this timing. Lewis, *The Four Loves*, 113–14: "In friendship . . . we think we have chosen our peers. In reality a few years' difference in the dates of our births, a few more miles between certain houses, the choice of one university instead of another, . . . the accident of a topic being raised or not raised at a first meeting—any of these chances might have kept us apart. But, for a Christian, there are, strictly speaking no chances. A secret master of ceremonies has been at work. Christ, who said to the disciples, 'Ye have not chosen me, but I have chosen you,' can truly say to every group of Christian friends, 'Ye have not chosen one another but I have chosen you for one another.' The friendship is not a reward for our discriminating and good taste in finding one another out. It is the instrument by which God reveals to each of us the beauties of others."

a gift of sorts. Such hearts lanced as they are by the loss of the other, who was the recipient of our self-gift of love, are broken and stretched on the rack by many and various things. But the most interior rupture is that we are forced to release: their deaths and our living mean these releases are the inevitable pattern for the rest of our lives.

The wound of the loss of the child is a perpetually re-inflicting wound. To believe it will get better is—with careful clarification—an unfair burden to put on oneself. Much of this involves clarifying the word "better." And in the strict sense of things, it cannot get better as if returned to what life was before the levy broke. The heart is, again, so finely grounded into a powder and the dust has been scattered into every memory, into every nook where hope still resides. It is not right that we should outlive the holy innocents. The climate is more violent, and the shifting seasons jagged and unfriendly. We open our eyes to an ugly world, one utterly off kilter, and one that reminds us of all the beauty that went before.

We are faced with a startling reality: in the death of the loved one we *have* lost heaven. More specifically, we have lost a foretaste of the heaven with which Christ invested the earth when he was born of the Virgin Mary. Heaven has indeed visited the earth, and the unrepeatable dignity of *each* person is a participation in that heaven that has visited the earth, and her death is, for us, the empty tabernacle on Good Friday.

> The Incarnation is the mystery of a God who travelled the entire road toward us, and who was not only one of us during His mortal life but has remained with us, and that is not all: He dwells within us. This being so, how could we aspire to find Him elsewhere if we possess Him here on Earth? I recall the Canticle of my First Communion: "Heaven has visited the Earth." ... Yes, and it has done more than visit the Earth, it has merged in it without annihilating itself, so that to die will be not only for us to leave the Earth but also to leave the Heaven we have possessed in the flesh even in the humiliation of sin and its tears.[17]

Part of grief's virulent stubbornness is because our faith is too weak to envision heaven, and thus too weak to sustain genuine hope in the afterlife. We think, believe, feel, viscerally experience, that we have lost it all in the death of the other—and part of this kind of grief does come from an infirmed understanding of the "better place." But we also grieve

17. Mauriac, *The Inner Presence*, 57.

with such awful humbling violence because we *have* been torn from the union that gives us a foretaste of heaven. We are the body of the church and Christ is its head, and through the head the body has possessed in the flesh heaven. And yet: "As it is written, eye hath not seen, nor ear heard, neither have entered into the heart of man, the things which God hath prepared for them that love him. But God hath revealed them unto us by his Spirit; for the Spirit searcheth all things, yea, the deep things of God."[18]

The Rosary of Tears: Two Worlds Living as One

> Certainly there was an Eden on this very unhappy Earth. We all long for it, and we are constantly glimpsing it: our whole nature at its best and least corrupted, its gentlest and most humane, is still soaked with the sense of "exile." . . . As far as we can go back the nobler part of the human mind is filled with the thoughts of *sibb*, peace and goodwill, and with the thought of its loss. We shall never recover it, for that is not the way of repentance, which works spirally and not in a closed circle; we may recover something like it, but on a higher plane.[19]

In the grief that places us within the incommunicability of death, the only way the mind functions is to be memorial. Catholic teaching is a paradox undergirded by contradictory levels of nature: death is both natural, since we all die, and yet also and more primally an unnatural state due to original sin. And we can see that profound unnaturalness in all of human reaction. Should we learn that an old mutual long-out-of-touch friend who was long believed to have few prospects and little motivation is a highly successful lawyer or an astronaut, we are surprised, interested to learn more, shocked even, but never the dumbfounded repetitive shock of death. Why is that? Why is the friend becoming an astronaut less shocking than learning of his death, given the odds are far more astronomical for the former as opposed to the latter? If we reside within the strict confines of a logical system, an announcement of death should not promote such unnerving shock. But death always carries an odd speechlessness about it. Perhaps this shock, when faced with the one inevitability of every single life, is the implicit recognition of our own

18. 1 Cor 2:9–10.
19. Tolkien, *Letters*, 110.

interior sense of immortality. But death does not give us that recognition with any ease, it both takes away what it gives, and then gives again what it takes away. Death *as death* appears to contradict our immortality, while at the same time confirming it. And we must live out that contradiction. Or is it a paradox? A contradiction ends in despair and in the nothingness of a dead end. A paradox, on the other hand, places us squarely within the incarnation and the events of the passion and, we hope, the resurrection. In other words, the contemplation of death is not in opposition to eternal life, but its handmaiden. The longing for heaven is always present in the shock of death. We are unable to process death due to its intrinsic unnaturalness; a state that does not reflect the grace God intended for us before the fall. And yet, we must attempt to process it because we do die, and we are not so wounded by original sin that we cannot understand our natures, even and especially in their defection. More still, and simultaneously to complicate and alleviate things, our deaths, now experienced through Christ's death and resurrection, become a supernatural good, a journeying process contributing to our redemption. Thus, every human life must experience the twofold charter of death: death as unable to be processed, as it throws us into the unnaturalness of the unretrieved; and yet now it must be dwelt upon, perhaps more than anything else, since it also unlocks the gates to human life as most profoundly realized in heaven. These conflicting layers—the unnaturalness of death and the supernatural contributive good of death as journey—do not destroy each other but appear, impossibly so, to live, if not in harmony, in a conversation that alone realizes our highest happiness. We experience the agony of grief, and it does not cancel or mute the experience of the joy of passive purification intrinsic in dying; both experiences are fully present and define the meaning of our transcending human flesh. We do not simply "get better" from the grief over the loss of the child—the natural order has and will always be on this earth inverted, and everything on earth serves to remind us of what is missing.[20]

At the same time, the cross has lifted us out of that unnaturalness of death, but this transcendence is not magic, it does not wipe away the

---

20. Cf. Shakespeare, "King John," *Complete Works* III, iv 93–99:
  Grief fills the room up of my absent child,
  Lies in his bed, walks up and down with me,
  Puts on his pretty looks, repeats his words,
  Remembers me of all his gracious parts,
  Stuffs out his vacant garments with his form;
  Then, have I reason to be fond of grief?

reality of the world as irredeemable without the grace and mercy of Christ. This is the risk to which grief opens one who must live again when the child is beyond earthly reach.

The healing that comes from faith always springs from the recognition that death is and will always be a gaping wound. We can say without contradiction: the holy innocents are home, and with God they miss nothing and gain everything, while affirming the sheer immeasurable loss and alienation housed in death, and localized in Christ, when he asks if the cup can be passed.[21] Otherwise, what do we make of the millions of aborted babies, of the lives lost before they began? Heaven is home, but earth is always the *way* home. With the poet Rilke:

> There is death in life, and it astonishes me that we pretend to ignore this: death, whose unforgiving presence we experience with each change we survive because we must learn to die slowly. We must learn to die: That is all of life. To prepare gradually the masterpiece of a proud and supreme death, of a death where chance plays no part, of a well-made, beatific and enthusiastic death of the kind the saints knew to shape. Of a long-ripened death that effaces its hateful name and is nothing but a gesture that returns those laws to the anonymous universe which have been recognized and rescued over the course of an intensely accomplished life. It is this idea of death, which has developed inside of me since childhood from one painful experience to the next and which compels me to humbly endure the small death so that I may become worthy of the one which wants us to be great. I am not ashamed, my Dear, to have cried on a recent early Sunday morning in a cold gondola which floated around endless corners through sections of Venice only so vaguely visible that they seemed to branch out into another city far away. The voice of the *barcaiolo* who called out to be granted passage at the corner of a canal received no answer, like in the face of death. And the bells that I had heard in my room only moments before (my room where I have lived a whole life, where I was born and where I am preparing to die) seemed so clear to me; those same bells dragged their sounds like rags behind them over the swirling waters only to meet again without any recognition. It is still always that death which continues inside of me, which works in me, which transforms my heart, which deepens the

---

21. Cf. Matt 26:39: "He went a little farther and fell on His face, and prayed, saying, 'O My Father, if it is possible, let this cup pass from Me; nevertheless, not as I will, but as You will.'"

red of my blood, which weighs down the life that had been ours so that it may become a bittersweet drop coursing through my veins and penetrating everything, and which ought to be mine forever. And while I am completely engulfed in my sadness, I am happy to sense that you exist, Beautiful. I am happy to have flung myself without fear into your beauty just as a bird flings itself into space. I am happy, Dear, to have walked with steady faith on the waters of our uncertainty all the way to that island which is your heart and where pain blossoms. Finally: happy.[22]

This is how we live out the paradox of death as simultaneously a natural experience and a profoundly unnatural state. All of us experience a degree of this paradox since we live and die, and none is immune to it. But death of the great love places us within that gaping wound that is ever un-healing and simultaneously healed, but only through Christ. We often forget that Christ overcame it through his death, which reflects how we must follow suit. He had to die to overcome it, he had to die to be resurrected. That is why grief is a participation in crucifixion, and it is this saddest of all states that alone brings us into the meaning of heaven, not merely as "better place," but in all its hard-won and gifted majesty. Each of us is already inside the twofold nature of death as simultaneously the experience of horrendous loss, and the confirmation of our immortality, and neither experience expels the other. And this odd, often unforgiving experience, will be with us for the rest of our lives. It is the death sentence releasing us from death! It is loss as loss, while being gain, and neither does the loss outwit the gain, nor the gain undercut the loss on this side of eternity. Christ's love gifts us with the way through that wound, and the way *is* the wound, for Christ has indeed risen with his scars.[23] We receive salvation hiding in his wounds. This is the rosary of tears that begins in the memory of innocence and in the blood shared by all.

> For the word of God is alive and active. Sharper than any double-edged sword, it penetrates even to dividing soul and spirit, joints and marrow; it judges the thoughts and attitudes of the heart.[24]

We never overcome that tragic sense on this side of eternity. We carry both of those experiences and, again, recognizing that neither experience cancels out the other is the first insight into recovering paradise

---

22. Rilke, *The Dark Interval*, 103–5.

23. Cf. ST II, 4.

24. Heb 4:12.

from merely the unexamined festival. Only in a life where the terror
of the loss of the loved one is felt as irremediable, and yet experienced
through the gift of the cross as immeasurable gain and loving, delightful
joy, can we approach what is won for us in our permanent home. That
is our cross; neither experience debrides the other, which means both
experiences are felt in their dramatic power and exigency. Only in paradise, through Christ's grace, is the experience of loss—or so we hope and
trust[25]—finally canceled out; that it is not merely a bloodless utopia but
the font of healing water in which our whole beings emerge, the estuary
of release that finally *does* release, the dance with laughing and singing
and praise, so ebullient, that tears of sheer nectar spring forth. "My son,
eat honey, for it is good, and the drippings of the honeycomb are sweet
to your taste. Know that wisdom is such to your soul; if you find it, there
will be a future, and your hope will not be cut off."[26]

25. Cf. Verweyen, "The Life of All as the Outermost Horizon of Christology," in
Balthasar, *Dare We Hope*, 58: "Whoever reckons with the possibility of even only one
person's being eternally lost besides himself is unable to love unreservedly." See also
Bloy, "Méditations d'un Solitaire," in Balthasar, *Dare We Hope*, 133: "No creature is
excluded from redemption, for otherwise there would be no community of saints. The
exclusion of a single soul from the wondrous concert of the world is inconceivable and
would pose a threat to the universal harmony."

26. Prov 24:13–14.

Acknowledgments

THANK YOU TO THE community at University of Holy Cross for your support, especially and including the awarding of the Holy Angels Endowed Professorship, which assisted in the formation and completion of this work. I am especially grateful to Professors Claudia Champagne and Juyanne James, whose invaluable literary insights have opened new worlds of nuance and meaning. A debt of gratitude must be paid to Professor Cyril O'Regan, who encouraged me to put these painful and obstinate grieving words down on paper, and whose kindness had such timing and wisdom. Thank you also to Dr. Herb Hartmann, Ms. Jane Simoneaux, Fr. Michael O'Connor, Kathleen, Irina, Rhonda, Cindy, Mia, Nancy, Jackie, Ralph, most especially to Gabriel, and to all my remarkable MAH students. And finally, to my husband, Fred, whose editorial care over the years is *non pareil*, coming always from the depths of love and intelligence.

List of Abbreviations

St. Thomas Aquinas:

Summa Contra Gentiles:	*SCG*
Summa Theologiae:	*ST*
Scriptum Super Sententiis:	*In Sent.*
De Veritate:	*DV*

"As the deer pants for water, so I long for you, O God. I thirst for God, the living God. Where can I find him to come and stand before him?"
—Psalm 42

Introduction

Returning to the Order of Heaven

THROUGH A GENERALLY THOMISTIC understanding of the unity of body and soul, and in conversation with selected literature and mystic traditions of East and West, this book will address and interrogate various questions about the nature of the afterlife, and propose various paths to answers. The scholarship will inform, but will be carried by the tone of natural conversation. In doing so, we seek to enable the work to unfold within the honesty of sheer, needful reflection upon the dearest of all things. For indeed, we are talking about that sacred innermost promise: the hope of paradisal reunion most secret and yet most universal, never abstract and shapeless, but embodied and individual. And through it all, we must wonder whether our casual forgetting of this estuary of human hope, the resurrected life, has caused us to lose ourselves in such a way that we do not even know what we have lost. Are we akin to Plato's prisoners in the allegory of the cave?[1] Should one be released and run to the light in thanksgiving, such a one would only have been imprisoned bodily but

---

1. Cf. Plato, *Republic*, 515b-e: "To them, I said, the truth would be literally nothing but the shadows of the images. . . . And now look again, and see what will naturally follow if the prisoners are released and disabused of their error. At first, when any of them is liberated and compelled suddenly to stand up and turn his neck round and walk and look towards the light, he will suffer sharp pains; the glare will distress him, and he will be unable to see the realities of which in his former state he had seen the shadows; and then conceive some one saying to him, that what he saw before was an illusion, but that now, when he is approaching nearer to being and his eye is turned towards more real existence, he has a clearer vision, —what will be his reply? And you may further imagine that his instructor is pointing to the objects as they pass and requiring him to name them, —will he not be perplexed? Will he not fancy that the shadows which he formerly saw are truer than the objects which are now shown to him?"

never entrapped in heart and mind. But the prisoner who is released is so spiritually blinded that he turns back, preferring his prior infirmity: this shows us the terrifying profundity of true lostness. It is a debilitating form of forgetfulness that renders us unable to recall that we ourselves are amiss, and missing the most precious of possessions. By losing any genuine sense of paradise, are we making ourselves into the image of something degrading because fleeting and failing?

> You have made my days a few handbreadths, and my lifetime is as nothing in your sight. Surely everyone stands as a mere breath. Surely everyone goes about like a shadow. Surely for nothing they are in turmoil; they heap up, and do not know who will gather.[2]

When we look at the many things that bring us joy in this nomadic world, whether it be laughter, intimacy, childhood, we find that these things are dependent upon a human nature built in layers of conflicting fabric. Each of us is:

A. a yearning remembrance for a pre-fall state we cannot quite recall, let alone recover. We glimpse it in childlike innocence and yet long for this strange, un-known, un-grasped state with a stubborn and persistent wantonness that itself becomes either the terrible hubris within all human goals and motivations, the resignation to the meaningless labor of Sisyphus, or the holy *eros* that leads to the sheer *agapetic* sublimation necessary for faith:

B. in a fallen state that struggles to make good out of evil, so that the things we cherish have their goodness spread, indeed woefully diluted, among natures and conditions that must be transformed to a state of perfection and, to our fearful minds, may not survive such a vast transformation;

C. a participant in the flesh and blood of Christ within the twofold reality of resurrection as hope-filled promise and certitude as trust. This mystery unites the theological certitude of faith as grace with love as the offer of the highest, truest, most beautiful union of lover and beloved, and hope as *kenotic*, utterly emptying itself, denoting "a movement or a stretching forth of the appetite towards an arduous good."[3] The Christian is both certain and in total longing, in the

---

2. Ps 39:5–6.

3. ST I-II, 17, 3, *resp.*

presence of Christ who has already run to us, and running towards him all the same.

And the paradox of it all is that in order for us to long genuinely and fiercely for these transformations, we must recover how they are not vitiated or lessened presences, while at the same time we must systematically let go of every earthly love up until the moment of death. The recovery of paradise in our hearts is a strange and potentially unforgiving affair, but perhaps the most meaningful act of our lives, for through it we can understand the meaning behind the first commandment: "love the Lord your God with all your heart, and with all your soul, and with all your mind."[4] Somehow, we must simultaneously experience a letting-go, a type of holy forgetfulness that transgresses and reshapes all things, while hoping for union and reunion with *our* loves not in a vague form of all-ness, but in a dramatic uniqueness particular to the drama of each human person. How is that possible? And how is it to be lived out? Both unobtainable and necessary, we must find ourselves inhabiting an impossible yet essential harmony: we must be transported to the best of what life is in all its beauty, exotic and familial, but from within the very pulse of a non-annihilating sense of relinquishing everything that we are, with rapt exactingness and relentless precision. We must understand with joy that to relinquish, and to be relinquished, is bliss itself while that very bliss is perfumed with the transcendent incarnation of all of earth's beautiful things.

> I think there is no suffering greater than what is caused by the doubts of those who want to believe. I know what torment this is, but I can only see it, in myself anyway, as the process by which faith is deepened. A faith that just accepts is a child's faith and all right for children, but eventually you have to grow religiously as every other way, though some never do. What people don't realize is how much religion costs. They think faith is a big electric blanket, when of course it is the cross. It is much harder to believe than not to believe. If you feel you can't believe, you must at least do this: keep an open mind. Keep it open toward faith, keep wanting it, keep asking for it, and leave the rest to God.[5]

Heaven is the summit and joy of human existence and, at the same time, strangely neglected. We understand it to be the estuary of the Good

---

4. Matt 22:37 (quoting Deut 6:5).

5. O'Connor, *The Habit of Being*, 353–54.

in which we shall have no other desire than to remain there eternally;[6] that while unseen at present, it is, in fact, the only reality truly experienced *as is*;[7] that paradise is the precious crown and treasure;[8] and that either we suffer here in this world through our ardent yearning for God, or suffer in the next through our obstinate denial of him.[9] Yet still, in all of this, heaven escapes us. And by this, I mean that the very texture, the filling, the tender incarnality of the place or state or realm or habitation eludes capture with a pervasive and abrupt persistence. And because we are unable to focus our lens to get a substantial glance, we are historically tempted to focus our belief on those so-called "more important" things, which are important to the faith but only within the context of salvation, and salvation is homecoming, and homecoming is heaven. All roads lead to heaven, from the *exitus* to the *reditus*. And it is the little things, the specifics, the minutiae that have *always* characterized a human life embodied by finitude and the longer way[10] of flesh and blood. Thus, the lon-

6. Alighieri, "Paradiso," *The Divine Comedy* I, 64–87.

7. Cf. St. Augustine, Sermon 22a.4, *The Works of Saint* Augustine, 53: He is keeping himself for those who love him. He wants to show his face to those who have purified, not their eyes of flesh but the eyes of their hearts. Blessed, you see, are the clean of heart, for they shall see God (Matt 5:8). Love, in order to see, because what you will see is neither trash nor triviality. You will see him who made whatever else you love. And if these are lovely, what must he be like who made them? God doesn't want you loving the Earth, he doesn't want you loving the sky, those are things you can see, but himself whom you can't see. . . . Love him absent, to enjoy him present. Long to hold him, to embrace him. First cling to him by faith, then afterward you will cling to him by sight. Now, as a traveler, you are walking by faith and by hope. When you arrive, you will enjoy him whom you have loved as you traveled on your journey. It's he who founded the native country to which you should be hurrying to come. He has sent you a letter from there, not to put off returning from your travels." See also 1 John 3:2: "For we shall see him as he is."

8. Cf. Matt 6:19–20: "Do not lay up for yourselves treasures on earth, where moth and rust destroy and where thieves break in and steal, but lay up for yourselves treasures in heaven, where neither moth nor rust destroys and where thieves do not break in and steal."

9. Cf. St. John Vianney, "Catechism of Suffering," *The Little Catechism*, 54: "Whether we will or not, we must suffer. There are some who suffer like the good thief, and others like the bad thief. They both suffered equally. But one knew how to make his sufferings meritorious, he accepted them in the spirit of reparation, and turning towards Jesus crucified, he received from His mouth these beautiful words: 'This day thou shalt be with Me in Paradise.' The other, on the contrary, cried out, uttered imprecations and blasphemies, and expired in the most frightful despair. There are two ways of suffering—to suffer with love, and to suffer without love."

10. Cf. ST I, 62, 5, ad. 1: "Man was not intended to secure his ultimate perfection

ger way of embodied human life cannot be bypassed in the architecture of heaven because heaven is realized in Christ. In unity with Christ, our flesh and blood are incarnated beyond transitoriness, and shot through with a durational eternity.[11] The radicality of such *kenosis* is stunning: because Christ is God and flesh, heaven itself is transcendentally incarnated. Wounded as it may be, our own flesh still has the signatories, the *entelechy*, to give us a glimpse into heaven's fitting abode.[12] We are neither angels nor beasts, instead we stand on the horizon between time and eternity.[13] What can we grasp of heaven that properly befits the created nature God gave us and that Christ realized in the incarnation? Perhaps, though, this state of blindness, this unclarified texture, is precisely the point; we are to be in the dark, we are not ready, nor worthy, and ever in

at once, like the angel. Hence a longer way was assigned to man than to the angel for securing beatitude."

11. See Newsome Martin's cogent and nuanced reflections on Henri "Bergson's distinctive notion of pure duration (*durée*), a non-linear, indivisible, mobile and metaphysical reality where being is not static but a pulsating, dynamic mobility and multiplicity of qualitative states" in "The Christian Future of Metaphysics" and in "Memory Matters"; Bergson, *An Introduction to Metaphysics*, 43–49.

12. Cf. SCG I, 8: "Now, the human reason is related to the knowledge of the truth of faith (a truth which can be most evident only to those who see the divine substance) in such a way that it can gather certain likenesses of it, which are yet not sufficient so that the truth of faith may be comprehended as being understood demonstratively or through itself. Yet it is useful for the human reason to exercise itself in such arguments, however weak they may be, provided only that there be present no presumption to comprehend or to demonstrate. For to be able to see something of the loftiest realities, however thin and weak the sight may be, is, as our previous remarks indicate, a cause of the greatest joy."

13. Cf. SCG II, 68: "Dionysius says: Divine wisdom has joined the ends of the higher to the beginnings of the lower. Thus in the genus of bodies we find the human body, composed of elements equally tempered, attaining to the lowest member of the class above it, that is, to the human soul, which holds the lowest rank in the class of subsistent intelligences. Hence the human soul is said to be on the horizon and boundary line [*Confinium/aeviternity*] between things corporeal and incorporeal, inasmuch as it is an incorporeal substance and at the same time the form of a body." SCG III, 61: The human person, by virtue of his intellectual soul stands on the borderline, the horizon or *confinium* between eternity and time. St. Thomas stresses this point throughout his works emphasizing that the soul is shown to hold the last place among intellectual things. See SCG II, 80–81; SCG II, 80; DV X, 8 resp. See also Pseudo-Aristotle, *Book of Causes* §22: "Indeed, the being that is after eternity and beyond time is Soul, because it is on the horizon of eternity from below and beyond time." §84: "And indeed, Intelligence encompasses the things it produces, both Nature and the horizon of Nature, namely, the Soul, for it is above Nature." See also É. Gilson, *History of Christian Philosophy*, 235–37.

need of grace. But at the same time, if we leave that sightlessness unnurtured, unattended, un-wrestled, does heaven, the only place we will ever truly see *as is*, devolve into emptied abstractions? And then what shall we see? This *kenosis* is, again, innumerably wondrous: when Christ realizes heaven for human beings, he does so by merging—and without annihilation of their dramatic differences as such—the presence of heaven on earth and even, and more secretly, the presence of earth in heaven. In heaven resides the taste, the hunger for the earthy, the carnal, the dust and the clay, transfixed and transposed.

> I am their father, says God. *Our Father who art in Heaven.* My son
> told them often enough that I was their father.
> I am their judge. My son told them so. I am also their father.
> I am especially their father.
> Well, I am their father. He who is a father is above all a father. *Our*
> *Father who art in Heaven.* He who has once been a father
> can be nothing else but a father.
> They are my son's brothers; they are my children; I am their father.
> *Our Father who art in Heaven,* my son taught them that prayer.
> *Sic ergo vos orabitis.* After this manner therefore pray ye.
> *Our Father who art in Heaven,* he knew very well what he was doing
> that day, my son who loved them so.
> Who lived among them, who was like one of them.
> Who went as they did, who spoke as they did, who lived as they did.
> Who suffered.
> Who suffered as they did, who died as they did.
> And who loved them so, having known them.
> Who brought back to Heaven a certain taste for man, a certain taste
> for the Earth.
> My son who loved them so, who loves them eternally in Heaven.
> He knew very well what he was doing that day, my son who loved
> them so.[14]

This twofold union of heaven's foretaste on earth and earth's carnality permeating heaven impresses upon us the distinctive anti-fantasist, fully substantialized drama of our human natures always stretching and inclining towards heaven. The desire for heaven is not a peripheral yearning, an *accoutrement* to life's goals, a wish-fulfilling sentiment soon left at the wayside from childhood to maturity; instead, it is what finally unveils and completes our open human nature. More still, as the Father is *only* Father in relation to the Son, and the Son is *only* Son in relation

14. Péguy, "I am their Father," *God Speaks*, 71–72.

to the Father, then the Father, like the Son, has given himself *need*. That need is for their home to be our home, that God is only home because we, in our flesh and blood realized in Christ, audaciously co-substantiate heaven undergirded by God's sheer eternalizing presence—this is the true "happily ever after."[15] Christ has given to human beings far more than we deserve: "we are not worthy for you to enter under our roof, but only say the word." The Word has been incarnated and the roof is formed in this unity of spiritual eternity and bodily duration. What Christ has given us is himself and thus a co-substantiating power within the very architecture of paradise!

Thus, the wellspring of resources, particularly theological and philosophical discussion on the nature of the human person in relation to God, have not been thoroughly applied to a dwelling on the concrete questions each human person raises when confronted with death. What St. Paul understood to be truly our home is set aside, and this causes a loss in genuine belief in God, and in the formation of a Christian community. Tertullian's *credo quia ineptum* loses all its invitational ardor and then becomes what it opposes: a literal defense that belief itself is unworthy of belief. How can we search for heaven if it is not dreamt of? When undreamt by our flesh and blood we deny ourselves, we deny our humble but central role in the co-substantiating power that gives heaven its erotic presence, degrading paradise into an empty and spaceless vortex of onticity.

When the afterlife is no longer strained to be imagined, fleshed out in our longings, envisioned as a dramatic commingling of *philia*, *eros*, and *agape*, its architecture recedes only to the depository of thoughtlessness, the unthought festivity that secretly begins the turn away from God more primordially than any atheistic philosophical system. All atheisms begin in a misunderstood human nature, and that error of all errors originates in the loss of heaven, for our human nature is realized only in our permanent home.[16] While the human soul does have a mode of knowledge

15. See Tolkien's letter to his son, Michael, during WWII. Tolkien, *Letters*, 45: "Still, let us both take heart of hope and of faith. The link between father and son is not only of the perishable flesh: it must have something of *aeternitas* about it. There is a place called 'Heaven' where the good here unfinished is completed; and where the stories unwritten, and the hopes unfulfilled, are continued. We may laugh together yet . . . ."

16. Is it not interesting how so many utopic ideologies force into political existence a heavenly dressed earth, far more synonymous with hell as "state of definitive self-exclusion from communion with God" (*Catechism*, §1033)? This state of self-exclusion opposes Bergson's intensifying duration and is an anti-dialogic stasis where,

separate from the body,[17] we are not angels, and to mis-envision heaven as if we were unembodied angelic intellects would relinquish the true joy and the engagement of happiness and community befitting the embodied natures endowed by our Creator. Furthermore, our souls were not produced before our bodies, for such a production would undermine the very nature of the soul *for* the benefit of the body and the body *for* the benefit of the soul.[18] Any sense of heaven that undercuts this created unity is far more Cartesian than Catholic and thus far more unworthy of belief.

While mindful that heaven is no mere better dressed earth, we must also see what *is to be seen* in this penultimate world of penultimate joys, as an inkling of the paradisal home to come.[19] We must recover the unbroken thread within our flesh and blood that connects us to the one truly Good Reality, the fairy tale to end all fairy tales that may be too good for us, but not too good to be true. We must recover this thread from its opposition—the thoughtless "better place," which hasn't enough substance to be the estuary where all desires flow in ecstasy and surrender.

> If you read fairy-tales, you will observe that one idea runs from
> one end of them to the other—the idea that peace and happiness

ultimately, nothing more can be said or contemplated, no growth can be achieved, only dissipation and loss. The fact that the denial of God places us in a dystopian unreality, actually tells us a good deal about the pervasiveness of heaven, of its inescapability. Deny God, and one does not claim earth, but claims hell. Downward into the den of iniquity, of the so-called real world of unreality, we find ourselves surrounded by another sort of flesh. The incarnation that gifts our human nature as fulfilled in heaven and nomadic on earth, the essential guardian to combat the academic and political strangleholds that demand, to the death, another sort of body *politique*, one of plasticine flesh enclosing the mannequin anatomy of misremembering that lurks in identity politics, critical race theory, and all the succubant variants so preoccupied by flesh but haven't a clue what it is—no blood or water flows from those sides.

17. Cf. ST I, 89, 1.

18. Cf. ST I, 90, 4, *resp*; ST I, 118, 3, *resp*.

19. Cf. Pope John Paul II, "General Audience," (07/21/99) §5: "This final state, however, can be anticipated in some way today in sacramental life, whose centre is the Eucharist, and in the gift of self through fraternal charity. If we are able to enjoy properly the good things that the Lord showers upon us every day, we will already have begun to experience that joy and peace which one day will be completely ours. We know that on this earth everything is subject to limits, but the thought of the "ultimate" realities helps us to live better the 'penultimate' realities. We know that as we pass through this world we are called to seek 'the things that are above, where Christ is seated at the right hand of God' (Col 3:1), in order to be with him in the eschatological fulfilment, when the Spirit will fully reconcile with the Father 'all things, whether on Earth or in Heaven' (Col 1:20)."

can only exist on some condition. This idea, which is the core of ethics, is the core of the nursery-tales. The whole happiness of fairyland hangs upon a thread, upon a thread. . . . This great idea, then, is the backbone of all folk-lore—the idea that all happiness hangs on one thin veto; all positive joy depends on one negative.[20]

Christ is the great idea, the backbone of existence, the greatest story ever told precisely because he radically fulfills the innermost yearning of the fairy tale. Our thread is trust, the painful and purgative grace of trust that rises like fragrance within us. Happy are we who trust in Christ: all positive joy rests on his story that ends all stories:

> Happy are those who trust in the LORD, who rely on the LORD. They will be like trees planted by the streams, whose roots reach down to the water. They won't fear drought when it comes; their leaves will remain green. They won't be stressed in the time of drought or fail to bear fruit.[21]

Christ alone achieves what they anticipate, seek, and yearn for: the *happily ever after*, substantiated through his *consummatum est,* wherein suffering as totalizing abandonment becomes impossibly but essentially so, the place for union, joy, peace, and play.[22] When Christ realizes heaven through his incarnation, he gives us so much more fertile ground in which to long for our home than the superficial celebration. The latter functions on an unthought acceptance of the soul as accidentally united to the body. This serious misunderstanding generationally vacates the sense of flesh ennobled by Christ which is far more than transitoriness and is, instead, the saturated presence of the divine—with rivers as bright as crystal, and trees yielding fruit, where there is no longer any night

20. Chesterton, *All Things Considered,* 256.

21. Jer 17:7–8.

22. Cf. Norwich, *Revelations of Divine Love,* 74: "I saw, while looking at the same cross, that His blessed expression changed. The changing of His blessed expression changed mine. . . . Then our Lord made me think happily, 'Where is there not one jot of your pain or your sorrow?' And I was very happy. I understood that we are now, as our Lord intends it, dying with Him on His cross in our pain and our passion; and if we willingly remain on the same cross with His help and His grace until the final moment, the countenance He turns on us will suddenly change, and we shall be with Him in Heaven . . . and everything will be turned to joy . . . ."

because the face of God will be brighter and warmer than the light of lamp or sun.[23]

The laborer may finally put down his axe and shovel, and enter the field of play, where walking turns into leaps and dancing, and words meld into singing and praise.[24] The fairy tale senses perfection in the most liminal manner, but must leave it undefined, framed by the closing lines "happily ever after." The story of Christ's gift is the happily ever after because he breaks the chains of death and thus breaks all stories, and invites us to share in his glorified body. When we do not pant like the deer for heaven, we unknowingly reduce the Christ-event to a narrative of wishes and ideals. We place Christ within the "better place" that cannot capture or enrapture a heart, that cannot raise even the most horrendous suffering into its dignity. We have lost Christ as the very story of life itself. Our faith is for the childlike, not the childish, for the warrior, not the coward. And this is so often misunderstood. What we are called to recover is the dramatic desire to enter into the beauty of the truest story, and through it, the love, hope, and redemption of transfigured souls.[25]

23. Cf. Rev 22:1–9: "Then the angel showed me the river of the water of life, bright as crystal, flowing from the throne of God and of the Lamb through the middle of the street of the city; also, on either side of the river, the tree of life with its twelve kinds of fruit, yielding its fruit each month. The leaves of the tree were for the healing of the nations. No longer will there be anything accursed, but the throne of God and of the Lamb will be in it, and his servants will worship him. They will see his face, and his name will be on their foreheads. And night will be no more. They will need no light of lamp or sun, for the Lord God will be their light, and they will reign forever and ever."

24. See Chesterton, the great prophet of common—yet rarefied—sense. *All Things Considered*, 96: "It might reasonably be maintained that the true object of all human life is play. Earth is a task garden; Heaven is a playground. To be at last in such secure innocence that one can juggle with the universe and the stars, to be so good that one can treat everything as a joke—that may be, perhaps, the real end and final holiday of human souls."

25. Cf. Chesterton, *Collected Works Vol. I*, 60: "Because children have abounding vitality, because they are in spirit fierce and free, therefore they want things repeated and unchanged. They always say, 'Do it again'; and the grown-up person does it again until he is nearly dead. For grown-up people are not strong enough to exult in monotony. But perhaps God is strong enough to exult in monotony. It is possible that God says every morning, 'Do it again' to the sun; and every evening, 'Do it again' to the moon. It may not be automatic necessity that makes all daisies alike; it may be that God makes every daisy separately, but has never got tired of making them. It may be that He has the eternal appetite of infancy; for we have sinned and grown old, and our Father is younger than we."

The boy eating some one's apples in some one's apple tree should be a reminder that he has come to a mystical moment of his life, when one apple may rob him of all others. This is the profound morality of fairy-tales; which so far from being lawless, go to the root of all law. Instead of finding (like common books of ethics) a rationalistic basis for each Commandment, they find the great mystical basis for all Commandments. We are in this fairyland on sufferance; it is not for us to quarrel with the conditions under which we enjoy this wild vision of the world. The vetoes are indeed extraordinary, but then so are the concessions. The idea of property, the idea of some one else's apples, is a rum idea; but then the idea of there being any apples is a rum idea. Not only can these fairy-tales be enjoyed because they are moral, but morality can be enjoyed because it puts us in fairyland, in a world at once of wonder and of war.[26]

The Hunt for Heaven

Let us now apply many of the meaningful contributions of the Christian enterprise to the essential and often uncharted territory of the afterlife. If heaven is our home, then I hope that the teachings of Christian philosophy and theology, when applied to their *proper* home, will serve to illuminate and guide our intellectual and spiritual conversations. In particular, the difficult metaphysical and phenomenological implications of the afterlife will come to the forefront of our discussions. We shall address whether or not there is a profound inconsistency when we posit St. Thomas's substance-based metaphysics and a disembodied state as posed in heaven. In order authentically to address such a critique and others, we will clarify the distinctions between heaven as the pre-resurrected state, and then the resurrected state of the glorified body, as discussion will naturally straddle these two states of being. Thus, ours is an intensive meditation on the loss of any substantial sense of heaven and its vast consequences. The notion of *mythos*, even and especially imagination and fiction, not as falsehoods but as primal compact expressions of the inexpressible, will be addressed. What happens to a culture, particularly a religious culture, when its underlying *mythos* is diminished? And this question gets us to the core of the unfortunate separation between the theologian and the saint which von Balthasar had raised years ago.

26. Chesterton, *All Things Considered*, 257–58.

> In modern times, theology and sanctity have become divorced, to the great harm of both. Except in a few cases, the saints have not been theologians, and theologians have tended to treat their opinions as a sort of by-product, classifying them as *spiritualité*, or at best, as *théologie spirituelle*.[27]

After Anselm, Bonaventure, and Aquinas, how strange—and yet is it not a critical indicator that something is amiss—that so few theologians have been saints? The practice of theology and the quest for sanctity have not only undergone a trial separation, seen other people, explored life apart, but have even accepted their divorce with the pride of a secularist badge of honor.

The deepest *mythoi* permeate the soil of existence and direct culture to flower, and through it the transcendent expressions of faith and sanctity deepen every facet of life. Western civilization is most deeply an expression of the Christian *mythos*, and we can see today why the Catholic Church is so much under attack, both from within and without. If one is to change, overcome, "cancel" Western culture, it must attack and subvert Judeo-Christian values, first intimidating them into a private-only existence, and then through a hostile neglect that causes these values to wither away, because their roots, their *mythos*, died without the sunlight of natural public practice. When virtues are exercised only privately, they are no longer virtuous and instead will inevitably become the basis for a deceitful civilizational decline, one that dresses up mob-mentality as wisdom and prudence.[28] What we seek to express through our dwelling on heaven is that Christianity is the greatest *mythos* of all myths, because it is the transcendent Truth itself that enables all other myths, fables, hopes, and dreams to spring up and yearn for sunlight like the winter's tulip. Chesterton again reminds us of these long untended roots:

> About all these myths my own position is utterly and even sadly simple. I say you cannot really understand any myths till you have found that one of them is not a myth. Turnip ghosts mean nothing if there are no real ghosts. Forged bank-notes mean nothing if there are no real bank-notes. Heathen gods mean

27. Balthasar, *Two Sisters in the Spirit*, 26. See also "Theology and Sanctity," *Explorations in Theology I*, 180–81.

28. Cf. Pieper, *The Four Cardinal Virtues*, 51: "Perhaps when all the consequences of a false presupposition suddenly become a direct threat men in their great terror will become aware that it is no longer possible to call back to true and effective life a truth they have allowed to become remote—just for the sake of their bare survival."

nothing, and must always mean nothing, to those of us that deny the Christian God. When once a god is admitted, even a false god, the Cosmos begins to know its place: which is the second place. When once it is the real God the Cosmos falls down before Him, offering flowers in spring as flames in winter. "My love is like a red, red rose" does not mean that the poet is praising roses under the allegory of a young lady. "My love is an arbutus" does not mean that the author was a botanist so pleased with a particular arbutus tree that he said he loved it. "Who art the moon and regent of my sky" does not mean that Juliet invented Romeo to account for the roundness of the moon. "Christ is the Sun of Easter" does not mean that the worshipper is praising the sun under the emblem of Christ. Goddess or god can clothe themselves with the spring or summer; but the body is more than raiment. Religion takes almost disdainfully the dress of Nature; and indeed Christianity has done as well with the snows of Christmas as with the snow-drops of spring. And when I look across the sun-struck fields, I know in my inmost bones that my joy is not solely in the spring, for spring alone, being always returning, would be always sad. There is somebody or something walking there, to be crowned with flowers: and my pleasure is in some promise yet possible and in the Resurrection of the dead.[29]

The Christian faith has always been a faith practicing death, but now we are practicing something quite other altogether—the death of the faith. At present, such a lamentable conflation exists throughout our culture and has taken stronghold in academia. The faith is being hounded out of existence by a tidal wave of vicious concessions that render it meaningless, dulling its beauty, and whitewashing its teachings. How then can we evangelize effectively, and reinvigorate the goodness of this salvific faith? There are no easy ways and means and, again, we are, each of us, lost in varying degrees, many to the point of believing our fallenness to be the new lodestar of virtue. We are all nomadic because this earth, while at times a loving promise to be our home, is itself not. This means, indeed necessitates, that all the teachings of the faith, from the theology of the body, to the sanctity of life, to the last things, lose their ardor and magnetic power when they are not presented within their proper place, within the abode of salvation. How can we promulgate the beauty of the faith if we haven't tended to its roots, to the beauteous, awe-inspiring mythic pattern of paradise? And by *mythos*, we do not mean an invented

29. Chesterton, *A Miscellany of Men*, 120–21.

narrative, fable, or tale that ends only as a narrative, fable, or tale atop existence but that cannot complete these yearnings. We mean the mystical wisdom so holy, inviting, and pure that it is understood only through consecrated experience. And when glimpsed, it is the ground from which spring all tales and all love songs. Until we recover a fleshed-out vision of paradise, we may indeed have theologians, doctors, maids, accountants, lawyers, plumbers, farmers, but we will not have saints, we will not have faith that drips like sap from the maple, and nectar from comb.[30] What is the good of a proclaimed "good life" if such goodness does not saturate our very being? To find this permeated soil, we must return to our roots, to the *alpha* and *omega*, to the heaven that Christ's flesh realizes within our own flesh.

Many of the chapters will be presented in the form of a question in keeping with our struggle to recover this most essential and beautiful home. The underlying interrogative tension of our spiritual appetite in relation to our physical process of decline—our embodied nature that must experience the immaterial through the longer way of the sensible in confrontation with our necessity to let go of all earthly loves—will play devil's advocate in our discussions on the nature of paradise. Any genuine appreciation of eternal happiness that elevates us beyond the well-intended but nullifying utopia requires an in-depth reflection on purgation both before and after death. Paradise cannot be a cosmetically better earthly existence, nor can it be so estranged from what embodiment denotes. Thus, what can and must we say of our home that for so long has been a strange and foreign land?

---

30. Cf. Balthasar, "Theology and Sanctity," *Explorations in Theology I*, 192–93: "The impoverishment brought about by the divorce between the two spheres [theology and sanctity] is all too plain, it has sapped the vital force of the Church today and the credibility of her preaching of eternal truth, This impoverishment is felt considerably more strongly by those who have to preach to modern pagans than by professors in their seminary lecture rooms. It is the former who look round for some example of the conjunction of wisdom and holiness. They long to discover the living organism of the Church's doctrine, rather than a strange anatomical dissection: one the one hand, the bones without the flesh, 'traditional theology'; on the other, flesh without bones, that very pious literature that serves up a compound of asceticism, mysticism and spirituality and rhetoric, a porridge that, in the end, becomes indigestible through lack of substance. Only the two together (corresponding to the prototype of revelation in scripture) constitute the unique 'form' capable of being 'seen' in the light of the faith by the believer, a unique testimony, invisible to the world and a 'scandal' to it."

Part I:

Heaven and the Transcendental Meaning of Death

1

Do We Lack and Long in Heaven without Our Bodies?

W ITH ST. THOMAS:

> For the human soul is immortal, and continues after its separa-
> tion from the body. Yet union with body is essential to it, for
> by its very nature soul is form of body. Without body it is in an
> unnatural condition; and what is unnatural cannot go on for-
> ever. Therefore the soul, which is perpetual, is not for ever apart
> from the body, but will be united with it. The soul's immortality,
> therefore, seems to demand the eventual Resurrection of body.[1]

Perhaps the hesitancy we face when attempting to dwell on heaven
is rooted in the crisis of the separated soul, which conjures an anti-phenomenological state uncomfortably closer to non-being than to the concrete life of carnal existence. If we take the dry Thomistic language that
the soul is the form of the body and realize it in its luminous radicality,
not only is the body for the benefit of the soul, but the soul also achieves
its perfection and *raison d'être* in the body. If the soul is the form of the
body, how can it be claimed that we do not lack and long in heaven and
yet how *can* we lack, and audaciously claim such a possibility, now wholly
united with God?[2] The state of the separated soul is, indeed, the crisis that

1. SCG, 4, 79.

2. When Aquinas speaks of the state of the glorified body, we see that the work-
ings of the soul through the divine vision are organized *through* a perfecting of the

19

hits at the very core of our unrepeatability as persons within the dignity of human nature. The objector in *prima pars* question 90 argues a neat solution: "the end is proportionate to the beginning. But in the end the soul outlasts the body. Therefore, in the beginning it was created before the body."[3] To which St. Thomas responds briefly, clearly, incisively. Through it, the sheer directionality is manifest: humans who seek heaven, more interiorly yearn for the paradisal abode of the resurrected state: "That the soul remains after the body, is due to a defect of the body, namely, death. Which defect was not due when the soul was first created."[4] Are we to concede then that the end in heaven, as a separated soul, is *not* proportionate to the beginning, united to a body, since the soul was not created before the body, but conjointly with it?[5]

St. Thomas in *prima pars* question 89 goes to great explanatory lengths to show that in our separated state, contrary to the objectors (including Aristotle), we do in fact have knowledge. This is necessary if he is to claim heaven as the perfected state for humans. But the Angelic Doctor well understands the delicacy, almost impossibility, of clarifying such a position:

> Hence it is as natural for the soul to understand by turning to the phantasms as it is for it to be joined to the body; but to be separated from the body is not in accordance with its nature,

body, in its action, passion, movement, and bodily qualities. See SCG, IV, 84: "Grant, of course, that in the Resurrection the merit of Christ does remove the deficiency of nature commonly from all men—from both the good and the evil; nonetheless, a difference will persist between the good and the evil in respect to what is suitable to each group personally. Now, it is an essential of nature that the human soul is the form of the body which vivifies the body and preserves it in being, but by its personal acts the soul merits to be elevated to the glory of the divine vision or to be excluded from the order of that glory by reason of its sin. The body, then, will be commonly disposed in all men in harmony with the soul, with this result: The incorruptible form bestows an incorruptible being on the body in spite of its composition from contraries, because in respect to corruption the matter of the human body will be entirely subject to the human soul. But the glory and power of the soul elevated to the divine vision will add something more ample to the body united to itself. For this body will be entirely subject to the soul—the divine power will achieve this—not only in regard to its being, but also in regard to action, passion, movements, and bodily qualities."

3. ST I, 90, 4, obj. 3.

4. ST I, 90, 4 ad. 3.

5. ST I, 90, 4 *resp*: "For it is clear that God made the first things in their perfect natural state, as their species required. Now the soul, as a part of human nature, has its natural perfection only as united to the body. Therefore, it would have been unfitting for the soul to be created without the body."

and likewise to understand without turning to the phantasms is not natural to it; and hence it is united to the body in order that it may have an existence and an operation suitable to its nature. But here again a difficulty arises. For since nature is always ordered to what is best, and since it is better to understand by turning to simply intelligible objects than by turning to the phantasms, God should have ordered the soul's nature so that the nobler way of understanding would have been natural to it, and it would not have needed the body for that purpose.[6]

The body is not united to the soul accidentally; if it were, such difficulties as to how we have knowledge in our separated state would quickly vanish. But because it is of the soul's very nature, for its very good, to be united to a body, and to phantasms and sensible examples for its knowledge, St. Thomas must illustrate how the soul within the line of created substances is the lowest of intellectual substances and as such has intellective power by the influence of the divine light. Aquinas' resolution never forsakes the predicament, the paradox, the ever-present crisis inherent in the state of the separated soul—a crisis for too long sidestepped by the "better place." In the line of beings, truly it is higher and nobler to be like the angels who receive knowledge by turning to intelligible objects, rather than having to deal with the exhaustive *longer way* of the flesh, which understands by turning to phantasms. But the former, while befitting an angel, does not befit a human soul. This would render the body accidental to the soul, which would wholly undermine the integrity of human nature and material creation. With the nihilists, what then would be the point of it all? But at the same time the strength of their unity, where the soul is the form of the body, poses the threat that the interior principle is corrupted with the death of the body and the loss of the phantasms, since turning to the phantasms is essential to human knowledge. Nor can heaven be a state of quasi-inactivity, where memories of one's human life, the imprint of the intelligible species from a lifetime's embodied experience with the phantasms, somehow sustains the soul. Such a state seems to be more the foundation for hell rather than heaven and itself poses problems since, at least, human memory does not function outside a repeated turning to the phantasms. If God had willed human souls to attain knowledge in like manner as the angelic species, then, for St. Thomas, human knowledge would become unclarified, non-specific generalities. The human soul is not the right template to understand separated substances. Could it?

6. ST I, 89, 1 *resp.*

Perhaps. But should this be its perfection? No. A thin un-waxed paper cup given at the dentist for gargling is not the proper container for hot coffee. It may hold the coffee briefly, but the experience of it would be fraught with fear of spillage, and be a distracted and caustic state, less perfect than its designed and intended use.[7] And herein again lies the problem, the crisis, of the state of the separated soul, which is so masked by the "better place" mantra. And that very masking perniciously heightens the loss of credulity in the faith, subsequently degrading and deforming the proper theology of the body that opens the door to a proper glimpse of the heaven that visited earth.

How then does the Angelic Doctor authentically resolve such a difficulty, one that influences every arena of human life? We have learned a number of intensifying but essential realities:

1. If heaven necessitated a form of knowledge equivalent to the angels' direct turning to the spiritual substance, then we would be in an existential impasse: heaven would not be a state of perfection for the human person. If heaven were a state void of knowledge, this would be plainly absurd. We are clearly walking an existential and conceptual tightrope, particularly when St. Thomas navigates the related question as to whether the sensitive powers remain in the separated soul.[8]

7. Cf. ST I, 89, 1 *resp*: "Therefore to make it possible for human souls to possess perfect and proper knowledge, they were so made that their nature required them to be joined to bodies, and thus to receive the proper and adequate knowledge of sensible things from the sensible things themselves; thus, we see in the case of uneducated men that they have to be taught by sensible examples."

8. Cf. ST Suppl. 70, 1, *resp*: "Now it is evident that certain operations, whereof the soul's powers are the principles, do not belong to the soul properly speaking but to the soul as united to the body, because they are not performed except through the medium of the body—such as to see, to hear, and so forth. Hence it follows that such like powers belong to the united soul and body as their subject, but to the soul as their quickening principle, just as the form is the principle of the properties of a composite being. Some operations, however, are performed by the soul without a bodily organ—for instance to understand, to consider, to will: wherefore, since these actions are proper to the soul, the powers that are the principles thereof belong to the soul not only as their principle but also as their subject. Therefore, since so long as the proper subject remains its proper passions must also remain, and when it is corrupted they also must be corrupted, it follows that these powers which use no bodily organ for their actions must needs remain in the separated body, while those which use a bodily organ must needs be corrupted when the body is corrupted: and such are all the powers belonging to the sensitive and the vegetative soul. On this account some draw a distinction in the sensitive powers of the soul: for they say that they are of two kinds—some being acts of

2. Faith and reason are not opposed, faith enables reason to gain humbling access into the mystery because, while beyond reason, the mystery is profoundly reasonable, identical with Truth, Beauty, and Goodness.[9] If this be the case, then the trust that situates revealed knowledge as guide to natural reason must not be merely acknowledged but be the informing principle of any dwelling upon the afterlife. We understand, by faith, that heaven is a state of the blessed, a state of perfection, that there is no lacking in heaven. This line must be held, and we must see how it *is* reasonable.

3. Paradoxically, we must recognize that the state of the separated soul of the blessed must be both a concession that denotes reference to a nobler state, and one that does not denote any lacking whatsoever. If the concession is not present, then the theo-drama of created existence becomes a nuisance, a meddlesome distraction to human transcendence in the way the Platonists envisioned embodiment as a prison house for the spirit. And if such a state denotes lacking, then God would not be *esse ipsum subsistens*, in which all perfections are identical to him and ever directed towards him.

God is his own existence and not merely his own essence;[10] he is Being *qua* pure Act. It is not sufficient to call God a beautiful, or good,

---

organs and emanating from the soul into the body are corrupted with the body; others, whence the former originate, are in the soul, because by them the soul sensitizes the body for seeing, hearing, and so on; and these primary powers remain in the separated soul. But this statement seems unreasonable: because the soul, by its essence and not through the medium of certain other powers, is the origin of those powers which are the acts of organs, even as any form, from the very fact that by its essence it informs its matter, is the origin of the properties which result naturally in the composite. For were it necessary to suppose other powers in the soul, by means of which the powers that perfect the organs may flow from the essence of the soul, for the same reason it would be necessary to suppose other powers by means of which these powers flow from the essence of the soul, and so on to infinity, and if we have to stop it is better to do so at the first step. Hence others say that the sensitive and other like powers do not remain in the separated soul except in a restricted sense, namely radically, in the same way as a result is in its principle: because there remains in the separated soul the ability to produce these powers if it should be reunited to the body; nor is it necessary for this ability to be anything in addition to the essence of the soul, as stated above. This opinion appears to be the more reasonable."

9. Cf *Fides et Ratio*, §13: "our vision of the face of God is always fragmentary and impaired by the limits of our understanding. Faith alone makes it possible to penetrate the mystery in a way that allows us to understand it coherently."

10. Cf. ST I, 3, 4 *resp.*

or true being, as if these are each one of his additions, as if he possesses only a degree of participation in the transcendentals. He is, instead, the uncreated *To Be* of all created things. God is Being itself: all perfections are directed to Being, and Being is directed to God who is Being itself, containing all perfections. "Can any hide himself in secret places, that I shall not see him?" saith the Lord. "Do not I fill heaven and earth?" saith the Lord.[11] God fills heaven and earth, and this truth of all truths must not be overlooked. It would be improper for heaven to necessitate that the human soul assimilate knowledge in like manner to the angels' non-embodied possession of intellectual objects, and this is not what occurs in heaven. The metaphysics of uncreated *To Be* truly unveils the reasonableness within the mystery of the faith's understanding of heaven. Our human nature seeks out spiritual existence, but unlike angels must go by way of the most unique compositeness. We have always been yearning beings *as* open natures, outside ourselves, because creationally open to the un-created. And through the recognition of that uncreatedness, which is the divine *To Be* most interior to all things, we are also inwardly dwelling within ourselves to the point where our own otherness is not our own, but rather a supernatural gratuity, always a participation in God. Earth has never fully revealed our human nature because it *cannot*. The human person is a being in active *wait*; both inwardly and outwardly we are beyond ourselves by virtue of this existential dis-possession—for no creature can possess the un-created source of God's reflection which is intrinsic to beings who can realize the root of their own createdness.

> The mystery of man is that he cannot know himself until he discovers that his compositeness is the vehicle of an intellectual nature living within a spiritual existence. Even though man stands on Earth, like any other composite, his intellectual nature stands ultimately and finally before God and nowhere else. Man stands there, he must learn to stand there, and he cannot discover himself or be himself unless and until this presence that is his spiritual existence recognizes and expresses the presence of God to him. It is not easy to think with St. Thomas about the nature of man. To be a man, as I think I have learned from him, is to be a witness to the creative presence of God in the universe and in man himself.[12]

11. Jer 23:24.
12. Pegis, "St. Thomas and the Meaning of Human Existence," 63–64.

God need not turn to phantasms nor to the more exalted intellectual object like the angels; none is appropriate for God's nature. God *Is*: every being in the line of createdness turns to him to receive knowledge in varying modes and degrees peculiar to their species. God is the Divine Light, one simple indivisible first principle, and by his own essence knows all things. Instead of the phantasms, the separated soul turns to God. As Creator, the very foundational *To Be* within the line of all creaturely beings—as God fills heaven and earth—he can appropriately take the place of the phantasms for us. Grasping the intellectual object in the manner befitting the angels would be woefully inappropriate. It would be a looking through the glass even more darkly than on earth,[13] for what use is the greatest sonata to the stone, or angelic knowledge to the human, or human carnality to the angel? We cannot square this circle. But the separated soul turning to God—who is the *To Be* of all things, who substantializes the phantasms, intellectual objects, and all created beings—is *most* fitting. Here, we retain the proper order that must not be bypassed, for faith is not magic, but rigorous truth endowed with perfect love.

> The separated soul does not understand by way of innate species, nor by species abstracted then, nor only by species retained, and this the objection proves; but the soul in that state understands by means of participated species arising from the influence of the Divine light, shared by the soul as by other separate substances; though in a lesser degree. Hence as soon as it ceases to act by turning to corporeal (phantasms), the soul turns at once to the superior things; nor is this way of knowledge unnatural, for God is the author of the influx of both of the light of grace and of the light of nature.[14]

Yet, still, the concession must be present, for original sin was not necessary, was not what the Creator intended. Death has hereditary consequences that are not removed by what would amount to an anti-phenomenological fiat, one that degrades flesh to the vessel and not the very substance of human life, affirming the intrinsic dignity of the composite unity.[15] The soul outlasts the body due to the disease of our sin, which removes the grace that held us from death:

13. Cf. 1 Cor 13:12.

14. ST I, 89, 1 ad. 3.

15. See also ST I, 118, 3, *resp*: "For if it is natural to the soul to be united to the body, it is unnatural to it to be without a body, and as long as it is without a body it is

> It is . . . evident that the first cause of the absence of grace is
> purely and simply on the side of man to whom grace is lack-
> ing because he had not been willing to receive it. On the side
> of God, there is no cause of the absence of grace, except once
> admitted that which is the cause on the side of man.[16]

While heaven is surely without deficit, there is an integral directionality within that blessedness where the nobler embodiment of the
resurrected state creates an anticipation and a purified yearning born not
of emptiness or a will opposed to God's, but of abundance and peace.
This heavenly yearning comes from a quieted will, a will at rest, a will that
is one with God's will, who eternally wills the good for each of us. Our
will rests in God's and is not static—for God is pure *Actus*. Unified, it is
actively geared to the intrinsic intimacy and singularity of each person's
relationship with God, so that each glorified body, even its vestments and
walk and posture, communicate the once incommunicable singularity[17]
of his or her relationship with God fulfilled, via grace, to its particular
perfection. And because of this, heaven becomes *more* of a community
than any earthly version could ever achieve.[18] The spiritual bloodlines
that Plato sought to universalize in the *Republic*, so as to create genuine
communal bonds beyond the family, but as indelible as familial affection
and intimacy,[19] are finally made manifest, are realized in the transition
from separated souls in heaven to glorified bodies in the resurrected
state. We see a sense of this paradoxical yearning of the unified will at

---

deprived of its natural perfection. Now it was not fitting that God should begin His
work with things imperfect and unnatural, for He did not make man without a hand
or a foot, which are natural parts of a man. Much less, therefore, did He make the soul
without a body."

16. St. Thomas, *Sententiarum*, I, dist. 40, 4, 2.

17. Cf. Baker, *Fundamentals of Catholicism,* 103.

18. So many earthly versions of community are susceptible to the most dangerous
forms of defection. Hubristically, they each think they have collected enough evidence
on the nature and motivations of mankind to resolve all longing within temporal and
material goods, and then subsequently suppress that spiritual incommunicability into
a perverted form of community. That incommunicability *as incommunicability* in one
respect is immune to that deforming suppression—the truth will out—but in another
respect, it only finds itself in the longer way of flesh and time as a longing for the inklings of the glorified body. The more community is deformed, the more the outlet for
the flesh's intimacy with God, when confronted with ubiquitous death, has nowhere
to go but the nonsense of the "better place" dressed up as mystery, confusing incommunicability with unknowability.

19. Plato, *Republic* 543a-576b.

rest, gifted with co-substantiating the architecture of God's infinity, in Canto I of *Paradiso*. Dante poses the most natural and earthbound question to the blessed Piccarda dei Donati. He is, after all, a visitor to heaven and has witnessed ascending orders to paradise: "But tell me, do you who are happy here desire a higher place, that you may see more and become more dear?" Piccarda's response, reflecting her seamless unity with God:

> Brother, the power of charity quiets our will and makes us will only what we have and thirst for nothing else. Did we desire to be more exalted, our desire would be in discord with His will who appoints us here, which thou wilt see cannot hold in these circles if to be in charity is here necessary and if thou consider well its nature. Nay, it is the very quality of this blessed state that we keep ourselves within the divine will, so that our wills are themselves made one; therefore our rank from height to height through this kingdom is pleasing to the whole kingdom, as to our King who wills us to His will. And in His will is our peace. It is that sea to which all things move, both what it creates and what nature makes.[20]

Our recoil at the emptiness of the celestial utopia is more than understandable, it is true to form and to embodied being. This must not be forgotten. To ignore the unease, the sense that something does not compute within this mystery, is to deform the promise of paradise into unreasonable unknowability, and to a sense of embodiment incapable of genuine *eros* and *agape*, and to a faith so regrettably unworthy of belief. Charles Péguy sets out what distinguishes us, and in a strange way elevates us above the angels,[21] and it is through this flesh that we will find our way home:

20. Alighieri, "Paradiso," *The Divine Comedy* I, 64–87.

21. While angels are far closer in image to God, St. Thomas deeply acknowledges the dignity of the human person, who, relatively speaking, by likeness or a likening power befitting intellectual substance and embodiment, is higher than the angels. See ST I, 93, 3 *resp*: "We may speak of God's image in two ways. First, we may consider in it that in which the image chiefly consists, that is, the intellectual nature. Thus, the image of God is more perfect in the angels than in man, because their intellectual nature is more perfect, as is clear from what has been said (I:58:3; I:79:8). Secondly, we may consider the image of God in man as regards its accidental qualities, so far as to observe in man a certain imitation of God, consisting in the fact that man proceeds from man, as God from God; and also in the fact that the whole human soul is in the whole body, as God from God; and also in the fact that the whole human soul is in the whole body, and again, in every part, as God is in regard to the whole world. In these and the like things the image of God is more perfect in man than it is in the angels. But

The Franciscan Nun tells young Joan
"What those that are carnal lack, as we know, is being pure.
But what we ought to know is that those that are pure lack being carnal.
The angels are certainly pure, but they aren't the least bit carnal.
They have no idea what it is to have a body, *to be* a body.
They have no idea what it is to be a poor creature.
A carnal creature.
A body kneaded from the clay of the earth.
The carnal earth.
They don't understand this mysterious bond, this created bond,
Infinitely mysterious,
Between the soul and the body.
This my child is what the angels do not understand.
I mean to say, that this is what they haven't experienced.
What it is to have this body; to have this bond with this body; to be this body,
To have this bond with the earth, with this earth, to be this earth, clay and dust, ash and the mud of the earth,
The very body of Jesus."[22]

these do not of themselves belong to the nature of the Divine image in man, unless we presuppose the first likeness, which is in the intellectual nature; otherwise even brute animals would be to God's image. Therefore, as in their intellectual nature, the angels are more to the image of God than man is, we must grant that, absolutely speaking, the angels are more to the image of God than man is, but that in some respects man is more like to God."

22. Péguy, *The Portal of the Mystery of Hope*, 45–46.

2

Incarnated Intentionality as Crucial
Signatory of the Afterlife

WITH PÉGUY, WE SEEK to clarify the importance of our integral humanity when unpacking the conceptual and existential difficulties in justly raising heaven above a phenomenal vacuity. It is critical that we recognize the unbroken thread in all human experience: any act of thought, engagement, experience places us simultaneously *inward*—through and beyond ourselves into our originary filiation with the uncreated as mystery at root in all things, and *outward*—into the other *as other* of our shared world of incarnality. It is never one or the other, all human experiences place us within this dynamic twofold intentionality that stretches human persons beyond themselves in order to be themselves.[1] No human person is a static entity, a closed essence; the union of body and rational soul, flesh and spiritual *tending*, allows us to experience, to be experienced, and to experience being experienced.[2] To think is to think

1. Merleau-Ponty sensed this intensifying, layered tending when critical of the Cartesian view of epistemology. See Merleau-Ponty, "Eye and Mind," *The Primacy of Perception*, 170: "A Cartesian does not see *himself* in the mirror; he sees a dummy, an 'outside,' which, he has every reason to believe, other people see in the very same way but which, no more for himself than for others is not a body in the flesh. His 'image' in the mirror is an effect of the mechanics of things. If he recognizes himself in it, if he thinks it 'looks like him,' it is his thought that weaves this connection. The mirror image is nothing that belongs to him."

2. Cf. Engelland, *Phenomenology*, 5–6: "But as obvious a point as it is, it must nonetheless be made: there would be no science if there were no scientists. And there would

of things, to be a being *of* and in the midst of presences, persons, places, relations. This interiorization of the other, which includes the form of self that the other has previously exteriorized, and the exteriorization of the self, which includes a form of the other previously interiorized, evokes the very essence of conversation.[3] This inward and outward process of becoming the other *as other* is grounded on our participation in God's uncreated *To Be*, which is epiphanically experienced in us as moving and incarnated images of eternity.[4] This is the intentional or *tending* structure inherent in all human acts[5] and only by grasping this thread can we encounter what eludes us in death, and understand why the "better place" terribly undercuts the magnificent fulfilment of intentionality in heaven, more magnified in the resurrected state. This understanding of a genuine phenomenologically informed Thomistic view of human nature retains the notion of nature so viciously deconstructed within postmodernity— and to its detriment, rendering philosophy varying degrees of sophistic dress up. It also refuses to reduce that nature to the failed juxtaposition of form and matter, act and potency, which cannot set up the crisis of death as torn separation of the human essence and experience. Nor can it approach, let alone encounter, the dramatic courtship with our nature that

---

be no scientists without the peculiarly human way of wondering why something is the way it is rather than other, and this very act of wondering which gives rise to science, is unthinkable apart from a general account of presence and the way we are able to experience and express the truth of things. The blind spot of contemporary science, an inability to locate itself in the picture it generates, serves as a primary focus for the field of philosophy called phenomenology. No account of the whole can be complete if it doesn't make sense of our curious wonder about the whole. And no account of wonder can be complete if it doesn't explain the presence of perception, not as the juxtaposition of two things, but instead as our openness to a field of experience." If the natural world is naturally supernatural, and revelatory in its cruciform incarnation, then phenomenological *intentio* as recovering our openness to the ground of experience has a unique role to play in revealing heaven as the only permanent home for beings who have such a peculiar wonder, activity, and receptivity.

3. Cf. Levinas, *Totality and Infinity*, 51: "To approach the Other in conversation is to welcome his expression, in which at each instant he overflows the idea a thought would carry away from it. It is therefore to receive from the Other beyond the capacity of the I, which means exactly: to have the idea of infinity. But this also means: to be taught. The relation with the Other, or Conversation, is a non-allergic relation, an ethical relation; but inasmuch as it is welcomed this conversation is a teaching. Teaching is not reducible to *maieutics*; it comes from the exterior and brings me more than I contain. In its non-violent transitivity the very epiphany of the face is produced."

4. Plato, *Timaeus*, 37c-d.

5. Cf. ST I, 85

human persons are granted through the body and blood of the God-man.[6]

> Believe with Saint Thomas that the intellectual incompleteness
> of the human soul needs the body in order to become an intel-
> lectual whole, and you are forced to believe both that the unity
> of human nature is intellectual and that death is—may I say
> it—an offense against that unity. . . . Why should Saint Thomas
> have said that for the soul of man to be separated from its body
> is against its nature, unless the human essence requires both
> body and soul for the constitution of that essence? What is death
> then? Is it simply a separation of the soul from the body, or is
> it the breakup of the human essence? On purely philosophi-
> cal grounds, Saint Thomas stands in the way of conceding the

6. Cf. Hume, *Human Understanding*, 77–94. With all of Hume's reaction to the rationalist's reduction, through his epistemological modesty, his could never be the gatekeeper of genuine mystery. Beings in flesh are not such nominal and private experience that any universality to things is agreed upon by convention. To concede to such a position may allow a pseudo-conserving sociological religion, but it could never reflect the relationality within Christianity, nor approach the *kenotic* and theological powerhouse of human relationships with the God-man which intrinsically direct us to heaven. "Nothing can ever be present to the mind but an image or perception, and that the senses are only the inlets, through which these images are conveyed, without being able to produce any immediate intercourse between the mind and the object." In the Humean project, there is always an irreconcilability between the perception of any object and the independent reality of the object. And because of this unseemly incongruity, what we call knowledge is weakened to a relativized perception and what perception is, is not the real thing, but the private mental image that is, again, something *other* than the thing itself. If it is not knowledge, what can we know? We can certainly have a nomadic life of horizontal and cyclical perceptions as mental images that guide our preferences and normative value systems, and we may also assign conventional patterns to them, but the question of knowledge as foundational, grounding, eternal, transcendent is a non-starter, an impossibility, a vestige of an irrelevant philosophical and theological past. Here we can recognize why phenomenology was so instrumental in dilating again the once closed question of divine meaning. How someone like St. Edith Stein converted from an absentee and atheistically inclined Jew to a Catholic and a nun killed in Auschwitz. Husserlian phenomenology with its celebrated "turn to the things themselves" recognized that so-called incongruity between the changing perception of the object and the real object as steady and unchanging. Instead of forming the same solipsistic and reductive conclusion as Hume, which wholly subordinated knowledge to a positivistic shadowland, Husserl envisioned a process of knowledge where the changing perception participates in, and actually unveils, the unchanging object, presenting it in many degrees of the object's reality. In doing so, his intentionality recovered the classic Aristotelian and Thomistic principle that the soul *is* in a way all things. See Husserl, *Cartesian Meditations*, 147. For Husserl, human beings are intentional or *tending* beings, co-extensive with the world, and it must be "recognized that the otherness of 'someone else' becomes extended in the whole world as its "Objectivity," giving it this sense in the first place."

second alternative, and the question is to know how to understand this formidable philosophical fact. Indeed, we seem to
be in a dilemma. We cannot deny death as a fact of nature, but
neither can we deny that, in constituting the human essence,
soul and body belong together. They belong so much so that the
Saint Thomas who said that it was against the nature of the soul
to be without the body has also said that the separated soul was,
according to its nature, in an unnatural condition. Thus, the
more we see immortality and death in the light of the unity of
man's nature, the more we wonder what to say about either one.
Can we simply let the parts of human nature go their respective
ways? Saint Thomas the metaphysician is saying we cannot. Immortality, even when it involves the separation of the soul from
the body, cannot include that separation as part of its meaning.
After all, what is an immortality that includes an unnatural condition? And what can we say about the death of the body, even if
it be called a natural event in the world of bodies, if that death is
against the nature of the soul and therefore the economy of the
human essence? Admit the unity of human nature, therefore, as
Saint Thomas conceives it, and you cannot think of either the
death of the body or the separation of the soul from the body
as natural.[7]

The intentionality we seek is a robust and fully existential realism
wherein knowledge's immaterial mode of existence does not imply divorce from the embodied givenness of the world.[8] Intentionality is quite

7. Pegis, "St. Thomas and the Meaning of Human Existence," 63.

8. Cf. Searle, *Intentionality*, 230: "My basic assumption is simply this: . . . The brain
is all we have for the purpose of representing the world to ourselves and everything we
can use must be inside the brain. Each of our beliefs must be possible for a being who
is a brain in a vat because *each of us is precisely a brain in a vat*; the vat is a skull and
the "messages" coming in are coming in by way of impacts on the nervous system." In
terms of the question of death, if we take the understanding of knowledge in Hume's
sense and extend it to its natural and regrettable end, we have a bedfellow of the sci-
entism to which so much of society is held hostage. In John Searle's understanding of
knowledge, we are a series of sensory impulses so that the brain is no longer a tool for
reasoning but equivalent to reasoning itself. Searle makes a category mistake, never
questioning how we can *experience* experiences, and denudes the person from the
biological process, from the genuine two-fold tending of beings in flesh. Just as the
hammer or a lamp is a tool, neither the hammer or the lamp captures the experience
or reality it produces, it may serve to issue those experiences, but it cannot experience
them. So is the difference between the brain as processor of stimuli, and the person
who utilizes the tools the brain gives and can *experience* those experiences. Should we
be purely passive, we would be a living receptacle for particular sense impressions,
but we would not be able to initialize or actualize an event where these meanings

dramatically that capacity to become the other *as other* immaterially, unified inwardly toward the uncreated, and outwardly within the flesh which seeks the divine. It refers to the immaterial mode of existence and to the soul's capacity to assume, and to put on the world (the other, created and uncreated); it is intrinsically relational.[9] Recovering this incarnational two-fold intentionality will also help us to place flesh at the center of any understanding of death, hell, purgatory, as fully realized only in the resurrected state.

---

take place. In a word, we would not be able to evoke the experience *as experience*, thus unable to understand the intelligibilizing unity related to those sense impressions. Passivity is an important part of our human experience since it involves an intrinsic openness to take in the vast dimensions of earthly experience and, more so, entails that these experiences are inherently *particular* insofar as it is one's own sense organs receiving the world. But to call impressions genuine experiences without any active sense of agency is seriously misleading and precisely what occurs in such scientisms, which equate biochemical signals of the brain with understanding and personhood. This, again, conflates the tool that aids to issue experiences with the very persons who experience the tool, *experience* the experiences, and experience themselves, who in the act of knowledge must necessarily and primordially transcend themselves. The act of knowledge is no mere "brain in a vat," this would perhaps raise us to the level of a world-less sensing, but not knowledge. There would be the tools for processing but nothing to engage those tools. Knowledge is the *under*-standing of sensation and experience within the step-back structure of consciousness. And it is precisely this step-back that reveals knowledge *as* knowledge, and persons *as* persons, and it is this knowledge that grants us a true glimpse of paradise.

9. Through this *intentio*, the knowability of that material reality has been objectified in the intelligible species and by which the soul is objectified, becoming the other as other. Phenomenologically, we can see this in the intensifying depth of shared human experience, that evokes time, memory, contingency, intimacy, and universality. The child, for instance, shows her father the fresh scrape received from slipping on the damp fallen autumn leaves, and his memories can well transport him to a nearly identical experience. In knowledge, we take in the phenomena of the skin tattered on the heels of the palm and on the knees, and we can recreate in our affective imagination the sting of the disinfectant poured over the sink, and also the wincing hesitancy as one waits for the sting to commence, as well as the relief that such pain is over far quicker than expected. What occurs in the father is not only an empathetic act which can be shared with animals, but a resurrecting of a knowledge present within him. Human knowledge places us on the horizon between time and eternity, it an immanent act that abstracts the real things itself from the material world. We know the real thing immateriality, not estimations, or sensible images, or caricatured emotions, but the fundamental totality of the thing in its *thingness* and the event in its *eventfulness*. In being, we are always extending beyond ourselves in relation to the world. For all the claims that an idea or position or view is "universal" or "global," only the act of human knowledge places the human person within that global habit of Being.

When we speak of intentionality as the knowledge of the other *as* other, what do we mean? We mean that, contra Cartesianism in all its forms, we know the other *as* other, not *as* ourselves, not subjective servants to the ego, but in its alterity and unique existence. We are *in* the world, *of* the world, and even *as* the world in its radical *To Be*. This is not mere "objectivism" but the soul's unique participation in the mysterious otherness of the world, and particularly the irreducible otherness of human persons, and the absolute Otherness of God. We are all responsible *for* others because each of us is a result of responding to others in such a way that our very temporality is altered, i.e., how we see ourselves in the past, in shifting memories, in the anticipated future and our power to cultivate said future or not. This primordial intentionality is not something we are able to choose or refuse; it naturally/intrinsically occurs by virtue of being ourselves in action. Recognizing this community of beings changes the understanding of what constitutes personhood. Our thought processes are not a compilation of vaguely phenomenal egos, somehow independent and distinct. Instead, what we call "our own thoughts" are always manifestly tied and bonded to others/otherness as inward towards the un-created and outward amidst finite beings. This tending is a spiritual and familial scaffolding (*oikos*), we graft the very architecture of the world, foreshadowing the hope that, through Christ, we co-substantiate the architecture of paradise, befitting the shared unrepeatability of our human natures. Only when we recognize that sheer primal interconnectedness of intentionality can we approach human flesh[10] as signatory of Christ's flesh. Only when we experience that that which lays at the center of our own soul has always laid in the center of another, can we encounter how Christ's incarnation brought a glimpse of heaven to earth through love and responsibility. The human soul here is not something poured into the body, but a dual unity of *tending* flesh. This incarnational

---

10. Cf. Engelland, *Phenomenology*, 45–46: "Flesh is the living body, which both feels and can be felt, both sees and can be seen. As we experience the world, flesh advertises to others our experiential engagement with things. By opening the world for us and for each other together, it readies us to speak about things and register them in their truth. Pick up a stone in your hand. It's cold and smooth. Turn it over, grasp it. Note how it feels good to finger its rounded contours. Plunge it in the water; feel the coolness of the water on your hand but also see how the wetness brings out vividly the stones natural coloration; the light plays so beautifully off the glossy finish. Your own flesh allows this lifeless thing to be made manifest as it is. . . . Flesh opens us up to explore the world and meet with not only things but also fellow explorers of things."

intentionality, where we become the other *as other*, involves every avenue of human comportment. It is:

A. a *metaphysical phenomenology* as the simultaneous two-fold tending towards otherness, inwardly in filiation with the uncreated *To Be*, and exteriorly within the netting of finite beings; this is the first scaffold of our being-in-the-world.

B. an *epistemological ethics* as a lifetime's interiorization of the other, which includes the form of self the other has, repeatedly in varying degrees, previously exteriorized. And the exteriorization of the self, which includes a form of the other has, repeatedly in varying degrees, previously interiorized.[11] This is the daily scaffold of being-in-the-world.

C. a *theological mystique* as co-substantiating the ethical, spiritual, moral, and aesthetic architecture of the world as foreshadowing the gift of co-substantiating, through union with Christ's flesh, the architecture of heaven. This is the intentional fulfillment of our being-in-the-world.

Incarnational intentionality is realized in the *apokálypsis* of Christ as bread of life. Christ who is one in being with heaven, entered the world, descended into hell—making hell *real*—and resurrected in his glorified body to complete the transcendental Beauty of intentionality, which death interrupts. How can we complete becoming the other *as other*, how can we know ourselves, if death is the torn separation of the

---

11. Cf. Levinas, "Meaning and Sense," *Basic Philosophical Writings*, 54: "Let us for the moment attend to the sense which the abstraction or nudity of a face which breaks into the order of the world involves and the overwhelming of consciousness which corresponds to this 'abstraction'. Stripped of its very form, a face shivers in its nudity. It is a distress. The nudity of a face is a denuding, and already a supplication in the straightforwardness that looks at me. But this supplication is an exigency; in it, humility is joined with height. The ethical dimension of visitation is thereby indicated. . . . A face imposes itself upon me without my being able to be deaf to its call or to forget it, that is, without my being able to suspend my responsibility for its distress. Consciousness loses its first place. The presence of the face thus signifies an irrecusable, a command, which puts a stop to the availability of consciousness. Consciousness is called into question by the face. Being called into question is not the same as becoming aware of this being called into question. The 'absolute other' is not reflected in consciousness. It resists it to the extent that even its resistance is not convertible into a content of consciousness. Visitation consists in overwhelming the very egoism of the I which supports this conversion. A face confounds the intentionality that aims at it."

human person, the rupture of the human essence? Christ's flesh completes what ours could not, it completes the *intentio* where ours stalls again and again, experienced in grief over the death of the other: "ring out the grief that saps the mind for those that here we see no more."[12] We tend toward the uncreated and toward the finite, and through both, we find Christ as the revelation of a redeemed intentionality, as the Other which can enable us to complete otherness and thus become ourselves. Christ not only completes in us what we have failed to complete, but gifts us with co-substantiating his wounds, which are the architecture of the church and family, the glimpses of heaven on earth, and through them we traverse the celestial architecture to come: "Now I rejoice in my sufferings for you, and I am completing in my flesh what is lacking in Christ's afflictions for His body, that is, the church."[13]

> For my flesh is real food and my blood is real drink. Whoever eats my flesh and drinks my blood remains in me, and I in them. Just as the living Father sent me and I live because of the Father, so the one who feeds on me will live because of me. This is the bread that came down from heaven. Your ancestors ate manna and died, but whoever feeds on this bread will live forever.[14]

12. Tennyson, *In Memoriam*, 167.

13. Col 1:24.

14. John 6:56–58.

3

Intentionality Denied
as Threshold to Hell

L'oeil était dans la tombe et regardait Cain

Cain, sleeping not, dreamed at the mountain foot.
Raising his head, in that funereal heaven
He saw an eye, a great eye, in the night
Open, and staring at him in the gloom.
"I am too near," he said, and tremblingly woke up
His sleeping sons again, and his tired wife,
And fled through space and darkness. Thirty days
He went, and thirty nights, nor looked behind;
Pale, silent, watchful, shaking at each sound;
No rest, no sleep, till he attained the strand
Where the sea washes that which since was Asshur.
  . . .
"You see naught now," said Zillah then, fair child
The daughter of his eldest, sweet as day.
But Cain replied, "That Eye—I see it still."
And Jubal cried (the father of all those
That handle harp and organ): "I will build
A sanctuary;" and he made a wall of bronze,
And set his sire behind it. But Cain moaned,
"That Eye is glaring at me ever." Henoch cried:
"Then must we make a circle vast of towers,

So terrible that nothing dare draw near;
Build we a city with a citadel;
Build we a city high and close it fast."

. . .

It seemed a city made for hell. Its towers,
With their huge masses made night in the land.
The walls were thick as mountains. On the door
They graved: "Let not God enter here." This done,
And having finished to cement and build
In a stone tower, they set him in the midst.
To him, still dark and haggard, "Oh, my sire,
Is the Eye gone?" quoth Zillah tremblingly.
But Cain replied: "Nay, it is even there."
Then added: "I will live beneath the earth,
As a lone man within his sepulchre.
I will see nothing; will be seen of none."
They digged a trench, and Cain said: "'Tis enow,"
As he went down alone into the vault;
But when he sat, so ghost-like, in his chair,
And they had closed the dungeon o'er his head,
The Eye was in the tomb and fixed on Cain.[1]

SUCH A DEMANDING INTENTIONALITY, as we have struggled to describe, has the very real power to be experienced as a liminal hell. Because it involves such relationality, responsibility, trust—particularly theological trust, and surrender, those that seek to gain the upper hand in this courtship, to alienate its givenness, or shirk its demands, experience its ubiquitous presence as entities ever in the throes of death, as caricatures hollowed out by their refusal to bear the otherness of Being. In Hugo's poem, Cain and his brethren have attempted to disconnect the incarnational intentionality at root in all human identity and experience. But because this *intentio* is primordial and intrinsic to our personhood, Cain is haunted by the uncreated Otherness of God, both in himself and through his relations with others. Ontologically, his attempts to sever the bonds of otherness have promoted an unravelling of his very being, for that which is foundational will only return as a haunting presence, realizing the threat of willful death that Cain has placed upon himself. Because Cain has attempted to sever the relationalities that make us, for we are always the other *as other* and thus *responsible*, the tomb symbolizes his ethical emptiness: the

1. Hugo, "La Conscience," *La Légende des Siècles*, Bk. II.

emptying of his personhood when being confronted by the faces—most especially God's—that he failed to escape, and that helped form his self as guilty conscience. Cain is attempting to complete in himself his nature outside of the otherness that always points through our flesh to the Divine, to heaven as permanent home. In doing so, this uproots his specifically human comportment and temporality as an *intentio* resolved only beyond himself. It curls temporality back upon that vacated self, creating another kind of time, deforming us from "moving images of eternity" to static glaciers of anti-eternality. Cain has become the torn separation of soul from body, *before* his death. He has, in his refusal to acknowledge the responsibility of his incarnational *tending*, dissolved any access into true freedom. The ever-following eye is viewed as threat, carrier of doom, but it is for the truthful other *as other*, the purgative invitation to our two-fold intentionality. But Cain refuses to look interiorly, or stretch himself exteriorly; he and his tribe run from the very sight needed in order to claim themselves as their own.

Their efforts to build walls, cities, cultures are not unlike the attacks on Western culture that demand the death of the family and of the church. But there is no remolding or making of a utopia on the rubble of a so-called post-Christian world. No matter where Cain travels, the eye *apocalyptically* follows him and remains with him, hollowing him out within the tomb. His disintegration is his own doing, as hell is always our own project.

> It is terminologically misleading to speak of the eternity of Hell. Eternity, in the strict sense, applies only to God, who stands above time and is Lord over time. A created being can participate in God's eternity if it receives from God a share in His glory. The damned, by contrast, is not eternal, nor does God grant him a share in glory. His lot is another form of being, which is an expression of his despair and hopelessness: endlessness, everlastingness. Thus, sin does not live eternally, but fixates man in such a way that he is trapped in an unchangeable rigidity that no longer desires conversion and no longer seeks forgiveness.[2]

Cain has, indeed, trapped himself in such an "unchangeable rigidity" that he vitiates the desire for conversion and forgiveness. And today, we see this anti-intentionality as precursor to hell in the many forms of failed conscience that flirt with the un-person that Balthasar describes as

2. Remarks by Otto Betz in Balthasar, *Dare We Hope*, 101–2.

Satan.[3] Below are four forms of failed conscience, where intentionality has been denied, obscured, wounded, even razed to the ground.[4] Each form represents aspects of hell realized on earth and of the twilight of Christ within the culture. Our fourth form—*the conscience of failed love*—to which I will devote the most attention, carries with it profound layers of suffering and, because of this, it still has access to an intentionality that is salvific rather than damning. In order for us to encounter and appreciate how heaven fulfills our nature, how genuine intentionality has *always* been the signatory of our paradisal home, we must, like Christ, descend a little into the earthly hells we have created by our self-imposed exiles from God and otherness.

The Sophistic Conscience

This is reserved for those who give a great deal of thought to how they are perceived while sidestepping any purgative sense of goodness. They shirk the idea of being viewed as callous, conscienceless, or cowardly; such views would render them naked, and expose them in their state of phenomenal vacuity. There is a recognition of incarnational *intentio*, but it is always viewed as a more troublesome than worthwhile pursuit. Such a one pantomimes a pseudo-intentionality misconceiving this "going through the motions" as the way to navigate or outwit death. This inability to bear the gaze of the other is what enflames hell as self-alienation.

---

3. Balthasar, *Dare We Hope*, 114: "To what extent the concept 'person' can still be applied to the satanic being. For being a person always presupposes a positive relation to some fellow person, a form of sympathy or at least natural inclination and involvement. Precisely this, however, would no longer be predicable of a being that had, in its entirely made a radical decision against God, or absolute love; thus, we would have to join J. Ratzinger in speaking of an 'un-person,' of the 'disintegration and collapse of personhood,' for which reason it is characteristic of the devil 'appears without a face and why his being unrecognizable is his real strength.' . . . 'He works in an impersonal, indeed, in a virtually person-dissolving way.'"

4. Nietzsche has an apt image of such denuding and destructive intentionality. See Nietzsche, *Aphorisms on Love and Hate*, 49: "*Too Close.* If we live in too close proximity to a person, it is as if we keep touching a good etching with our bare fingers; one day we have poor, dirty paper in our hands and nothing more. A human being's soul is likewise worn down by continual touching; at least it finally *appears* that way to us—we never see its originary design and beauty again. One always loses by all-too-intimate association with women and friends; and sometimes one loses the pearl of his life in the process."

Polus, the obsequiously sycophantic student of the notable rhetorician Gorgias, exudes this type of failed intentional conscience, most particularly in his embarrassing defense of his teacher.[5] Polus admonishes Socrates for bad form, for not following the unwritten rules of civil society; Socrates should not have raised the question as to whether the rhetorician could and should teach justice. For Polus, it is an inappropriate question aimed to hurt precisely because no sensible civil person would ever deny that he knows what justice is and that he can teach it![6] Polus is accusing Socrates of manipulating Gorgias into a corner, asking Gorgias to defend his good values; this is in poor taste, it is a boorishness (*agroikia*) on the part of Socrates. Towards the end of their exchange, Socrates gets the upper hand on Polus, because the latter cannot bear the gaze of the other. Socrates begins by getting Polus openly to agree that rhetoric would only be doing good if it helped to enable the guilty to accuse himself and to seek his punishment.[7] But because it is used often to defend the criminal and to secure gains from injustice, rhetoric becomes ignoble.[8] Polus cannot publicly deny that the conclusions follow from the premises, but the results are absurd (*atopa*) and secretly contrary to the very aims of his "art" or profession. Polus, though, is embarrassed not by his conscience, like Gorgias, but merely by the sting of defeat. He is bound to the so-called rules of "polite" society—that it is better always to appear just. The just man who looks guilty for Polus is foolish and in a worse position than the unjust man who appears just. Polus, as sophistic conscience, pantomimes agreement, feigns intentionality, in order to satisfy the appearance of justice.

> SOCRATES: Then for the purpose of defending one's own guilt
> or that of his parents or friends or children, or his country when
> guilty, Polus, rhetoric is of no use whatever—unless we should
> on the contrary assume that a man ought to accuse himself first

5. Plato, *Gorgias*, 461b-481b.

6. Cf. Plato, *Gorgias*, 461b-c: "What, Socrates? Is what you are saying your true opinion about rhetoric? Or do you imagine just because Gorgias was ashamed not to admit that the rhetorician will know the just also and the honorable and the good, and that, if any man came to him without this knowledge, he himself would instruct him, and then, as result, I suppose, of this admission a contradiction arose in the argument —which is just what you love and you yourself steer the argument in that direction— why, who do you think will deny that he himself knows the right and will teach it to others? But it is the height of bad taste to lead discussions into such channels."

7. Plato, *Gorgias,* 480b-d.

8. Plato. *Gorgias.* 480e-481b.

and foremost, and then his kinsfolk and any friend who at any time is guilty of wrongdoing, and that he ought not to hide the evil away but bring it to light in order that the culprit may be punished and regain his health. And he should prevail upon himself and the others not to play the coward but to submit as a patient submits bravely with closed eyes to the knife or cautery of the surgeon, ever pursuing what is good and honorable and heeding not the pain, but if his guilty deeds be worthy of flogging, submitting to the lash; if of imprisonment, to bonds; if of a fine, to the payment thereof; if of exile, to exile; if of death, to death. He should be the first to accuse himself and his kinsmen, and should use rhetoric for the sole purpose of exposing his own misdeeds and ridding himself of the greatest of all evils, wickedness. Are we to accept this or not, Polus?

POLUS: To me it seems fantastic, Socrates, but I suppose it is consistent with what was said before.

SOCRATES: Then surely we must disprove that, or else this view must follow.

POLUS: Yes, that is so.[9]

The Parasitical Conscience

This predatory form of anti-intentionality is strange and unnerving, for it is often the most honest with respect to its condition, and the least in bad faith.[10] Such a failed conscience understands the power of forming perspectives, the place of opinions in manipulating others. The parasitical conscience recognizes intentionality—much like the demons recognize Christ[11]—but chooses to create a fully opposed form of it, one where we do not know ourselves in the face of otherness, but subsume the other in order to cut off the possibility of knowledge, to immanentize transcendence, to alienate selves out of existence.[12] This conscience only exists

9. Plato, *Gorgias*, 480b-e.

10. Cf. Sartre, "Patterns of Bad Faith," *Being and Nothingness*, 96–111.

11. Matt 8:28–30; Mark 1:34.

12. Cf. Sartre, remarks on *No Exit* in 1965 (reference in Grippe, "The Hell of Our Choosing: Sartre's Ethics," *Ethics and Phenomenology*, 118): "'Hell is other people' has always been misunderstood. It has been thought that what I meant by that was that our relations with other people are always poisoned, that they are invariably hellish relations. But what I really mean is something totally different. I mean that if relations

by feeding on others; rather than relationality, one has a host and vector entrapment, where the parasitical conscience forms hell in the diminishing returns of undone otherness.

> When I say I'm cruel, I mean I can't get on without making people suffer. Like a live coal. A live coal in another one's heart. When I'm alone I flicker out. For six months I flamed away in her heart, till there was nothing but a cinder. One night she got up and turned on the gas while I was asleep. Then she crept back into bed. So now you know.[13]

The Conscience of Unreflected Desire

One often sees little threat in those void of reflective depth, and exuding shallowness, and yet it is precisely because of this anti-reflexive conscience that genuine intentionality is at its most perilous state. This is a state of almost primordial conscienceless. Here, the person does not think or give a second glance to any actions beyond herself. She does not think in terms of the presence of conscience as the others do. The sophistic conscience may fail in conscience but has reflected on how it should "look," and the parasitical conscience is indifferent to its own failure, but well knows what happens to those around her. But the conscience of unreflected desire is something different altogether. Usually, all human desire must somehow be reflective, turn towards itself and decide to have or enact conscience in relation to that desire, to increase, transform, or cease that desire. But a vacant will-based conscience has almost instinctively avoided the ever-present demands of intentionality, and codified its pure unexamined desires by never enacting the self-with-others reflection that develops conscience. Such a person desires, as if without thought, the continuation of her desire to be desired in all things as her sole desire. And unnervingly, this conscience is at ease with becoming

---

with someone else are twisted, vitiated, then that other person can only be Hell. Why? Because . . . when we think about ourselves, when we try to know ourselves, . . . we use the knowledge of us which other people already have. We judge ourselves with the means other people have and have given us for judging ourselves. Into whatever I say about myself someone else's judgment always enters. Into whatever I feel within myself someone else's judgment enters. . . . But that does not at all mean that one cannot have relations with other people. It simply brings out the capital importance of all other people for each one of us."

13. Inez in Sartre's *No Exit*, 27.

an object for others, and fine with them making her an object in turn, as long as that ever-forward desire remains intact. This is Kierkegaard's "vain and wanton woman"[14] whose use of the reflective mirror is not a parable for intentionality but its very opposite. We tend to think of mirrors as a window to the soul, to conscience, but here the paradox is that the mirror is the opposite of conscience, it is the presence of pure appearance reflected back, with nothing other than conscienceless appearance, and unexamined or unreflected desire. Such a conscience has the least depth and yet this poses little problem for she hasn't given it a thought. To do so would be to lessen that desire of hers, to open it to the question of conscience, potentially to stop the forward movement of her being desired in all others as her desire. But again, such a conscience hasn't given that any examined/reflective thought. Such a conscience of unreflected desire is the perfect template for political upheaval and for cultural discord and disintegration.[15]

> The polis offers the opportunity for full actualization of human nature. The fully actualized man is the *spoudaios*, the mature man, who has developed his *dianoetic* excellences and whose life is oriented by his noetic self. . . . Under pretext of respect for the freedom of conscience they ignore the fact that conscience, however "good" it may be putatively, can only be as good as the man who has it. A theory of conscience that shies away from ontology, and in particular from a theory of the nature of man, is empty; it is a parlor game in which one can indulge as long as the surrounding society contains enough Christian substances to make at least the worst sort of good consciences socially ineffective; but even under such favorable conditions . . . this nihilistic theory of conscience contributes to the intellectual and moral confusion that paves the way for the best of all consciences, viz., that of the totalitarian killers. All men are equal, to be sure, or they would not be individuals of one species; but sometimes it is forgotten that the point in which they most certainly are equal is their capacity for evil. Enough of that evil is rampant; and this is no time to pat the viciously ignorant on the back for being "sincere," or abiding by their "conscience." This is a time for the philosopher to be aware of his authority, and to assert it, even if that brings him into conflict with an environment infested by

14. Kierkegaard, "The Quiet Despair," *Parables*, 87.

15. Today, we see it everywhere, under the banners of woke ideology, abortion on demand, critical race theory; it is a lethal dose performed while asleep. And here hell marches forward and intoxicates the soul with an unknowing but accepting rapidity.

dubious ideologies and political theologies—so that the word of
Marcus Aurelius will apply to him: "The philosopher—the priest
and servant of the gods."[16]

The Conscience of Failed Love: Long Day's Journey into Night

In our three previous failed forms of intentionality, where consciences
create precursors to the self-alienation in hell, we have seen little legacy
of love in relationships with others; there is a dearth of good desire for the
best in the other. At each of their cores, these consciences are irremedi-
ably cruel and, again, approach something of the existential "un-person"
found in the metaphysics of the satanic. But what about the conscience
that *tends* towards love, but tends in failed ways, in partial truths, in lies
hoping to bring about good ends?[17] Such a conscience seems always to
revolve around families—perhaps because heaven, embodied in the Holy
Family, is the pulse and heart of all happy families and the aching fable
for unhappy ones, permeating them with equal parts of hope and neglect,
love and ruin.[18] Let us remember that what shines forth in the Holy Family is the visible flesh of Trinitarian intentionality. Each is knitted into
the other, and through that fabric of body and spirit, of uncreated and
creational tending, of repeated interiorization and exteriorization of the
self and other, the very glory of heaven streams forth, heaven visits earth
in the flesh. This is the model of family to which we are invited.

> Mary was a peerless model of contemplation of Christ. The face
> of the Son belonged to her in a special way because he had been
> knit together in her womb and had taken a human likeness from
> her. No one has contemplated Jesus as diligently as Mary. The

16. Voegelin, *Published Essays: 1953–65*, 45–46.

17. Cf. Dostoevsky, *Demons*, 25–26: "You cannot imagine what sorrow and anger
seize one's whole soul when a great idea, which one has long and piously revered, is
picked up by some bunglers and dragged into the street, to more fools like themselves,
and one suddenly meets it in the flea market, unrecognizable, dirty, askew, absurdly
presented, without proportion, without harmony, a toy for stupid children."

18. So much of Dostoevsky's writings revolve around such a conscience of failed
loves, as if grafted into the family unit and a crucible of divine relationality. See Dostoevsky, *The Brothers Karamazov*, 268: "Nothing is more seductive for man than his
freedom of conscience, but nothing is a greater cause of suffering. And behold, instead
of giving a firm foundation for setting the conscience of man at rest for ever, Thou
didst choose all that is exceptional, vague and enigmatic; Thou didst choose what was
utterly beyond the strength of men."

gaze of her heart was already focused on him at the moment
of the Annunciation, when she conceived him through the action of the Holy Spirit; in the following months she gradually
became aware of his presence, until, on the day of his birth, her
eyes could look with motherly tenderness upon the face of her
son as she wrapped him in swaddling clothes and laid him in
the manger. Memories of Jesus, imprinted on her mind and on
her heart, marked every instant of Mary's existence. She lived
with her eyes fixed on Christ and cherished his every word. . . .
Mary's ability to live by God's gaze is, so to speak, contagious.
The first to experience this was St Joseph. His humble and sincere love for his betrothed and his decision to join his life to
Mary's attracted and introduced him, "a just man" (Matt 1:19),
to a special intimacy with God.[19]

To examine the intentionality of the conscience of failed love—and
failed returns—let us tread carefully within Eugene's O'Neill's veiled autobiographical tragedy[20] *A Long Day's Journey into Night*. In this play, we
have a family as failing image of the Holy Family, and by "failing" we
do not mean the sophistic, parasitical, or the failed desire variants that

19. Pope Benedict XVI, "General Audience," (12/28/11) §1.

20. The play parallels O'Neill's own life, with the character of Edmund patterned
after O'Neill. The summer house style and location correspond with his own actual
summer residence. The surname "Tyrone" in the play is a veiled reference to the surname "O'Neill," as it is the name of the earldom granted to Conn O'Neill by Henry
VIII. In the play Eugene is the middle child who died at a very young age of measles,
and Edmund is the third child of a very difficult birth. Autobiographically, the order is reversed, Edmund died, and Eugene is the third child born in those difficult
circumstances. His mother, Mary Ellen "Ella" Quinlan, reflects the character, Mary
Cavan. And the ages of the persons in the play are the actual ages of the members of
the O'Neill family that Summer of 1912. Eugene O'Neill's father, James O'Neill, was
an actor, he did share the stage with Edwin Booth mentioned in the play. He also did
gain financial success in the title role of Dumas in The Count of Monte Cristo, playing
the title role six thousand times, and was criticized for "selling out." Eugene's mother
Mary attended Catholic school in the Midwest, Saint Mary's College, of Notre Dame,
Indiana. Eugene's older brother Jamie whom he became very close with, did drink
himself to death in 1923. Regarding O'Neill, much of what is described of Edmund
reflects his life. By 1912 he had attended a Princeton for only a single year, spent several years at sea. He also suffered from depression and alcoholism. Like Edmund, he
also contributed to the local newspaper, the *New London Telegraph*, writing poetry as
well as reporting. And O'Neill did go to sanatorium in 1912–13 due to suffering from
consumption/tuberculosis. During that year in the sanatorium, he focused entirely on
playwriting. The events in the play are set immediately prior to O'Neill beginning his
career in earnest and he asked that this play not be published until twenty-five years
after his death (which did not happen).

willfully defect from the womb of that image and likeness. Instead, we are in the presence of a family that desires the good, craves, with disquieting sadness, incarnational intentionality, but fails in their spiritual resources to recover the thread of likenesses that help us to sustain the image of Holy Family. Even the play's opening dedication sets ups this most tragic of human relationality:

> For Carlotta, on our 12th Wedding Anniversary: Dearest: I give you the original script of this play of old sorrow, written in tears and blood. A sadly inappropriate gift, it would seem, for a day celebrating happiness. But you will understand. I mean it as a tribute to your love and tenderness which gave me the faith in love that enabled me to face my dead at last and write this play—write it with deep pity and understanding and forgiveness for all the four haunted Tyrones. These twelve years, Beloved One, have been a Journey into Light—into love. You know my gratitude. And my love! Gene, Tao House July 22, 1941.[21]

Each member of O'Neill's Tyrone family has confused the shadows of Plato's cave with proper likenesses, but even shadows, as Plato knew, bear resemblances to the Good.[22] What is striking about this family is that Mary Tyrone, the mother in the play, reflects in failed form and failing and flailing love, that she is the womb of that family; like Our Lady she is the source that knits the men of the family in likeness, in hope, and every instant of their exchanges is imprinted in her as the mediatrix of their desired redemption.

> In the practical proportions of human history, we come back to that fundamental of the father and the mother and the child. It has been said already that if this story cannot start with religious assumptions, it must none the less start with some moral or metaphysical assumptions, or no sense can be made of the story of man. . . . If we are not of those who begin by invoking a divine Trinity, we must none the less invoke a human Trinity; and see that triangle repeated everywhere in the pattern of the world.[23]

21. O'Neill, *Long Day's Journey into Night*, dedication.

22. Cf. Plato, *Republic* 516b-c: "Last of all he will be able to see the sun, and not mere reflections of him in the water, but he will see him in his own proper place, and not in another; and he will contemplate him as he is. He will then proceed to argue that this is he who gives the season and the years, and is the guardian of all that is in the visible world, and in a certain way the cause of all things which he and his fellows have been accustomed to behold?"

23. Chesterton, *The Everlasting Man*, 44–45.

Long Day's Journey into Night is a sort of foretaste of hell because it is a looking glass through to the estranged heaven within those many "might have beens" that populate all human exchanges. In this domestic tragedy, hidden within the hours of one languishing day, incomplete and partial loves inaugurate both person-dissolution and the art of survival unique to familial love. Unlike the prior three failed forms of conscience, each of our four main characters[24] is heartrendingly permeated with aspects of genuine love for the others, heartfelt concern, and an intentionality desirous for the good in the other. Thus, there is present a *positive* relation and inclination towards the good essential to persons, which was mostly absent in the prior three forms of failed conscience. In this long day, we have a far more frightful version of Sartre's *No Exit* and its secular hell. The Tyrone family are persons seeking to be, to become, to recover, to discover their transcendent personhood. Each is knitted into the lives of the other through love, memory, time, history, space, but the thread unravels as quickly—more quickly perhaps—than can be stitched, rendering each the person-dissolving force for the self and for the other.[25] Here we witness Edmund losing the very hope that keeps him soldiering on in *positive* relationality; he has placed his personhood in the *other* who cannot bear the otherness of selfhood, as he cannot bear the selfhood derived from otherness. If only his mother is still keeping to her drug rehabilitation, if only that glassy, dissociating look in her eye is not what he knows it to be. Can she not gaze at him with redeemed love and through her he will be redeemed? The facade begins to break, he asks her: "What can he believe?" to which Mary responds:

24. James Tyrone, or Tyrone, the father, Mary the mother, Jamie, the eldest son, and Edmund the youngest son born after the death of their middle child who died of measles at age two. The whole tragedy is one of failing love interlaced with both goodwill and lies, blame, guilt, and shame. Each family member has his own netting of love interlaced with unresolved guilt, and lies as protective coverall, directed towards each other member. This is coupled with his own excoriating self-loathing. Mary, for example, blames young Jamie for entering the child's room when he had measles. She blames the husband for always skimping on costs and not getting a top-quality doctor and medical treatment for her. She loves Edmund but nevertheless looks at him with guilt, as the accident, the replacement for the unreplaceable child. Most of all, with a relentlessly quiet destruction, she blames herself: if only she had kept her guard up, had not become comfortable leaving the child in the care of others, he would not be dead.

25. Cf. Dostoevsky, *Demons*, 708: "In sinning, each man sins against all, and each man is at least partly guilty for another's sin. There is no isolated sin. And I am a great sinner, perhaps more than you are."

Nothing, I don't blame you. How could you believe me—when I can't believe myself? I've become such a liar. I never lied about anything once upon a time. Now I have to lie, especially to myself. But how can you understand, when I don't myself. I've never understood anything about it, except that one day long ago I found I could no longer call my soul my own. *She pauses— then lowering her voice to a strange tone of whispered confidence.* But some day, dear, I will find it again—some day when you're all well, and I see you healthy and happy and successful, and I don't have to feel guilty any more—some day when the Blessed Virgin Mary forgives me and gives me back the faith in Her love and pity I used to have in my convent days, and I can pray to Her again—when She sees no one in the world can believe in me even for a moment any more, then She will believe in me, and with Her help it will be so easy. I will hear myself scream with agony, and at the same time I will laugh because I will be so sure of myself. *Then as Edmund remains hopelessly silent, she adds sadly.* Of course, you can't believe that, either. *She rises from the arm of his chair and goes to stare out the windows at right with her back to him—casually.*[26]

To be a person invokes this intrinsic and essential relationality fully realized in the love born of our two-fold *tending*. We acquire our identity through the relationships we have with each other, so much so that there is no stabilized innate nucleus to each person that exists outside that intentionality. And herein lies the drama and danger of human existence, the precarity of human flesh, and of the power of human bonds either to elevate or annihilate the other. This precarity is precisely what Eugene O'Neill unveils for us. Human persons never persist in their own mode of thinking because their beings are always in dynamic phenomenological conversation. Through this incarnating intentionality, we build a profound picture of all human virtues and vices existing only as shared and co-substantiated through Christ's flesh, the salvific experience of love. Love that does not fail is simultaneous with eternity and responsibility. What we mean in love at its highest, deepest, truest, most beautiful is how Boethius describes eternity as identical with his divine love: "The complete and perfect possession of unending life."[27] When we love, we seek the best for the other, not the perishable, but the enduring and perfecting happiness that will fulfill the other. In goodness, we embody

26. O'Neill, *Long Day's*, 96.

27. Boethius, *Consolation*, V, 6: "Aeternitas igitur est interminabilis uitae tota simul et perfecta possession."

true eternity for the other, as the other unveils that goodness for us, and because the *longer way* of likenesses is how we find our *imago dei*, we intensify that love each time we interiorize and exteriorize ourselves in the simultaneous exchange of self and other.[28] To think, for example, of myself in heaven without my children and my husband would cease to be heaven altogether.[29] I would simultaneously not be in heaven, which is no heaven at all, for who I am is wholly bound up in the gifts and love they brought into me and formed through each of their lives of two-fold tending. I would not be I without them, and they would not be they.[30] This is the unbearableness of being-in-the-flesh, but also its song and its poetry. In ways as heartbreaking as deformed, the Tyrone family have pinned their hopes on the others who comprise their little family nucleus. And while they sense the genuine netting of a heaven always forged in the bonds of incarnational intentionality, and cling to its memorial pattern within their beings, they choose the perishable, the lie, the kindly deceit, the denial that shifts responsibility, as the vehicles of their intentionality and familial love.

The Tyrone family members are the most intimate of personal unities, each with a partial view to eternal life, love, happiness. As readers, we experience our own failed intentionality, the relationality of wounded beings, with every instantiation of love and happiness they express for the other. How true it is that persons cannot meaningfully persist without seeking the happiness of the other! So, we witness in them, in spite of themselves, how their spiritual appetites survive because they seek the good. We watch helplessly as each member is given enough substance to reanimate, a little less formed than before, that spiritual ardor, that desire for heaven. And each time it is cut down in all their wrong avenues

28. See 1 Cor 15:55: When St. Paul mockingly taunts death, "O, Death where is thy sting?" this is because he believes with all his body and soul that his relationship with Christ is saturated with such transformative love, that Christ as supreme person completes what is lacking in us. The Son of Man has realized intentionality, as he realizes hell and heaven. He bears that responsibility of our failed love and incomplete otherness, and through his crucifixion, brings his flock into eternal love, life, happiness. True personhood is at its root the loving reality that our happiness and/or fulfillment is always bound up in the other.

29. Cf. Balthasar, *Dare We Hope*, 60: "Can a man be lost if another, anchored in God, is bound to him? To be lost would mean resisting love so violently that it is no longer possible to stay attached to him. But will the refusal to love ever be stronger than the infinite love of the Spirit?"

30. Cf. Waugh, *Brideshead Revisited*, author's note: "I am not I; thou art not he or she; they are not they."

undertaken in the name of love. Each Tryrone attempts to claim responsibility for himself, and for the other, and each recognizes his failures to bear things through, turning to alcohol and drug abuse, to escape the gaze of incarnated intentionality. There is no monster lurking in the corner of that summer house, there is no sinister plot deforming that long day into night. We cannot pin all the failure and all the injustice on some evil outside the intentionality of their failed loves.[31] Each has good intentions that extend forward each day and recede back into incompletion as evening draws to a close. They are, in various ways, exhausted by hopes that cannot be fulfilled and re-animated each day by a far-off sense of liberation that lingers in the air and draws them into bondage. Every day is the promise of resurrection and the descent into hell. Each holds the other captive, not out of lovelessness and cruelty, but out of love that cannot complete, and responsibility that confuses itself with lies. They are persons, not anti-persons entrapping themselves at the threshold of hell, fighting against the loss of their collective personhoods but with spiritually insufficient tools. They can now only love by avoiding, at all costs, the penetrating gaze into the other *as other*. Or if they do, what they see as true must dissolve and become the lie; it must not, cannot, be borne.

> *Frightenedly—with a desperate hoping against hope*
> He's a liar! It's a lie, isn't it, Mama?
> *Keeping her eyes averted.*
> What is a lie? Now you're talking in riddles like Jamie.
> *Then her eyes meet his stricken, accusing look. She stammers.*
> Edmund! Don't!
> *She looks away and her manner instantly regains the quality of strange detachment—calmly.*[32]

31. Cf. Solzhenitsyn, *The Gulag Archipelago*, 168: "If only there were evil people somewhere insidiously committing evil deeds, and it were necessary only to separate them from the rest of us and destroy them. But the line dividing good and evil cuts through the heart of every human being. And who is willing to destroy a piece of his own heart? During the life of any heart this line keeps changing place; sometimes it is squeezed one way by exuberant evil and sometimes it shifts to allow enough space for good to flourish. One and the same human being is, at various ages, under various circumstances, a totally different human being. At times he is close to being a devil, at times to sainthood. But his name doesn't change, and to that name we ascribe the whole lot, good and evil. . . . Socrates taught us: 'Know thyself.' Confronted by the pit into which we are about to toss those who have done us harm, we halt, stricken dumb: it is after all only because of the way things worked out that they were the executioners and we weren't. From good to evil is one quaver, says the proverb. And correspondingly, from evil to good."

32. O'Neill, *Long Day's*, 67.

Our Tyrones are children of Cain entombing themselves as the Eye pursues. We see clearly now how tragic human love really is; how every failure to remain *remains* within us as a failure to remain; something more sacred, more lonely, and wild remains.[33] Shifting between person-dissolution and relentless efforts to undo that disintegration, something nevertheless must remain. They seek to redeem themselves and the others *as* they are being vitiated, because the love in them that makes them relational remains—remains as failure, remains as memory, remains as *ennui*, but remains stained, grafted, transposed, and transfixed within their flesh and blood. It remains in a form muted, muffled, unable to be extracted in any sense of undiluted goodness, and we, like them, stumble around in the basement of Being excavating within ourselves the tiresome litany of wrong words and times.[34] Stubborn and fighting for survival, this hollowed memorial failing love, even in its impotency, enables the Tyrones to retain ghosts of personhood within their collective dissipation. And it is here, with Edmund, that we witness the specific corrupted intentionality that acts out our generationally inherited original sin. Each of us is with him walking into the fog where he can longer see the house, no longer recognize the relationality, where everything can hide within itself as if ghosts can take refuge within ghosts:

> The fog was where I wanted to be. Halfway down the path you can't see this house. You'd never know it was here. Or any of the other places down the avenue. I couldn't see but a few feet ahead. I didn't meet a soul. Everything looked and sounded unreal. Nothing was what it is. That's what I wanted—to be alone with myself in another world where truth is untrue, and life can hide from itself. Out beyond the harbor, where the road runs along the beach, I even lost the feeling of being on land. The fog and the sea seemed part of each other. It was like walking on the bottom of the sea. As if I had drowned long ago. As if I was the ghost belonging to the fog, and the fog was the ghost of the sea.

33. Cf. Levinas, *Totality and Infinity*, 146: "Suicide is tragic, for death does not bring a resolution to all the problems to which birth gave rise, and is powerless to humiliate the values of the Earth—whence Macbeth's final [sic] cry in confronting death, defeated because the universe is not destroyed at the same time as his life. Suffering at the same time despairs for being riveted to being—and loves the being to which it is riveted. It knows the impossibility of quitting life: what tragedy! what comedy! The *taedium vitae* is steeped in the love of the life it rejects; despair does not break with the ideal of joy."

34. Cf. Lewis, *Till We Have Faces*, 293–95.

It felt damned peaceful to be nothing more than a ghost within a ghost.[35]

These ghosts of personhood are a danger to the relational and potentially redemptive love that paradoxically helped create them. This wounded intentionality unveils ghosts of the past that afflict and will not lay buried, phantoms of an unbearable present knocking about upstairs, and specters of a future unworthy of anticipation but anticipated with costly obedience. The Tyrones' tortured temporality is created by bonds fighting to survive the lies, fighting to redeem the family. But these ghosts are as much phantasm as fantasy, they are woven by semblances of truth and this means they are also woven by lies, lies that degrade what remains into shadowy semblances. In this family-conscience of failed love, we recognize in each of us the marriage of lies and truth: it is why the lights must be lowered, why eyes must be averted, why water must replace the dwindling whiskey in the decanter, why confrontations are only made in detachment and anger or drunkenness—in some vehicle that must obscure the truth.

> *Mechanically*. Drink hearty, lad. *They drink. Tyrone again listens to sounds upstairs—with dread*. She's moving around a lot. I hope to God she doesn't come down. *Dully*. Yes. She'll be nothing but a ghost haunting the past by this time. *He pauses—then miserably*. Back before I was born—
> Doesn't she do the same with me? Back before she ever knew me. You'd think the only happy days she's ever known were in her father's home, or at the Convent, praying and playing the piano. *Jealous resentment in his bitterness*. As I've told you before, you must take her memories with a grain of salt.[36]

The term "Mechanically," used several times throughout the play, is in sharp contrast to the raw and primal desires that dominated the dialogue. "Mechanically" gives us an allusion that each family member has surrendered the tools to fight the lies that overtake them. This is not quite true: like hands lobbed off, but still grasping for their weapon of choice, the hearts of the Tyrone men are so wounded, perhaps terminal, but they are still grasping for hope, impossible, absurd hope. The three men hinge everything on Mary somehow not relapsing back into addiction.[37]

35. Edmund to his father. O'Neill, *Long Day's*, 133.

36. O'Neill, *Long Day's*, 139.

37. Cf. O'Neill, *Long Day's*, 78: "The cures are no damned good except for a while, The truth is there is no cure and we've been saps to hope."

If Mary survives, if she accomplishes this sobriety she has never once before completed, somehow their remaining relationality to her that keeps each of them afloat—each as persons with a glimmer of *positive* relationality—could enable them to survive with something *more* substantial. As if she could bring each of them out of the abyss . . . as if the happily ever after of paradise is not the wish of fools, the aged, and the dying.

> It's all right. Glad you did. My dirty tongue. Like to cut it out.
> *He hides his face in his hands—dully.*
> I suppose it's because I feel so damned sunk. Because this time Mama had
> me fooled. I really believed she had it licked. She thinks I always believe
> the worst, but this time I believed the best.
> *His voice flutters.*
> I suppose I can't forgive her—yet. It meant so much. I'd begun to hope, if
> she'd beaten the game, I could, too.
> *He begins to sob, and the horrible part of his weeping is that it appears sober, not the maudlin tears of drunkenness.*[38]

Each Tyrone has unified the impossible: truth and lies, a chimera of failed love, relentlessly *tending* towards love and failure. O'Neill has shown a family thrown spiritually overboard in the storm, in the middle of the swollen ocean, clinging to the other, but oh how they cling! Simultaneously they are the other's life preserver and more secretly their anchor. Each drags the other, one after another, down into the depths. More furiously they grasp hold, seeking genuinely the life preserver of the other's relationality and love, which is still present by way of fallen forms. The Tyrones' grasp with such gutting force because they have each reckoned with the possibility that if even one person was eternally lost in hell, then he or she would be "unable to love unreservedly."[39] They instinctually recognize that something seemingly irremediable and unrecoverable would place itself within their breasts and in their hearts and lungs and every place where spirit dwells if the other sinks down beyond reach.[40] But, again, because their relationality lives by way of the uneasy

38. Jamie to Edmund. O'Neill, *Long Day's*, 165–66.

39. Verweyen, "The Life of All as the Outermost Horizon of Christology," in Balthasar, *Dare We Hope*, 58.

40. Edmund to Tyrone. O'Neill, *Long Day's*, 156: "I lay on the bowsprit, facing

union of truth and lies, each family member is for the other, the weighted chain that drags him down. Jamie's drunken speech to his brother warning him that he seeks his downfall heartrendingly admits so very much. It is a warning-truth *as love*, but wrapped in the nonsense of drunkenness, which can be set aside as falsehood. Edmund believes he mustn't give this nonsense a second thought. He must do so to survive the architecture of this inverted intentionality of failed love at the core of original sin, inherited by us all. The truth must be sidestepped for love's sake, for God's sake if one is to say the truth, packaged in the stuff of tomfoolery or more gravely made to act in the ways that lies behave, speak the truth while enacting a vice:

> What I wanted to say is, I'd like to see you become the greatest success in the world. But you'd better be on your guard. Because I'll do my damnedest to make you fail. Can't help it. I hate myself. Got to take revenge. On everyone else. Especially you. Oscar Wilde's "Reading Gaol" has the dope twisted. The man was dead and so he had to kill the thing he loved. That's what it ought to be. The dead part of me hopes you won't get well. Maybe he's even glad the same has got Mama again! He wants company, he doesn't want to be the only corpse around the house! *He gives a hard tortured laugh.*
>
> Jesus Jamie! You really have gone crazy!
>
> Think it over and you'll see I'm right. Think it over when you're away from me . . . tell people, "I had a brother, but he's dead." And when you come back, look out for me. I'll be waiting to welcome you with that "old pal" stuff, and give you the glad hand, and at the first good chance I get stab you in the back.
>
> Shut up! I'll be God-damned if I listen to you any more—

---

astern, with the water foaming into spume under me, the masts with every sail white in the moonlight, towering high above me. I became drunk with the beauty and singing rhythm of it, and for a moment I lost myself—actually lost my life. I was set free! I dissolved in the sea, became white sails and flying spray, became beauty and rhythm, became moonlight and the ship and the high dim-starred sky! I belonged, without past or future, within peace and unity and a wild joy, within something greater than my own life, or the life of Man, to Life itself! To God, if you want to put it that way. . . . And several other times in my life, when I was swimming far out, or lying alone on a beach, I have had the same experience. Became the sun, the hot sand, green seaweed anchored to a rock, swaying in the tide. Like a saint's vision of beatitude. Like the veil of things as they seem drawn back by an unseen hand. For a second you see—and seeing the secret, are the secret. For a second there is meaning! Then the hand lets the veil fall and you are alone, lost in the fog again, and you stumble on toward nowhere, for no good reason!"

As if he hadn't heard. Only don't forget me. Remember I
warned you—for your sake. Give me credit. Greater love hath
no man than this, that he saveth his brother from himself. *Very
drunkenly, his head bobbing.*[41]

In order to survive the heartaches, the losses, the disappointments,
the comparisons that degrade the other, as well as the exquisite armory of
hurts and sufferings that are inflicted by and on family members, we each
put on masks, the *prosopon* (πρόσωπον). This is the face, countenance,
or persona that aligns more often with appearance rather than reality,
that protects us from the penetrating gaze of our incarnation two-fold
intentionality.[42] The precarity of our embodiment is within the midst of
this mask. The longshot hope is that if we must put on a *prosopon*, which
appears inevitable for worldly survival, we put one on that is virtuous
and transcendent, so as to become one in being with us. Or we remain in
control and can take the mask on and off, deftly balancing reality and illusion, the person and the persona. Perhaps fortune favors us, and we put
on the mask of goodness and by enacting that goodness again and again,
by interiorizing and exteriorizing this mask, the face becomes us. We are
sublimated into its goodness, and we in turn speak *through*, in and to another's soul.[43] But in like manner, can we not also put the mask of lies on
in repeated fashion until we are unsure whether we'd survive without it?
Terror seeps into us: how could we survive without those immanentized
caresses that brush aside reality? Has it all become too indistinguishable,
the truth from the lies? Has the soul gone too far? Have we even forgotten

41. O'Neill, *Long Day's*, 169–70.

42. Cf. Levinas, "Meaning and Sense," *Basic Philosophical Writings*, 53: "The visitation of the face is thus the disclosure of the world. In the concreteness of the world a
face is abstract or naked. It is denuded of its own image. Through the nudity of a face
nudity in itself is first possible in the world. The nudity of a face is a bareness without
any cultural ornament, an absolution, a detachment from its form in the midst of
the production of its form. The face enters into our world from an absolutely foreign
sphere, that is, precisely from an ab-solute, which in fact is the very name for ultimate
strangeness. The signifyingness of a face in its abstractness is in the literal sense of
the term extra-ordinary, outside of every order, every world. How is such a production possible? How can the coming of the Other, the visitation of a face, the absolute
not be—in any way—converted into a revelation, not even a symbolism or a sugges-
tion. How is a face not simply a true representation in which the Other renounces his
alterity?"

43. Cf. Plato, *Alcibiades* cited in Robichaud, *Plato's Persona*, 35: "When Socrates
converses with Alcibiades through words, he isn't addressing your face (*prosopon*), it
seems, but Alcibiades, that is your soul (*psyche*, ψυχή, breath of life itself)."

that the mask is on, because life has come between us and what we'd like to be, so much so that we have become lost forever?

> But I suppose life has made him like that, and he can't help it. None of us can help the things life has done to us. They're done before you realize it, and once they're done they make you do other things until at last everything comes between you and what you'd like to be, and you've lost your true self forever.[44]

In *Long Day's Journey into Night*, each family member has a mask 1) to keep the relationality of family love intact through the meals together, drink comradery, living room conversations, the intimate pleasantries of family life, while 2) protecting oneself from the haunting truths that will immeasurably upend family bonds—Mary's abuse of morphine again; her resentfulness regarding Jamie's hand in the death of Eugene; her regret over having another child, Edmund, wishing he'd never been born; Edmund's disease that might kill him; Jamie's resentfulness of living in his brother's shadow within the family, and his father's shadow professionally; that James Tyrone is guilty for selecting the cheap treatment that promoted his wife's addiction, and on and on. But what happens when the masks are removed in such a circumstance as the Tyrone family? Especially when each mask has fastened itself onto the face, fused itself to the flesh, used the face's blood vessels to supply the mask with color, contour, and texture? How can it be pulled apart without destroying the bearer beneath? What happens when this wounded intentionality of failed love is interiorized on the basis of a vicious surrogate for the uncreated, such as false hope, where futurity doubles as spiritual stagnation and deadening indecision? And what happens when family members exteriorize their mask for the others, offering primarily heaping piles of defected love, boundless fear, self-loathing, regret, not only unresolved, but repeatedly hidden and brushed aside in order to protect the good? Where then can the good be found in such a circumstance as this? Faith is not, nor ever has been, magic. Where is the inkling of heaven on earth found in flesh, from God to man?

> Nothing, I don't blame you. How could you believe me—when I can't believe myself? I've become such a liar. I never lied about anything once upon a time. Now I have to lie, especially to myself. But how can you understand, when I don't myself. I've never understood anything about it, except that one day long

44. Mary to Edmund about Jamie. O'Neill, *Long Day's*, 65.

ago I found I could no longer call my soul my own. *She pauses—
then lowering her voice to a strange tone of whispered confidence.*
But some day, dear, I will find it again—some day when you're
all well, and I see you healthy and happy and successful, and I
don't have to feel guilty any more—some day when the Blessed
Virgin Mary forgives me and gives me back the faith in Her love
and pity I used to have in my convent days, and I can pray to
Her again—when She sees no one in the world can believe in me
even for a moment any more, then She will believe in me, and
with Her help it will be so easy. I will hear myself scream with
agony, and at the same time I will laugh because I will be so sure
of myself. *Then as Edmund remains hopelessly silent, she adds
sadly.* Of course, you can't believe that, either. *She rises from the
arm of his chair and goes to stare out the windows at right with
her back to him—casually.*[45]

If we can substantiate, time and time again, signatories of hell on
earth, thresholds of damnation in the very family womb where undiluted
love should dwell, then doesn't this speak more to the promise of heaven
within the worn patina of the earth, than to its denial as irrelevant, antiquated, non-essential to meaning and being? The existential depths in
which we can hurl ourselves, the ability for us to fuse the mask in such
a way that what has really occurred is the hell of our ruptured essences,
points by way of defection to our intrinsic supernatural destiny, to heaven
as the only satisfying home. We have never been purely natural material
beings directed towards natural material ends, the depths we descend to
when squandering our spirit-food are startling and terrifying.[46]

In the Tyrone family, the two goals of the mask—keeping relationality together while hiding haunting primal truths—have dueled with each
other, perhaps for too long, and now redemption may have no place, no

45. Mary to Edmund. O'Neill, *Long Day's*, 96.

46. Cf. Kreeft, *Every Thing You Ever Wanted to Know about Heaven*, 22–23: "My
greatness depends on reality's greatness. If reality does not extend to Heaven, I cannot
either. Even if I am a small fish, I am greater if I am a small fish in a big reality-pond
than if I am a big fish in a small reality pond. That is why C. S. Lewis makes the surprising judgment that 'it is more important that Heaven should exist than that any of us
should reach it.' . . . The ontological thirst, the thirst for being, is our deepest thirst. In
every desire, even for truth and goodness and beauty, we desire being; we desire that
the object be real. Self-generated fantasies satisfy only imaginary needs. Our spirit, unlike God, is not independent and self-contained; it cannot feed upon itself or fecundate
itself or actualize itself. We need reality as our spirit-food. We eat reality. Knowing is a
kind of eating: a spiritual assimilation."

avenue left salvifically to conquer the soul. This is the "precarity of the flesh."[47] The intentionality of failed love creates a chimerical being, where quite realistically "the true self is lost forever."[48] This is the torn separation of the soul from the body, and the body from the soul, and it happens here in the flesh. Christ realized this awful power when he realized hell in his descent. And hell can begin on earth, we witness it in the consciences of failed loves. The Tyrones' willingness to lie and to delude themselves, to keep loving relationality alive, breeds the simmering undercurrent of truth under the auspices of alienation as resentfulness. This renders that love unable to be seen *as* inviting, *as* good. And herein lies the potentially irremediable problem of the Tyrone family: the swirling miasma of lies they have inflicted on themselves and others in order to protect love, has enshrined a love that is both present and absent. Present—for they love each other, that's precisely what prompted the lies; they sought not only for themselves but for their family ways to avoid pain, to rewrite history as if to ease suffering, to circumvent its cost. But absent because this love they encased and entombed in lies is actually the failure to love completely, fully, honestly, authentically. Love is now the seething undercurrent that bursts at the seams throughout the play from every character who utters truth and then apologizes for his angered, unacceptable, and vitriolic remarks, thereby making the relating-of-truth the enemy of truth-telling. The irony is that the characters apologize for the truth, for goodness impossibly packaged in destruction, or more precisely for a love that has little ability to heal, transform, and redeem!

Because genuine truth as love has been suppressed by their masks, it only reveals itself as alienation and resentfulness, which takes on the appearance of the opposite of the truth, the very thing that needs to be suppressed. And this resentfulness is in one sense the just reaction of love squandered for so long, and also now part of the cycle of lies, for true love can no longer be seen as it should be—as a home, which Mary keeps seeking, as a place of consolation, of forgiveness and transformation. From the beginning to the end of this quiet tragedy, the need for home defines everything:

> *She pauses, looking out the window—then with an undercurrent of lonely yearning.*

47. Newsome Martin, "The Christian Future of Metaphysics: The Carnal Turn in Catholic Theology."

48. O'Neill, *Long Day's*, 65.

Still the Chatterfields and people like them stand for something. I mean they have decent, presentable homes they don't have to be ashamed of. They have friends who entertain them and whom they entertain. They're not cut off from everyone.[49]

Never mind. The summer will soon be over, thank goodness. Your season will open again and we can go back to second-rate hotels and trains. I hate them, too, but at least I don't expect them to be like a home[;] . . . it never has been and it never will be [a home]. . . . In a real home one is never lonely. You forget I know from experience what a home is like. I gave up one to marry you—my father's home.[50]

It was my fault. I should have insisted on staying with Eugene and not have let you persuade me to join you, just because I loved you. Above all, I shouldn't have let you insist I have another baby to take Eugene's place, because you thought that would make me forget his death. I knew from experience by then that children should have homes to be born in, if they are to be good children, and women need homes, if they are to be good mothers. I was afraid all the time I carried Edmund. I knew something terrible would happen. I knew I'd proved by the way I'd left Eugene that I wasn't worthy to have another baby, and that God would punish me if I did. I never should have borne Edmund.[51]

In the conscience of failed loves, the truth, so it seems, does not will out. What happens in such a lamentable situation where it seems there is no exit, no exit for the truth as love? The Tyrones have gone so far down a road of masks formed by lies under the auspices of protective love, which traded away truth for shades of truth. And then the actual truth—which is identical with genuine love—having little or nowhere to go, having been suppressed repeatedly, manifests itself as the opposite of love. If they continue to live by lies, they begin to die, but have some semblance of union punctuated by the truth manifesting as resentment. If they try to remove the masks and live by love, the existential death will

---

49. Mary to Edmund. O'Neill, *Long Day's*, 44.

50. Mary to Tyrone. O'Neill, *Long Day's*, 74.

51. O'Neill, *Long Day's*, 90. Cf. Lewis, *Till We Have Faces*, 86–87: "It was when I was happiest that I longed most. . . . The sweetest thing in all my life has been the long-ing—to reach the Mountain, to find the place where all the beauty came from—my country, the place where I ought to have been born. Do you think it all meant nothing, all the longing? The longing for home? For indeed it now feels not like going, but like going back."

be expeditiously fierce, and it will overwhelm them with the power of hell; what is up will be down and what is down will be up, each as blind as someone who never had sight.

> But don't get wrong idea, Kid. I love you more than I hate you. My saying what I'm telling you now proves it. I run the risk you'll hate me—and you're all I've got left. But I didn't mean to tell you that last stuff—go that far back. Don't know what made me.[52]

Here's the tragedy of the conscience of failed love, of the lost heaven it presents: they need to tear off their masks for love to grow and not to become squandered. But the masks must remain for them to survive, the Tyrones could not bear the truth for they *have rendered the truth unbearable*. The family has done the impossible and made survival opposed to love, when love is the only thing that endures. Each family member has entered into such a person-dissolving territory, that what remains of their personhood is bound up in the other who is also dissolving. But between each other they have enough substance to persist collectively. For one to risk tearing off the mask would be like existential death, creating a domino effect of spiritual demise in the others. It would quicken the protracted death that for now, as slow and languishing, keeps them this side of alive, as ghosts of memory and regret and familial bond and even love, yes love. Eugene O'Neill sought to create a tragedy where persons could no longer call their souls their own, where "everything comes between you and what you'd like to be, and you've lost your true self forever." Here love is so out of place that it seems it cannot be found again. Is this not the very risk of hell itself?

---

52. Jamie to Edmund. O'Neill, *Long Day's*, 169.

4

What Can We Say about the Experience-as-Non-Experience of Death?

Plato himself, however, is no Platonist. At any rate, in the late dialogue *Phaedrus*, when he launches on what seems a wholly fresh approach to the question of "in what sense a living being is termed mortal and immortal," he suddenly ceases to speak of the soul alone. We think, he says, "of a living being, spiritual and physical at once, but both, soul and body, united for all time." Moreover, he goes on, immortality is not to be regarded as a mere rational concept susceptible to demonstration; rather, we think of it with our minds on "the god whom we have never seen, nor fully conceived." . . . If ever immortality is conferred upon us, not just the soul but the entire physical human being will in some inconceivable manner participate in the life of the gods. . . . For what is in truth meant by this indestructability [of the soul] is the immortality, exceeding all conception—not of the soul, but of the whole man.[1]

THE DEATH OF THE other presents us with the one experience we ourselves cannot undertake or assimilate like all other earthly experiences. How does the "I" complete the task of intentionality, how do we become the other *as other*, especially when confronted with the non-experience of death *as death*? The living, and even the dying, do

1. Pieper, *Death and Immortality*, 104–5.

not experience death *per se*, and yet it invades all claimants, defines by demarcating and distinguishing all human experiences. We are haunted by our inability to know death, to conceive and take in its radical alterity, to become this most impermeable other *as other*. Yet we need to grasp this intractable shadow, for what we do know is that death is our lifelong companion, and the most pressing and defining experience of human existence. Thus, this repeated inability to assimilate death, most realized in grief, must be given its dwelling place before we can proceed faithfully into matters regarding human experience in the afterlife. If we are to make the connection that our experiences in the world, how we authentically know through embodiment, and the *processes* of thought are still naturally guiding and present in the afterlife—because grace *perfects* nature and does not destroy it—then the experience of death—which is most fundamental to us, as the horizon and crucible of our anthropology, especially realized in Christ[2]—cannot be side skirted.

The death of the loved one with all its abundance of grief and irresolution, is also a stumbling, non-experiential event. And grief is uniquely the experience of that non-experience, that inability to take-in the other whom we have always intentionally taken-in and exteriorized, and who in turn, has also taken us in repeatedly and exteriorized our otherness for us. What becomes of the other when she dies, and also what becomes of us? Haven't the dead, through a lifelong process of intentionality, taken something of us within them to the grave? And yet we cannot, it seems, take death in as we live and breathe. This is the very act of death, which takes us in as we live via the protracted act of intentionality, and then wrestles us away when we die, in the rupture of the human essence, as violent separation of body and soul. Death eludes all capture, and the hunted becomes the hunter.

---

2. Cf. Norwich, *Revelations of Divine Love*, 3–6: "It seemed to me that I could feel the Passion of Christ strongly, but yet I longed by God's grace to feel it more intensely. I thought how I wished I had been there at the crucifixion with Mary Magdalene and with others who were Christ's dear friends, that I might have seen in the flesh the Passion of our Lord which he suffered for me, so that I could have suffered with him as others did who loved him. . . . It suddenly occurred to me that I should entreat our Lord . . . so that he would fill my whole body with remembrance for the feeling of his blessed Passion . . . for I wanted his pains to be my pains, with compassion, and then longing for God. Yet in this I never asked for a bodily sight or any kind of showing of God, but for fellow-suffering, such as it seemed to me a naturally kind soul might feel for our Lord Jesus, who was willing to become a mortal man for love. I wanted to suffer with him, while living in my mortal body, as God would give me grace.

And suddenly I saw the red blood trickling down from under the crown of thorns."

The sheer *ennui* of the knowledge of grief *as un-knowingness*, is deftly framed by William Carlos William's *The Widow's Lament in Springtime*. Our widow recalls the beauty of the plumtree blossoms in her yard which furiously bloom and call into presence-as-absence her husband and their years together:

> Sorrow is my own yard
> where the new grass
> flames as it has flamed
> often before but not
> with the cold fire
> that closes round me this year.
> Thirty five years
> I lived with my husband.[3]

She cannot take-in those flowers in the way to which she was accustomed prior to his death. The blossoms are *of* her-with-him and because of his death she cannot become this other *as other* by which the flowers remind; it is epistemologically unbearable, the flower is and is no longer itself. Like the Host, its exterior form, the eucharistic species,[4] is unchanged, but the whole enactment of the blossoms for the intentional subject has existentially altered. In transubstantiation, God is acting in the Eucharist, effecting a change in the inner reality of the elements. Death, in a mirrored manner, effects the inner elements of the experience of our incarnational intentionality. Outwardly, it all looks the same, the world is exteriorly the same world, but within the two-fold process of interiorization of the other-with-self, and exteriorization of the self-with-other, the world has also become a foreign place. The salt loses its savor, and the beauty of the blossoms can no longer be appreciated *as is*, for they are tinged with the unassimilated presence of his death, reminding us of the tragic wisdom within finitude and flesh that outwits all intentionality. Yet the widow desires that union, cannot exist without this knowledge of unknowing union. She learns of other surrogate flowers growing at the edge of the heavy woods, down in the meadow, all white blossoms

---

3. Williams, *The Widow's Lament in Springtime*, 171.

4. Cf. *Catechism* §283: "What is the meaning of transubstantiation? Transubstantiation means the change of the whole substance of bread into the substance of the Body of Christ and of the whole substance of wine into the substance of his Blood. This change is brought about in the eucharistic prayer through the efficacy of the word of Christ and by the action of the Holy Spirit. However, the outward characteristics of bread and wine, that is the 'eucharistic species,' remain unaltered."

sinking into the marsh: she seeks out that un-knowledge as if to sink into it, to become inseparable from that unknowing, and then, perhaps only then, will she know the dearest other again. This knowledge is what death simultaneously cannot provide, but only death, compared to all worldly alternatives, can facilitate its foreshadowing:

> The plumtree is white today
> with masses of flowers.
> Masses of flowers
> load the cherry branches
> and color some bushes
> yellow and some red
> but the grief in my heart
> is stronger than they
> for though they were my joy
> formerly, today I notice them
> and turn away forgetting.
> Today my son told me
> that in the meadows,
> at the edge of the heavy woods
> in the distance, he saw
> trees of white flowers.
> I feel that I would like
> to go there
> and fall into those flowers
> and sink into the marsh near them.[5]

While in knowledge we put ourselves alongside the event, in the witnessing of death we are left at the precipice of meaning, enacting but not completely becoming this most particular other *as other*. We cannot assimilate the experience of being dead, for this takes on the gaze-less stare of non-experience. And this is the knowledge we so very much desire to complete, not only because we wonder whether such finality is, indeed, final, but because it has *always* been present as the very crux in which all things were magnified to us by their presence and their absence. We see the child grow from infant to toddler, to young adult, and all our seeing has been shaped and refined by the little deaths that occur along the way in the making of such a life. There are so many little deaths that make up the moments, the hours, the days of passing flesh. The last call, the last game, and all the firsts in existence, which cannot help but extinguish something older that had, in a way, put us closer to

5. Williams, *The Widow's Lament in Springtime*, 171.

our immortality. Every change is growth and death, every transcendence prepares us for dying, every union necessitates parting, ubiquitous death cannot be contained. Death is wordless speech and unreceived listening, its touch caresses all as it holds nothing, only to hold everything as its caresses go undifferentiated from living and breathing. To consider it would be to grasp hold of something more intimate to ourselves than ourselves.

> Consider the dying: do they
> not come at last to guess the hollowness
> of everything that we engage in here?
> Nothing is what it is! O Childhood hours,
> whose presences possessed behind them more
> than past . . . when future did not lie before us.
> We grew and grew, and even sometimes made
> haste to be fully-grown; half for the sake
> of those grown-ups . . . who owned so little else.
> Left to our own devices we were still
> made glad enough by all the things that stayed
> eternally the same, so that we lived
> within a borderland: between the hard World
> and our objects of Delight; inhabited
> a place that always, from the very first,
> has been reserved for innocent events.
> Who will show us what children really are?
> Who sets them in the constellations, puts
> a yardstick to tell *difference* in their hands?
> Who moulds the death of children, who makes death
> from that grey bread, leaves it to harden . . . ? Or
> sucks at it, roundmouthed, the core that's left
> of some sweet apple? Easy enough, to see
> into the hearts of murderers. But this:
> to bear all death, the whole of death; death even
> before life; and gently, without rancour,
> to keep it, contain it,
> is terrible beyond all language.[6]

This other-worldly moratorium on assimilative knowledge in relation to death must be given patient anthropological, metaphysical, and phenomenological care. We cannot take-in the one experience that provides the backdrop for everything we assimilate or take-in when knowing

6. Rilke, *Duino Elegies,* 43.

ourselves. In a way shocking and profound, while we know ourselves in these acts of knowledge, we are also held suspended from the completion of knowing ourselves because this non-assimilative reality of death has imprinted everything we have known. It is the unpacking of this uneasy mystery that provides us with a genuine accounting of the very real and relevant promise of the afterlife as a promise co-extensive with the deepest seat of our natures. Our epistemological activity shows us that we cannot rest or know ourselves most profoundly without what heaven gifts us—and most particularly what the resurrected state recovers within embodiment. Every act of human knowledge born from a backdrop of death-as-unknowing actually attests to this powerful truth. Again, with Rilke: "to bear all death, the whole of death; death even before life; and gently, without rancour, to keep it, contain it, is terrible beyond all language." Thus, if we bypass this uneasy reality of death as non-assimilative, we may be able to eulogize the so-called beauty of a happily ever after, but we will not be able to shirk the creeping suspicion that both the "beauty" and the "happily ever after" are very dear desires but cannot really be the *dearest* because not the *truest*. And without even knowing it, something occurs behind our backs in the twilight of our discontent: heaven fades from view.

Let us approach once more the world of embodiment in relation to the divine, let us "consider the dying" within the patterns of the natural world. God's creative action is not like our own—ours is the signatory of the protracted creaturely dying. When we create, there must always be this actualizing movement from potentiality to actuality, from incomplete to more completed knowledge.[7] But God who is purely actual does

---

7. Cf. ST I, 79, 2 *resp*: "In a wide sense a thing is said to be passive, from the very fact that what is in potentiality to something receives that to which it was in potentiality, without being deprived of anything. And accordingly, whatever passes from potentiality to act, may be said to be passive, even when it is perfected. And thus, with us to understand is to be passive. This is clear from the following reason. For the intellect, as we have seen above (I:78:1), has an operation extending to universal being. We may therefore see whether the intellect be in act or potentiality by observing first of all the nature of the relation of the intellect to universal being. For we find an intellect whose relation to universal being is that of the act of all being: and such is the Divine intellect, which is the Essence of God, in which originally and virtually, all being pre-exists as in its first cause. And therefore, the Divine intellect is not in potentiality, but is pure act. But no created intellect can be an act in relation to the whole universal being; otherwise it would needs be an infinite being. Wherefore every created intellect is not the act of all things intelligible, by reason of its very existence; but is compared to these intelligible things as a potentiality to act."

not create in a way that his knowledge depends on things other than himself for his action, he does not go from incomplete to completed creation,
there is no cycle of potentiality and actuality. The creative *actus* is always
present in him as identical to his Being, and that actuality is transferred
to creatures who themselves as finite creatures participate in it by way of
potentiality and actuality, particular to their natures. It is the creaturely
act that invokes potentiality, and that is why actuality *always* precedes
potentiality. God as creative source has enabled us to participate in his
own actuality, and so when we move and act and engage of our own accord, we are participating in that actuality by acting on the very *actus* or
body of God's Being as innermost in all things. This alone is an incredible
signatory of heaven as our permanent home: our dependency rises above
the constraints of materiality—of satisfaction in earthly termini—and
reveals itself to be a *knowing* participant on the body of the infinite and
uncreated, satisfied only with that which precedes, exceeds, and unveils
knowledge. No deconstructionism, secularism, postmodernist imagination can compare with, let alone approach, the power of participated
beings who realize themselves within the Godhead as most Free, True,
Good, Beautiful effulgent inexhaustibility.

> Everything participated is compared to the participator as its
> act. But whatever created form be supposed to subsist "per se,"
> must have existence by participation; for "even life," or anything
> of that sort, "is a participator of existence," as Dionysius says
> (Div. Nom. v). Now participated existence is limited by the ca-
> pacity of the participator; so that God alone, Who is His own
> existence, is pure act and infinite. But in intellectual substances
> there is composition of actuality and potentiality, not, indeed,
> of matter and form, but of form and participated existence.
> Wherefore some say that they are composed of that "whereby
> they are" and that "which they are"; for existence itself is that by
> which a thing is.[8]

8. ST I, 75, 5 ad. 4. See also Gilson, *Subordinated Ethics*, xxxi: "The soul is *already*
outside itself, it lives a radically exteriorized existence, so much so that what primarily
constitutes our own nature is also the site of our own surpassing of self. What we
own the least are our own selves, precisely because the soul in its innermost reality is
existentially dependent on Being for its existence, and this is manifested most acutely
in the act of knowledge. In knowledge, the human soul reveals itself to be the alterity
of the divine, becoming, in a way, all things. Because we are not separately existent, we
must arrive at ourselves by becoming identical with otherness."

If we were primarily passive receptacles—merely a series of synapses firing off in the brain when flooded with sense impressions—we would be forever affected by outside or external forces that alter, manipulate, change, and reduce us. The very notion of personhood would be realistically suspect and, at best, a vague convention—ontical ellipses connecting non-identities. The table exists but cannot of its own power preserve itself from being rotted, damaged, painted, or broken; this is certainly not analogous to a person. In other words, the soul needs something purely actual that confers intelligibility so that it rouses the passive soul to take-on that sensible knowledge in a personal and freeing way. Every natural thing comprises receptivity and activity, and no natural participant in this cycle of actuality and potentiality emancipates itself from their shared dependency to claim the status as truly a *first* efficient cause. Each moving thing is moved by another. So that the ear moved by the sound of the dog's barking is thus dependent on the barking to be roused from its passive state. The dog is roused to that active state when its eyes first *received* sight of the cat scurrying across the lawn. Furthering this dependency, every natural thing reveals itself to be a caused-cause or an effect of something prior by the diverse examples of generation and decay. Natural causes possess a degree of efficiency or "firstness," as an acorn is temporally and causally prior to the oak it subsequently causes. But because both the acorn and the oak go through growth and change, they are grounded in a cycle of non-emancipatory dependency that reveals them to be dependently caused. Every natural cause possesses potentiality, revealing that none is *truly* first, each is a secondary or dependent cause. Every natural cause may cause or generate something else and is thus prior to its effects in time but is at the same time wholly like its own effects. All these natural causes are themselves generated by something else which is prior to in time. Thus, all natural priority is relativized, revealing that these secondary causations cannot exist without a *true* first. This true first must be purely actual and because of that it is unrestrictedly innermost in all things as the primordial source of all actualizing. When we think of our intellects as receptive, we realize that the very *experience* of that reception fundamentally involves action, so much so that no receptive or passive state can fulfill itself without a prior activity as rousing agent. To remain within a cyclical and non-hierarchical set of active and passive states may be able to describe the immediately present phenomenal and temporal experiences but it cannot account for the origin of those experiences nor the maintenance of activity throughout them and beyond. It is no wonder that there is an aspect of our souls understood to be purely active and subsistent, containing no material and sensible potentiality. This *per se* operation is the aspect of us that is closest to the essence of God.[9] Heidegger describes such a unique privileged state as "world-forming."[10]

> In maintaining that animals are poor in world, Heidegger is clear that the environments of animals are not as such poor; they are poor only when those various environments are compared with the human world of linguistic experience and truth. The point is the richness of the human world rather than the poverty of the animal. Bees navigate and forage by living out a range of relevance specified by the good of the hive. They notice sources of nectar but they don't contemplate the intelligibility of the flower or the beauty of the bloom; there are no bee botanists or bee poets. Now, this might seem like a trivial point. After all, there are no human drones or human hives. But phenomenologists are not calling attention to random differences between bees and humans. They are highlighting the character of the fundamental difference that makes the observation of this difference possible. The bee or any other animal is inscribed within the domain of an environment. Humans, by contrast, can transcend

9. Cf. ST I, 75 2 *resp*: "It must necessarily be allowed that the principle of intellectual operation which we call the soul, is a principle both incorporeal and subsistent. For it is clear that by means of the intellect man can have knowledge of all corporeal things. Now whatever knows certain things cannot have any of them in its own nature; because that which is in it naturally would impede the knowledge of anything else. Thus we observe that a sick man's tongue being vitiated by a feverish and bitter humor, is insensible to anything sweet, and everything seems bitter to it. Therefore, if the intellectual principle contained the nature of a body it would be unable to know all bodies. Now every body has its own determinate nature. Therefore it is impossible for the intellectual principle to be a body. It is likewise impossible for it to understand by means of a bodily organ; since the determinate nature of that organ would impede knowledge of all bodies; as when a certain determinate color is not only in the pupil of the eye, but also in a glass vase, the liquid in the vase seems to be of that same color. Therefore the intellectual principle which we call the mind or the intellect has an operation per se apart from the body. Now only that which subsists can have an operation 'per se.' For nothing can operate but what is actual: for which reason we do not say that heat imparts heat, but that what is hot gives heat. We must conclude, therefore, that the human soul, which is called the intellect or the mind, is something incorporeal and subsistent."

10. Cf. Heidegger, *Fundamental Concepts*, 177: "The stone (material object) is worldless; the animal is poor in world; Man is world-forming."

their environment and dwell within the world. As a result, they can compare one environment with another.[11]

On earth, human nature comes closest to attesting to the pure actuality and power of that first cause. While we can clearly see the cycle of actuality and potentiality as wholly binding and determinative in the plant and animal, in ourselves we intensively and intentionally re-create the active power of a true first cause in our learning and creative action. Whereas the plant's cycle of actuality and potentiality is wholly united with an unfree materiality, we play and bring change into existence through our creative choices. We can, of our own actuality, place ourselves in positions of receptivity; our passive reception provides the framework for the active intellect to take in the object in the form of the knower. I can actively choose to go to the lecture and thus place myself in a state of receptivity by which my actualizing intellect can abstract the fundamental meanings and connections. My actuality has a priority and a primacy in that it can and must lead the receptive or passive aspects of my existence. It is this ability to lead that reveals my free will and intellectual comportment. Human beings have a principle of *actus* that, as immaterial, grants us unique privileges in existence. And yet, we are not without genuine life-affirming dependency which, in turn, particularizes us, making each of us in the image and likeness of God's unrepeatability. Our birth, maturation, and our death attest to our needful participation in this cycle of potentiality and actuality. It also reflects St. Thomas' remarks that a longer way was assigned to man than the angels for his beatitude.[12]

In the interiority of our intellectual substance, the composition is of actuality and potentiality, which reflects not form and matter, but form and participated existence. This is astonishing! Within our two-fold incarnational intentionality, this simultaneous tending points in every way beyond ourselves to heaven. Our intellectual substance's potentiality is predicated on participation within God's inexhaustible and uncreated

---

11. Engelland, *Phenomenology*, 102–4. Cf. Heidegger, *Fundamental Concepts*, 264: "For it is *not* simply a question of qualitative *otherness* of the animal world as compared with the human world, and especially not a question of quantitative distinctions in range, depth, and breadth—not a question of whether or how the animal takes what is given to it in a different way, but rather whether the animal can comprehend something *as* something, something *as* a being, at all. If it cannot, then the animal is separated from man by an abyss."

12. ST I, 62, 5, ad. 1.

To Be. When we are roused, through the longer way of matter, to take on the other *as other*, there is, more interiorly, a second layer of potentiality, an incarnational potentiality irreducible to material potentiality, and in the midst of that materiality. This is the powerhouse meaning of the flesh, not only as transience but as moving image of the eternal. This immaterial potentiality raises our embodiment to the dignity of divine participation.[13] As we repeatedly assimilate the other who has previously assimilated us within this repeated and intensifying cycle of a human life, we are revealing inklings of the glorified body, of the overflow of that person into each experience, and a testament of shared existence.[14] But death reminds us that these inklings are by dispossession, by our recognition that the other is everywhere and nowhere, is in all things, in the sunlight and the wood, in the unexpected bend of the road dappled in shadow, but nothing ever captures her overflow:

> At first I was very afraid of going to places where H. and I had
> been happy—our favourite pub, our favourite wood. But I

13. This is why the church speaks of the dignity of the body, of the sanctity of life from cradle to grave. No life is made of material disjecta. Every life has within it the openness, the receptivity to that obediential potency that animates the resurrected body. Aquinas speaks of obediential potency, this two-fold level of potentiality, in *De Virtutibus*, 1, 10, ad. 13: "*In tota creatura est quaedam obedientialis potentia, prout tota creatura obedit Deo ad suscipiendum in se quidquid Deus voluerit.*" (In every creature there is an obediential potency, insofar as every creature obeys God in receiving whatever God wills") and in ST, III, 11 1, *resp*: "It was fitting that the soul of Christ should be wholly perfected by having each of its powers reduced to act. Now it must be borne in mind that in the human soul, as in every creature, there is a double passive power: one in comparison with a natural agent; the other in comparison with the first agent, which can reduce any creature to a higher act than a natural agent can reduce it, and this is usually called the obediential power of a creature. Now both powers of Christ's soul were reduced to act by this divinely imprinted knowledge. And hence, by it the soul of Christ knew: First, whatever can be known by force of a man's active intellect, e.g., whatever pertains to human sciences; secondly, by this knowledge Christ knew all things made known to man by Divine revelation, whether they belong to the gift of wisdom or the gift of prophecy, or any other gift of the Holy Ghost; since the soul of Christ knew these things more fully and completely than others. Yet He did not know the Essence of God by this knowledge, but by the first alone, of which we spoke above."

14. Cf. ST Suppl. 85, 1, ad. 4: "Even as the clarity of glory will overflow from the soul into the body according to the mode of the body, and is there otherwise than in the soul, so again it will overflow into each part of the soul according to the mode of that part. Hence it is not unreasonable that the different parts should have clarity in different ways, according as they are differently disposed thereto by their nature. Nor is there any comparison with the other gifts of the body, for the various parts of the body are not differently disposed in their regard."

decided to do it at once—like a pilot up again as soon as possible after he's had a crash. Unexpectedly, it makes no difference. Her absence is no more emphatic in those places than anywhere else. It's not local at all. I suppose that if one were forbidden all salt one wouldn't notice it much more in any one food than in another. Eating in general would be different, every day, at every meal. It is like that. The act of living is different all through. Her absence is like the sky, spread over everything. But no, that is not quite accurate. There is one place where her absence comes locally home to me, and it is a place I can't avoid. I mean my own body. It had such a different importance while it was the body of H.'s lover. Now it's like an empty house.[15]

In knowledge we are always alongside the event of otherness. When we experience the death of the other, we are enduring the innermost nexus of intentionality. We are perpetually enacting the assimilative process of becoming the other *as other* but held suspended from completing it until our death, which we hope brings us, in grace, to heaven and to the gift of resurrection. In every epistemological act resides the shadow of a knowledge that has been unassimilated, has been held out from being taken-in. This fugitive essence, death, has been our companion in all human experience; it has demarcated, defined, distinguished, and delineated all events. From our first acts of knowing to our last, we have repeatedly engaged death *because* it first engaged us, and repeatedly inflicted its nearness. When the passive intellect is roused by the senses, it is roused more secretly by death, the death within life: the sensations of change, growth, decay, beginnings, ends, by everything that whispers and affirms the separation of things, the cessation of presence, the tearing apart of what was once enjoined. Once upon a time never comes again. Every act of knowledge is, in a way, sacred and profound, an act of death or more precisely, a reminder that one must go through death to live.[16] We must press on even further. Every act of knowledge taunts us with that unassimilated presence of death that first engaged us when our senses were roused in the longer way of knowledge. All acts of knowledge place themselves at our sides and whisper into our ears: *you have not learned it all, you have had the experiences, again and again, but missed the meaning; until you assimilate death, until you know it, you have not completed knowledge, nor known yourself.* But what must we conclude?

15. Lewis, *A Grief Observed*, 11–12.
16. Cf. Phil 1:21: "For to me, to live is Christ and to die is gain."

Earth cannot complete this knowledge and yet we are rational animals, *knowing* beings. If it is our very nature to know, then an earth void of the substantializing hope of heaven, as permanent home, is a frustrated end for us.[17] We live a life entwined in death, knowing there is something we cannot yet know.

Our intentionality—if not the consciences sown wholly of the sophistic, parasitical, unreflected desire, or failed love—has the audacious capacity to bring home within us the preambles of our glorified bodies![18] Heartrendingly it is in grief that we are lanced with the strange recollection of something like the glorified body by way of the other, by way of her absence as presence, by way of how the other who can no longer be assimilated, carries *all* things needful and good by way of dispossession. Death of the loved-other places who we are, as the once assimilated other, in exile. In grief, we experience the beginnings of the torn separation of body and soul, just as much as we sense the glorified body by way of this impossible state of existence, in which all things remind, all things overflow with her nearness. In grief, we are on the hunt for the one home that can offer the most impossible and needful of citizenships, one that can offer the type of body, the type of spiritual architecture, that can house our potency to be in a way *all things*, to complete what always, on earth, remains unresolved.

> But our citizenship is in heaven, and from it we await a Savior, the Lord Jesus Christ, who will transform our lowly body to be like his glorious body, by the power that enables him even to subject all things to himself.[19]

This potentiality to become in knowledge all things, has always had within it the protracted failure to become all things. Death, those repeated little deaths throughout life, suspend us from the completion of knowing ourselves. The non-assimilative reality of dying stamps everything we know with a penultimacy of real knowledge that simultaneously stops short of completion. This is the birthplace of *eros* and of grief. To transcend from the penultimate to the ultimate, from the created intellect's

17. Cf. Maritain's remarks on how no natural aim results in a frustrated end. *Approaches to God*, 111–12.

18. Cf. 1 Cor 15:42–44: "So is it with the resurrection of the dead. What is sown is perishable; what is raised is imperishable. It is sown in dishonor; it is raised in glory. It is sown in weakness; it is raised in power. It is sown a natural body; it is raised a spiritual body. If there is a natural body, there is also a spiritual body."

19. Phil 3:20–21.

erotic, grasping quasi-finality to the agapetic union with the uncreated, necessitates that God as Life overturns death and its trail of unassimilated meaning throughout our lives. Our interiorizing intentionality turns towards the uncreated, which, like death, cannot be assimilated via the created intellect,[20] and yet it recognizes by negation, nearness, and cosmogonic difference, this primal *Actus* within all things. In this sense our natural vision reaches for what it cannot see, because it can recognize its own blindness: "And we depart not from thee, thou shalt quicken us: and we will call upon thy name. O Lord God of hosts, convert us: and shew thy face, and we shall be saved."[21] Our created intellect participates in the uncreated via dispossession, as death participates in us by dispossession. Both the uncreated and death, now overcome through Christ, positively order our natural vision to put itself in the habit of yearning for what it cannot assimilate, to exile ourselves beyond ourselves. In heaven, we trust that God's essence will become the form by which our intellectual substances can take-in the unassimilated,[22] as Christ's body becomes for us, in the glorified state, the unseen made visible through the chorus of creatures in praise and joy, each thoroughly united to his body and blood. Our natural blindness is transformed into a unique sight, our earthly dispossession is repossessed in Christ whose flesh communalizes all things in the glorified state.[23] Our natural sight cannot encounter the uncreated

20. Cf. ST Suppl. 92, 1, *resp*: "Certain theologians held that the human intellect can never attain to the vision of God in His essence. On either side they were moved by the distance which separates our intellect from the Divine essence and from separate substances. For since the intellect in act is somewhat one with the intelligible object in act, it would seem difficult to understand how the created intellect is made to be an uncreated essence. Wherefore Chrysostom says (Hom. xiv in Joan.): 'How can the creature see the uncreated?'"

21. Ps 79:19–20.

22. Cf. ST Suppl. 92, 1, ad. 8: "In the vision wherein God will be seen in His essence, the Divine essence itself will be the form, as it were, of the intellect, by which it will understand: nor is it necessary for them to become one in being, but only to become one as regards the act of understanding."

23. Cf. ST Suppl. 92, 2, *resp*: "I say then that God can nowise be seen with the eyes of the body, or perceived by any of the senses, as that which is seen directly, neither here, nor in heaven: for if that which belongs to sense as such be removed from sense, there will be no sense, and in like manner if that which belongs to sight as sight be removed therefrom, there will be no sight. Accordingly seeing that sense as sense perceives magnitude, and sight as such a sense perceives color, it is impossible for the sight to perceive that which is neither color nor magnitude, unless we call it a sense equivocally. Since then sight and sense will be specifically the same in the glorified body, as in a non-glorified body, it will be impossible for it to see the Divine essence

as we cannot assimilate death. These two poles: the infinite, and the nothingness that cannot exist outside the infinite, precede all vision. On earth, our flesh—in grief, happiness, peace, heartache—turns to what it cannot see, unable to find a corresponding sensible image befitting such experience.[24] This turn of human sight into blindness, paradigmatic of every honest human life, illustrates the project of longing, which could only be resolved in the overflow that passes from a soul united to God in the beatific vision, rendering joy and happiness the visible imprint of that uncreated:

> Beatitude is the perfection of man as man. And since man is man not through his body but through his soul, and the body is essential to man, in so far as it is perfected by the soul: it follows that man's beatitude does not consist chiefly otherwise than in an act of the soul, and passes from the soul on to the body by a kind of overflow, as explained above (Supplement: 85:1). Yet our body will have a certain beatitude from seeing God in sensible creatures: and especially in Christ's body.[25]

---

as an object of direct vision; yet it will see it as an object of indirect vision, because on the one hand the bodily sight will see so great a glory of God in bodies, especially in the glorified bodies and most of all in the body of Christ, and, on the other hand, the intellect will see God so clearly, that God will be perceived in things seen with the eye of the body, even as life is perceived in speech. For although our intellect will not then see God from seeing His creatures, yet it will see God in His creatures seen corporeally. This manner of seeing God corporeally is indicated by Augustine (De Civ. Dei xxii), as is clear if we take note of his words, for he says: 'It is very credible that we shall so see the mundane bodies of the new Heaven and the new Earth, as to see most clearly God everywhere present, governing all corporeal things, not as we now see the invisible things of God as understood by those that are made, but as when we see men . . . we do not believe but see that they live.'"

24. Cf. *Confessions* X, xvii: "I will pass even beyond this power of mine which is called memory: yea, I will pass beyond it, that I may approach unto Thee, O sweet Light. What sayest Thou to me? See, I am mounting up through my mind towards Thee who abidest above me. Yea, I now will pass beyond this power of mine which is called memory, desirous to arrive at Thee, whence Thou mayest be arrived at; and to cleave unto Thee, whence one may cleave unto Thee. For even beasts and birds have memory; else could they not return to their dens and nests, nor many other things they are used unto: nor indeed could they be used to any thing, but by memory. I will pass then beyond memory also, that I may arrive at Him who hath separated me from the four-footed beasts and made me wiser than the fowls of the air, I will pass beyond memory also, and where shall I find Thee, Thou truly good and certain sweetness? And where shall I find Thee? If I find Thee without my memory, then do I not retain Thee in my memory. And how shall I find Thee, if I remember Thee not?"

25. ST Suppl. 92, 2, ad. 6.

Our beings, simultaneously exteriorized within the world via our finitude, and interiorized through the non-mediated union with the un-created, are also held suspended from reflecting on death's pre-reflective ground. We are left in a protracted completion, and yet again, is it not strange how all of life is defined through this protracted completion? Every act of assimilated knowledge is predicated on the experience-as-non-assimilative experience of death. This is the true revolution of Truth itself: All things learned *via* assimilation pay their dues by reminding us of the innermost and overarching protracted promise of knowledge not yet assimilated. All acts of knowledge instigate in us a seeking for its more dramatic completion. Everything groans for God; heaven is not a tributary to existence but its estuary. We genuinely know the real thing itself immaterially, but we do not complete the assimilation of the co-extensive experience of death within each object of knowledge, which would enable our own beings to know ourselves identical with Being, to know as the uncreated knows. We are not Christ, we cannot overcome death. Thus, in knowledge we know ourselves as knowing beings, as the beings who stand on the *confinium* between time and eternity. Because this knowledge unfolds on the more primordially protracted assimilation of death, which, again, does not as of yet complete itself, we are, as result, un-completed and un-finished. We are *knowers* held suspended from our ownmost *beings*: we know ourselves as beings unable completely to catch up to Being. We *knowingly* groan inwardly for God, knowing something is missing in our experience of knowledge; knowing the earth in its "bondage to decay" cannot provide it as assimilated, only unassimilated as death.[26] We know we have had the experiences, all our lives, but missed the meaning, and we are seeking that home that restores the experience in a different form altogether:

> The moments of happiness—not the sense of well-being,
> Fruition, fulfilment, security or affection,
> Or even a very good dinner, but the sudden illumination—
> We had the experience but missed the meaning,
> And approach to the meaning restores the experience

26. Cf. Rom 8:19–23: "For the creation waits with eager longing for the revealing of the children of God; for the creation was subjected to futility, not of its own will but by the will of the one who subjected it, in hope that the creation itself will be set free from its bondage to decay and will obtain the freedom of the glory of the children of God. We know that the whole creation has been groaning in labor pains until now; and not only the creation, but we ourselves, who have the first fruits of the Spirit, groan inwardly while we wait for adoption, the redemption of our bodies."

In a different form, beyond any meaning
We can assign to happiness.[27]

But Christ who turns the tables upside down[28] turned to Martha and said: "I am the resurrection and the life. Those who believe in me, even though they die, will live, and everyone who lives and believes in me will never die."[29] Thus death *should* be able to be taken-in, through Christ, and we *should* have the power to assimilate it into our beings and understand its length and breadth, what it is and what it is not, and what glimmers of the afterlife are present or absent. Christ has placed sin and death into his very being,[30] He has tasted death for all,[31] paid its once insurmountable wages, which did surrender all intentionality,[32] and overturned it, overcoming the world,[33] making "Heaven a house of bread."[34] Christ has revealed death as no longer the end, no longer emptied cessation, but *viatoric*, and thus open to persons assimilating its dispossession without

27. Eliot, "Dry Salvages," *Four Quartets*, 39.

28. Cf. Matt 21:12–13. See also Chesterton, "Jesus or Christ," 159: "If I say 'Suppose the Divine did really walk and talk upon the Earth, what should we be likely to think of it?' I think we should see in such a being exactly the perplexities that we see in the central figure of the Gospels: I think he would seem to us extreme and violent; because he would see some further development in virtue which would be for us untried. I think he would seem to us to contradict himself; because, looking down on life like a map, he would see a connection between things which to us are disconnected. I think, however, that he would always ring true to our own sense of right, but ring (so to speak) too loud and too clear. He would be too good but never too bad for us: 'Be ye perfect.' I think there would be, in the nature of things, some tragic collision between him and the humanity he had created, culminating in something that would be at once a crime and an expiation. I think he would be blamed as a hard prophet for dragging down the haughty, and blamed also as a weak sentimentalist for loving the things that cling in corners, children or beggars. I think, in short, that he would give us a sensation that he was turning all our standards upside down, and yet also a sensation that he had undeniably put them the right way up."

29. John 11:25–26.

30. Cf. 1 Tim 1:15: "This *is* a faithful saying, and worthy of all acceptation, that Christ Jesus came into the world to save sinners; of whom I am chief."

31. Heb 2:9: "But we see Jesus, who was made a little lower than the angels, for the suffering of death crowned with glory and honor, that he, by the grace of God, might taste death for everyone."

32. Rom 6:23: "For the wages of sin is death; but the gift of God is eternal life through Jesus Christ our Lord."

33. John 16:33: "I have said these things to you, that in me you may have peace. In the world you will have tribulation. But take heart; I have overcome the world."

34. St. Ambrose, *Letters*, XI, 13.

unravelling themselves in the process. In Christ, we can become the other as other so inexhaustibly that what is truly lost can be found again and, in a way, for the first time. Christ offers his body and blood at the Last Supper, knowing the death that awaits him, knowing the abandonment and godforsakeness that must unravel all epistemological recognition, placing terrorizing blinders on every act of intentionality. Christ knew that the way to salvation for all is not through a *fiat*, or a sidestepping of the consequences of human action, but *through* death, and *how* death is processed as inconceivability.

> Every soul which receives the bread which comes down from Heaven is a house of bread, the bread of Christ, being nourished and having its heart strengthened by the support of the heavenly bread which dwells within it. Hence Paul says: "We are all one bread." Every faithful soul is Bethlehem, just as that is called Jerusalem which has the peace and tranquility of the Jerusalem on high which is in heaven. That is the true bread which, after it was broken into bits, has fed all men.[35]

Transubstantiation, as supreme offer of life, mirrors as it overturns the epistemological power of death, because in his descent into hell death is the unwieldy tool Christ had to work with in completing the mission of salvation. It is through death that he unfastens the nails from the cross and chisels away at the stone across the tomb. Christ used death within his Being to overcome death within his Being. The Eucharistic species remains unchanged—we see the razed wheat, the temporality, the finitude, the flesh,[36] the brief life, the thin shell of a wafer that reflects the experience as non-experience of death. But inwardly, it is a superabundance of life. That which cannot carry life becomes the vessel *for* life, and that which cannot allow us to assimilate knowledge of death *as death*, interiorly, shows us that we already have assimilated death through partaking in his body and blood. In assimilating Christ's death within the Communion mystery, we have within and overflowing from us the glorified body of our Lord Jesus Christ, for we have always been his other *as other*.[37]

---

35. St. Ambrose, *Letters,* XI, 13.

36. Cf. Isa 40:7–8: "All flesh is like grass, and all its glory like the flowers of the field. The grass withers and the flowers fall when the breath of the LORD blows on them; indeed, the people are grass. The grass withers and the flowers fall, but the word of our God stands forever." See also 1 Pet 1:24–25.

37. Cf. St. Jerome, "Short Commentaries," §1390, *The Faith of the Early Fathers,* 203: "After the type had been fulfilled by the Passover celebration and He had eaten

To know the real thing itself immaterially lends startling credence to the idea of the resurrected state. While it is by no means *necessary* that we be resurrected, it is by no means *unnatural, nonsensical,* or opposing the ways in which human beings know. In fact, the way in which we know through assimilation points to the reality that all assimilated knowledge invites a deeper completion. In the resurrected state, the person is now re-granted his embodiment as truly co-extensive and co-substantiating participation, one with Being, and not divided by death as a result of original sin. Our sin cuts the knowing process short, rendering death, or the life past death, unassimilated. In knowing the real thing itself, we liberate the other from its materiality, which does possess that non-conceptuality of death. Knowledge is in inverse ratio to materiality; the greater the knowledge the greater the immateriality. To a certain degree, we are granted access into death's meaning by that materiality that first triggered but which alone cannot show. Christianity reveals the deeper meaning of flesh, through and past materiality. Flesh itself signifies eternal life.

> The Christian religion is the only one that, overlooking the supremely evident fact of the mortality of the flesh—which has pushed all other religions towards spiritualization as the only possible path to Salvation—has found in the flesh, in the mortal, eucharistic, mystical, resurrecting flesh, the unsurpassable end of the ways of God. This concrete, extremely problematic man who is imprisoned and sunk in his flesh: God has him and no other in view; he intends to become one, truly "one flesh," with him.[38]

the flesh of the lamb with His Apostles, He takes bread which strengthens the heart of man, and goes on to the true Sacrament of the Passover, so that just as Melchisedech, the priest of the Most High God, in prefiguring Him, made bread and wine an offering, He too makes Himself manifest in the reality of His own Body and Blood."

38. Balthasar, *Theo-Logic* II, 221.

5

Summary Remarks

THE TYPE OF SPIRITUAL life, and most especially afterlife, reflective of our carnality lends essential clarification to our discussions of the meaning of death, hell, and purgatory. Death is the torn separation of the body, which is unnatural *for* the soul, as the soul perfects itself *naturally* united to a body. Personal human death has dramatic competing layers of metaphysical and phenomenological unnaturalness that does not annihilate the spiritual super-naturalness won through the cross and resurrection, nor does the cross ever obscure the heartbreaking reality of death.

> My spirit is overwhelmed within me; my heart within me is desolate. I remember the days of old; I meditate on all thy works; I muse on the work of thy hands. I stretch forth my hands unto thee: my soul thirsteth after thee, as a thirsty land. Selah. Hear me speedily, O LORD: my spirit faileth: hide not thy face from me, lest I be like unto them that go down into the pit.[1]

In death, the nativity's Christ child is now liturgically, and in every unendurable sense of the literal, not too far removed to be recalled, but too near us, so tragically near that ours is his, that mine is thine. What an inheritance of impotence did our Christ take on to complete the distance that was ours to complete! The Psalmist's words echo *almost* its length

---

1. Ps 143:3–8. Cf. Matt 27:46: "And about the ninth hour Jesus cried with a loud voice, saying, *Eli, Eli, lama sabachthani?* that is to say, My God, my God, why hast thou forsaken me?" See also Ps 42:9.

in space and time: "Why art thou so far from helping me, and from the words of my roaring?"[2] How can we forget that the Son, pinned to the dead tree of fallen ends and failed deeds, not only aged all the ages, with skin broken, faded, parched, and bones quaking beneath, but did so as the joy within the womb, as the child nourished on the breast, who laid near his mother's heart, a holy innocent ever cradled in her embrace. His thirst in dying is his thirst in the manger. How impossible this is, and yet truly the only thing needful. From cradle to cross Christ becomes so profoundly our impotence. Here the beauty of the nativity is too near, the reality of love, as the total giving forth, is everything *because* it has pierced our sin so profoundly and entered its nothingness by means of abandonment and dispossession.

The only way is the way without power, becoming the surrender that prefigures all surrender. Yes, we wait without hope, for we are not ready for hope. My God, my God, this is the exquisite armory made by your absence, the exquisite gift of being forsaken. The Christ child is simultaneously the crucified one, and will bear what we cannot, will give up the only ghost worthy to inhabit flesh and blood, for unless we be like this child, we cannot enter the kingdom of heaven. Please make us ready for hope.

If death, and through it the state of the separated soul—in bruising separation—is not carefully clarified in its manifold tensions, then what is left to waste away is any genuine sense of, and yearning for, paradise.[3] As a result, we can see the fictionalizing escapism that renders the doctrine of hell a fable encouraging moral rectitude but that in fact does not have any existential relevance. If the sense of hell, that we are under threat

---

2. Ps 22:1.

3. We have seen this "laying to waste" in many other related arenas of human life. Take for example theology of the body, which is always on the defensive against the postmodernist revolution that sees such theological conceptions as not only antiquated but vicious, because un-freeing, and opposed to the dignity of secular autonomy. The arguments in theology of the body work to illustrate that it is in fact the secular conceptions of the flesh that obfuscate human dignity. I contend that theology of the body can *only* function from within a conception of the unity of body and soul that, while fully rooted in nature, is only fully realized in heaven as permanent home. It is this latter part that is mentioned but too quickly bypassed vis-à-vis the "better place," and to our detriment. If we cannot show how death is simultaneously an unnatural state now shot through with supernatural meaning through Christ's incarnation overcoming of the world—which gifts our own flesh and blood with the grace to co-substantiate the architecture of paradise—we do not have a leg to stand on that can vigorously counteract such virulent rationalisms and nihilisms.

of judgment, is diminished out of public discourse, and estranged from hearts and minds, or if hell is only for others[4]—with the kind of smug certainty that removes the existential risk involved in perfect love—then what results is a reduction of heaven to a thoughtless utopia caressing and substantiating our many ideological preferences. Are the notions that "all are saved" or "hell is for others," the unfortunate repercussion of our forgetting that earth is not our permanent home? Are such notions as blank and empty as the "off to a better place"? And more still, do they undermine the very *viatoric* nature of persons, as nomads wandering the earth, restless until our hearts rest in Christ?

> I accuse myself of having prayed but little or badly for the dead, of having thought of them only on certain days and along with the crowd, forgetting that they may need me every moment of the day, that they are more defenceless than children and that our thoughts should never abandon their painful cradle: forgetting that every single one of the dead needs every single one of us, and that a collective homage does not abate their suffering, which is still more individually felt than the suffering of the living. . . . I accuse myself of having practically forgotten the Dogma of Purgatory, of not having realized to what an extent it reveals the splendour of the divine justice, of not having realized that a too earthly soul, having caught a glimpse of heaven, itself experiences the admirable necessity of preparing itself the better therefore *by purifying itself*—that the dead are very great souls, which consider themselves not beautiful enough for the beauty of God, and which, like the Saints on Earth, but more than the Saints, are consumed with a sublime ferocity of desire to eradicate every imperfection in themselves and to burn the old Adam. . . . I accuse myself of having, in my own heart, allowed the dead to die.[5]

We seek throughout to glimpse the restlessness so deeply reflected in the teachings on purgatory, and its foretaste experienced on earth as sweet suffering antechamber to heaven. While disappointing, it is not surprising that prayers for souls in purgatory have diminished, it is an unmistakable symptom of the loss of heaven as simultaneously the loss of the powerful union of body and soul. We may then genuinely argue that when we lose heaven, our permanent home, we emaciate the transcendent figure at root which realizes human nature. When we lose

4. See Balthasar, *Dare We Hope*, 50–57.
5. Debout, *My Sins of Omission*, 14–17.

purgatory, then we lose the immediacy conditioning all human predicaments, losing arduous mystical hope,[6] and replacing it with either empty wish-fulfillment or nihilistic despair.[7] And when we lose the threat of hell, and by that I mean either encamping in the prideful certainty of its existence (more often for others) or equally false certainty of its irrelevance or non-existence, we become reflections of a diminished love, a vitiated love,[8] that has now traded itself for lies dressed up *as love*—lies that caress only to deform human nature, society, politics, and human relations.[9] The union of body and soul, of spirit and flesh, has always been the key to that essential and sustaining glimpse of paradisal perfection. Such a glimpse is far more joyful and needful than the traveler finding water in the desert. Only through it can we then encounter the mystery of death as passageway to what it is to be persons intentionally co-substantiating the very architecture of heaven.[10]

6. For an encounter with purgative and mystical hope, see St. John of the Cross, *Spiritual Canticle*, XXXVI–XXXIX

Let us rejoice, O my Beloved!
Let us go forth to see ourselves in Your beauty,
To the mountain and the hill,
Where the pure water flows:
Let us enter into the heart of the thicket.
We shall go at once
To the deep caverns of the rock
Which are all secret,
There we shall enter in
And taste of the new wine of the pomegranate.
There you will show me
That which my soul desired;
And there You will give at once,
O You, my life!
That which You gave me the other day.
The breathing of the air,
The song of the sweet nightingale,
The grove and its beauty
In the serene night,
With the flame that consumes, and gives no pains.

7. Cf. Camus, *Caligula*, 73.

8. We lose the sense of love as true self-giving, as *ekstasis*. See Pope Benedict XVI, *Deus Caritas Est* §6: "Love is indeed 'ecstasy,' not in the sense of a moment of intoxication, but rather as a journey, an ongoing exodus out of the closed inward-looking self towards its liberation through self-giving."

9. The terrible sin of abortion on demand is a powerful example of hell no longer bearing any relevance in human life.

10. Cf. Wolfgang Amadeus Mozart's letter to his father, the composer Leopold

Mozart, 4th of April 1787 in Steptoe, *Mozart-Da Ponte Operas*, 84: "As death, when we come to consider it closely, is the true goal of our existence, I have formed during the last few years such close relationships with this best and truest friend of mankind that death's image is not only no longer terrifying to me, but is indeed very soothing and consoling, and I thank my God for graciously granting me the opportunity . . . of learning that death is the key which unlocks the door to our true happiness. I never lie down at night without reflecting that—young as I am—I may not live to see another day. Yet no one of all my acquaintances could say that in company I am morose or disgruntled."

Part II

Heaven & the Mystery of Forgiveness

6

Forgiveness as Price of Admission

Four difficulties

> Therefore, if thou bring thy gift to the altar, and there remem-
> berest that thy brother hath ought against thee; leave there thy
> gift before the altar, and go thy way; first be reconciled to thy
> brother, and then come and offer thy gift.[1]

A S CHRIST IS HUNG on the cross, his first saying is one of forgiveness.
As Son, he asks with all children that our Father forgive us, for we
know not what we do.[2] This is one of the most enigmatic sayings in the
Gospel and central to the drama of salvation. There is no salvation, no
heaven, no resurrected state, no happiness without forgiveness. Before the
Son of Man offers up his spirit so that we may recover our true home,
before he descends into godforsakeness, suffering every human cruelty
to the bitter end of each of their non-sequiturs, he lays everything on

---

1. Matt 5:23–24.

2. Luke 23:34–37: "Then said Jesus, Father, forgive them; for they know not what
they do. And they parted his raiment, and cast lots. And the people stood beholding.
And the rulers also with them derided him, saying, he saved others; let him save himself, if he be Christ, the chosen of God. And the soldiers also mocked him, coming to
him, and offering him vinegar, and saying, If thou be the king of the Jews, save thyself."

the question of forgiveness. For us properly to encounter the inkling of heaven that visited earth, we must set out to understand the nature of forgiveness, separating the wheat from the chaff, the genuine lifesaving *kenosis* overflowing within each of us, as opposed to the multitudinous substitutes and surrogates through which we inoculate ourselves against the genuine experiences of guilt, penance, peace, and surrender. A mismanaged view of forgiveness is symptomatic of an emptied heaven, and even of a hell on earth. Let us diagnostically examine four difficult claims regarding forgiveness and penance, seeing which ones open up the door to our natures, and which ones block that passageway. In doing so, we hope to come closer to experience the forgiveness Christ offers to us as prerequisite to salvation and happiness.[3]

Listed below are five existential alternatives when confronted with the question of giving and receiving forgiveness. Our intention is first to skirt the surface of this difficulty, then enter the depths, and throughout play devil's advocate in our efforts to expose the rigorous forgiveness that is truly in the image and likeness of Christ's dying plea on our behalf:

A. *Why can't we resent and hold the grudge as recognition of injustice against us? Why are vengeance and resentment bad? Why is forgiveness the unqualified good?*

> The "humanitarian" blessings of Christianity forsooth! To breed out of *humanitas* a self-contradiction, an art of self-pollution, a will to lie at any price, an aversion and contempt for all good and honest instincts! All this, to me, is the "humanitarianism" of Christianity!—Parasitism as the only practice of the church; with its anemic and "holy" ideals, sucking all the blood, all the love, all the hope out of life; the beyond as the will to deny all reality; the cross as the distinguishing mark of the most

---

3. Cf. Chekhov, "The Student," *Selected Stories*, 266: "The student thought again that if Vasilisa wept and her daughter was troubled, then obviously what he had just told them, something that had taken place nineteen centuries ago, had a relation to the present—to both women, and probably to this desolate village, to himself, to all people. If the old woman wept, it was not because he was able to tell it movingly, but because Peter was close to her and she was interested with her whole being in what had happened to Peter's soul. And joy suddenly stirred in his soul, and he even stopped for a moment to catch his breath. The past, he thought, is connected with the present in an unbroken chain of events flowing one out of the other. And it seemed to him that he had just seen both ends of that chain: he touched one end, and the other moved."

subterranean conspiracy ever heard of,—against health, beauty, well-being, intellect, kindness of soul—against life itself.[4]

What worth or use is it adopting Christian values concerning forgiveness, when it likely exposes one to more pain, deception, distrust, and with little gain. Have we been conditioned, even historically indoctrinated within both East and Western spiritualities, to view the grudge as opposing value?[5] Perhaps the resentment is finally the purgative force strong enough to ensure we stick to so-called healthy boundaries, to provide the essential space that will allow us to avoid additional hurt and to re-evaluate the relationship with the other. When we take the claimed "noble or high road," are we constantly attempting to experience what the other is experiencing? Are we thwarting the potentially positive aspects of the grudge and its anger via the ubiquitous belief that said emotions are deleterious to our emotional health?[6] Are we neglecting the time needed to orient and know oneself, to understand what actions we should and should not bear? Perhaps by *not* holding the grudge, we are promoting anemic ideals that will only fester in the long run, that suck all the healthy and honest instincts out of human experience. Perhaps the grudge, in all its anger, will allow us to develop some self-love rather than pernicious self-pity.

In Euripides' *Medea*, the heart of the tragedy is the anger (*khólos*) and rage (*lyssa*) of Medea, a jilted and betrayed wife. The very power of

---

4. Nietzsche, *The Antichrist*, §62.

5. Cf. Buddha, *Dhammapada*, §231–34: "Beware of bodily anger, and control thy body! Leave the sins of the body, and with thy body practice virtue! Beware of the anger of the tongue, and control thy tongue! Leave the sins of the tongue, and practice virtue with thy tongue! Beware of the anger of the mind, and control thy mind! Leave the sins of the mind, and practice virtue with thy mind! The wise who control their body, who control their tongue, the wise who control their mind, are indeed well controlled."; Rom 12:19: "Dearly beloved, avenge not yourselves, but rather give place unto wrath: for it is written, Vengeance is mine; I will repay, saith the Lord."

6. Cf. Callard, "The Philosophy of Anger": "Suppose that you are angry on Tuesday because I stole from you on Monday. Suppose that on Wednesday I return what I stole; I compensate you for any disadvantage occasioned by your not having had it for two days; I offer additional gifts to show my good will; I apologize for my theft as a moment of weakness; and, finally, I promise never to do it again. Suppose, in addition, that you believe my apology is sincere and that I will keep my promise. Could it be rational for you to be just as angry on Thursday as you were on Tuesday? Moreover, could it be rational for you to conceive of a plan to steal from me in turn? And what if you don't stop at one theft: could it be rational for you to go on to steal from me again, and again, and again."

this anger gives Medea the strength to calculate levels of revenge that will destroy everything in her wake, including her own children; to punish cowardly Jason for his "shamelessness." Medea learns from her unfaithful husband, Jason (of the Golden Fleece), that he is arranging to marry Glauce, princess of Corinth, daughter of King Creon. To avoid Medea's wrath and her powers as a sorceress, King Creon arranges to send Medea into exile. Jason's enfeebled rationale for this betrayal is that this is an opportunity to elevate his standing; how can he pass up the opportunity to marry royalty—Medea is a barbarian, Glauce is a Princess, only through the latter can his family elevate their social standing. Jason alleviates any passageway into salvific guilt through a glut of promises: to keep her as a mistress, to figure a way to unite the families, to take care of her and the children, that he will not disown them.

> Worst of the Worst! I can say only this,
> the greatest insult I can offer for your cowardice.
> You have come here, my bitterest enemy, here.
> There is no sign of boldness or of courage,
> to stand and face the family you have wronged.
> It's the worst of all human diseases:
> Shamelessness.[7]

Medea, witnessing his shamelessness, does not see how she will "profit" from ending her anger (*khólos*) as Jason entreats her to do. And this question of "profit" is the prime question: in which respect does she actually profit, what choice or choices allow justice to take effect? How is it fair or just for her to bear the brunt of Jason's trickery dressed up as generosity?

> I'm not going to debate you anymore.
> If you want to accept the help my money
> can give you and the children in your exile,
> say so. I'm prepared to give without stint.
> I'll send tokens to my friends; they'll treat you well.
> You're a fool woman, if you're not willing
> to take it. You'll profit more if you end your anger.[8]

Euripides' Medea sees her plans to avenge this injustice as supported by the gods.[9] She is not only justifiable in anger, but justifiable in vengeance. Herein lies the difficulty: the offender should know not

---

7. Medea to Jason. Euripides, "Medea," *The Greek Plays*, §465–72.

8. Jason to Medea. Euripides, "Medea," *The Greek Plays*, §609–15.

9. Cf. Medea to Jason. Euripides, "Medea," *The Greek Plays*, §625–28.

abstractly but existentially—and into his spirit and sinews—the pain of being the author of injustice, otherwise the offender cannot learn. We can view vengeance in two ways: 1) as justice or a justifiable avenging that is instructive and necessary, or 2) an unjust revenge or retribution that further damages the delicate balances of human relationships. What then is the difference between the two, keeping in mind the education of the offender? It seems that this justifiable avenging evokes:

a) a proportionate response to the offense

b) the punishment/suffering given to the offender is properly measured and handed out by proper figures in society, by God, so that it can instruct and elicit moral virtue, and

c) the offender must experience the damage the sin/offense has caused in order to understand why it must be avoided.

Whereas unjust vengeance promotes:

a) a disproportionate response exceeding the original suffering of the offense

b) is handed out in a way that exceeds the authority/rights of the person doling out this vengeance (i.e., this person has not the right to exact this type of punishment) and

c) the disproportionate suffering overwhelms the eliciting of any moral lesson.

To play devil's advocate: If one murders another, why is execution of the offender unjust? Why is castration for the rapist unjust? Why *isn't* it unjust to give the sex offender a fifteen to twenty year sentence with a heaping of various behests for forgiveness? Doesn't such a form of justice carry more than a whiff of illegitimacy? More still, doesn't such a scenario seem disproportionate? If the difference between just and unjust vengeance is rooted in a proportionate response to the offence, wouldn't execution for the murderer be proportionate, and fifteen to twenty years jail and forgiveness for the pedophilia and rape potentially be woefully disproportionate, given what is taken away from the child? Does the so-called redeemed and healed offender make any whit of difference, help in any way, the one who was victimized? Perhaps it does, but the spiritual status of the two should not be so expeditiously conflated. Isn't the one who was victimized the *most* entitled to exact vengeance, to know when the punishment is proportionate to the offense?

> I don't want the mother to embrace the oppressor who threw her son to the dogs! She dare not forgive him! Let her forgive him for herself, if she will, let her forgive the torturer for the immeasurable suffering of her mother's heart. But the sufferings of her tortured child she has no right to forgive; she dare not forgive the torturer, even if the child were to forgive him! And if that is so, if they dare not forgive, what becomes of harmony? Is there in the whole world a being who would have the right to forgive and could forgive? I don't want harmony. From love for humanity I don't want it. I would rather be left with the unavenged suffering. I would rather remain with my unavenged suffering and unsatisfied indignation, even if I were wrong. Besides, too high a price is asked for harmony; it's beyond our means to pay so much to enter on it. And so I hasten to give back my entrance ticket, and if I am an honest man I am bound to give it back as soon as possible. And that I am doing. It's not God that I don't accept, Alyosha, only I most respectfully return him the ticket.[10]

If we avoid these difficulties, how can we envision heaven as anything other than the scrap heap for unresolved justice, love, and harmony? And while the earth and its passengers are *viatoric*, and heaven is the home that resolves all earthly irresolution, it cannot be done by way of fantastical dispensation. Heaven is not the dung-pile of worthless knowledge, but the mystery that fulfills every worthwhile yearning. Let us not neglect to recognize the dirty and difficult business of life. The right instruction—the proportionate justice—which has the power to elicit within the offender a remorseful recognition of his evil deeds— especially one so steeped in lies and self-delusion—is no easy feat. This proportionate response is full of risks that are messy, horrendous, and themselves costly, but then perhaps the cycle of vengeance and justice is so costly—so entrenched in generational original sin—that we can never excise ourselves from it.[11] Thus, weighing so many of these layered con-

---

10. Dostoevsky, *The Brothers Karamazov*, 245.

11. Cf. Girard, *Violence and the Sacred*, 15: "Precisely because murder inspires horror and because men must be forcibly restrained from murder, vengeance is inflicted on all those who commit it. The obligation never to shed blood cannot be distinguished from the obligation to exact vengeance on those who shed it." And Girard, *Violence and the Sacred*, 87: "Men cannot confront the naked truth of their own violence without the risk of abandoning themselves to it entirely. They have never had a very clear

flicts, is Medea correct in her rationale for vengeance? Is her response to Jason, which includes the murder of their own children, the death of Jason's father in-law and new wife, proportionate and just on the basis just set out? We respond with a resounding and confident "no," but still shouldn't we take a closer look at this whole question and why Medea felt driven to such lengths in her quest for justice.

The genesis of anger (*khólos*) in the tragedy foreshadows what is to come. Medea is filled with a heavy-hearted anger (*Baruthumon organ*). This is the type of anger that refuses at its core to accept the insults, the belittling, the diminishment Jason places upon her. He has wronged her, their children, and the bond they forged; he has forsaken them wholly, as if they had never played a consequential role in his life. Medea recognizes this and sees her anger as justifiable: she left Colchis, her homeland (where she is considered a semi-divine royalty descended from the sun god Helios) to marry Jason; she was instrumental in helping Jason obtain the Golden Fleece and preventing him from dying; she betrayed (even killed) her own family and people to protect Jason's life; she bore him children, which she rightly considers a fundamental gift and a core reflection of their indelible bond. But Jason's responses only inflame Medea's justifiable anger. He claims: a) she's irrational: he argues that Medea's whole exile and situation could have been avoided if she was not so unreasonable. If she had not, through her irrational and unpredictable rage, angered King Creon, all would be well; b) he's generous: that the marriage to Glauce (while still married to Medea) actually intercedes on her behalf and their children's by raising their social standing; c) he has no obligation towards her, in spite of years of marriage. Jason then tells Medea that all the sacrifices she made for him does not mean he shares a responsibility or obligation for them. Because she did them freely out of love, he does not bear responsibility for them; d) his actions benefit her and she should be grateful: he argues that he is being rational, thinking things through in a way that will benefit her and their entire family in the long run. In a word, he is being a friend to Medea. Jason reiterates how his actions benefit the standing of their family. He even argues that

---

idea of this violence, and it is possible that the survival of all human societies of the past was dependent on this fundamental lack of understanding." See also Girard, *The One by Whom Scandal Comes,* 18: "To escape responsibility for violence we imagine it is enough to pledge never to be the first to do violence. But no one ever sees himself as casting the first stone. Even the most violent persons believe that they are always reacting to a violence committed in the first instance by someone else."

marrying Glauce does Medea no wrong, that instead, it secures a place
for them in Corinth, that she can be his mistress, and over time both
families can unite (effectively with royal standing).[12] To all of this Medea
responds:

> I differ from many people in many ways:
> I think for instance, the unjust person who makes
> clever speeches deserves the harshest penalty.
> He's so sure he can deck out wrongdoing
> with pretty words that he'd do any crime.
> But he's not clever. Nor are you. Don't pretend
> with smart talk that you're on my side. One word's
> enough to flatten you.
> You saw in old age
> a foreign marriage wouldn't serve you well.[13]

Does Medea's justifiable anger translate into justifiable deceit? Does
it translate into the loss of lives, including her own children? It cannot.
But affirming that Medea takes the gravely wrong path does not resolve
the predicament over Jason's actions and his indifference to their evils.
It is his cowardice and indifference that drive Medea to such terrible
lengths. Thus, again, recognizing that Medea has made the worst choices
reacting against Jason's indifference and cruelty does not alleviate the
difficulty of justice and forgiveness when confronted with persons like
Jason. Jason has thoroughly inoculated himself against the experience
of genuine remorse and regret through his repeated betrayals. How is
he to *learn* the experience of the injustice he has caused unless it does
involve the glaring, galling, and messy business of life that Medea surely
seeks to offer him in return?[14] Medea's way is utterly sinful, but uneasily
effective in concretizing for Jason what it means to surrender one's family,
to forsake one's bonds. Medea disabuses him of the sin that one can exist
unscathed after having alienated the forms of intentional otherness that

---

12. Jason to Medea. Euripides, "Medea," *The Greek Plays,* §693–97:
Get this into your head: it wasn't for the woman
I made the royal marriage I now have.
As I said before, I wanted to protect you,
to father children from the same seed
as my two sons, a safeguard for my house.

13. Euripides, "Medea," *The Greek Plays,* §597–606.

14. Cf. Matt 25:12: "'Lord, Lord,' they said, 'open the door for us!' But he replied,
'Truly I tell you, I don't know you.'"

sustained him for so long. How, then, do we separate the sinfulness but retain the effectiveness?

How can justice walk that tightrope? Can we, in a world of dead ends, achieve such succinct moral calibration? Or are we to turn the other cheek?[15] But does that choice emancipate us from the difficulties of justice[16] and is it not even more fraught with its own difficulties? Does turning the other check allow justice to go on unchecked, or rather deferred as God's problem—and perhaps becoming the supreme problem, irreconcilable even for him?[17] Is the Christian choice only *tacitly* recognizing the injustice, is the score only settled with an insufficient, mediocre, and anemic justice that weeps like a gaping wound badly bandaged, where such a justice will soon turn septic? Or is our turning of the cheek the most powerful form of resistance,[18] the surrender to the divine form of justice, a way to halt the dying of the light within each of us?[19]

15. Matt 5:38–40: "You have heard that it was said, 'Eye for eye, and tooth for tooth.' But I tell you, do not resist an evil person. If anyone slaps you on the right cheek, turn to them the other cheek also. And if anyone wants to sue you and take your shirt, hand over your coat as well."

16. Bentham, "Principal of Penal Law," *The Works*, 382: "The forgiveness of injuries is a virtue necessary to humanity; but it is only a virtue when justice has done its work, when it has furnished or refused a satisfaction. Before this, to forgive injuries is to invite their perpetration—is to be, not the friend, but the enemy of society. What could wickedness desire more, than an arrangement by which offences should be always followed by pardon?"

17. How *would* God—as infinitely extending and relational Goodness—bear the separation of us from him, who sent his only Son on a rescue mission that cost him everything? How does the inflicting of such punishment as Christ no longer recognizing us as his beloved other, harmonize with such inexhaustible love? Are we to accept that the infinite will surrenders to the finite will, or that the infinite will violates the consequences of human free will to forsake God's love? Cf. St. John Chrysostom, Homily 23:9, *Nicene and Post Nice Fathers*, 10: "No doubt Hell, and that punishment is a thing not to be borne. Yet though one supposes ten thousand Hells, he will utter nothing like what it will be to fail of that blessed glory, to be hated of Christ to hear 'I know you not,' to be accused for not feeding him when we saw him [hungry]."

18. Cf. Girard, *Things Hidden Since the Foundation of the World*, 211: "But we must see that there is no possible compromise between killing and being killed. . . . For all violence to be destroyed, it would be sufficient for all mankind to decide to abide by this rule. If all mankind offered the other cheek, no cheek would be struck. . . . If all men loved their enemies, there would be no more enemies. But if they drop away at the decisive moment, what is going to happen to the one person who does not drop away? For him the word of life will be changed into the word of death. It is absolute fidelity to the principle defined in his own preaching that condemns Jesus. There is no other cause for his death than the love of one's neighbor lived to the very end, with an infinitely intelligent grasp of the constraints it imposes."

19. Cf. Tolstoy, *Father Sergius*, 39: "They told him that people needed him, and

Perhaps anger is the purifying emotion, the fundamental mechanism of morality that staves off apathy and indifference derived from the dry scholastic overly intellectualized theoretical view of life. If morality is derived from the social netting of how we feel about one another personally, politically, religiously, if our status as moral beings rests entirely on our ability to take a stance, to be affected, to be swept up and to fight for perceived goods and against perceived evils, then wouldn't morality be at root not an intellectual activity but an affective or sentiment-based exercise? If morality is rooted in what we care about, so much so that it is contingent upon those cares, then for Euripides' Medea, anger should not be suppressed but rather allowed to be our guiding emotion, fighting off the dryness of intellectual indifference.[20] The intensity of anger, directed toward a particular person, situation, perceived injustice, has that power to arouse feelings, to change minds, to shame those who do a perceived evil. But if justice and mercy are purely sentiment-based activities depositing themselves around the poisoned wells of subjectivism and relativism, then the need for salvation is overplayed and dried up. The question of forgiveness becomes one of relativizing stances, each with its own rules and absolutisms and hell or heaven, and all the utopic stances in-between are nothing more than derivatives of our affective imagination.

---

that fulfilling Christ's law of love he could not refuse their demand to see him, and that to avoid them would be cruel. He could not but agree with this, but the more he gave himself up to such a life the more he felt that what was internal became external, and that the fount of living water within him dried up, and that what he did now was done more and more for men and less and less for God. Whether he admonished people, or simply blessed them, or prayed for the sick, or advised people about their lives, or listened to expressions of gratitude from those he had helped by precepts, or alms, or healing (as they assured him)—he could not help being pleased at it, and could not be indifferent to the results of his activity and to the influence he exerted. He thought himself a shining light, and the more he felt this the more was he conscious of a weakening, a dying down of the divine light of truth that shone within him. 'In how far is what I do for God and in how far is it for men?' That was the question that insistently tormented him and to which he was not so much unable to give himself an answer as unable to face the answer. In the depth of his soul he felt that the devil had substituted an activity for men in place of his former activity for God. He felt this because, just as it had formerly been hard for him to be torn from his solitude so now that solitude itself was hard for him. He was oppressed and wearied by visitors, but at the bottom of his heart he was glad of their presence and glad of the praise they heaped upon him."

20. Cf. Russell, "Science and Ethics," *Ethical Theory*, 24: "Every attempt to persuade people that something is good (or bad) in itself, and not merely in its effects, depends upon the art of rousing feelings."

What's the universal good of forgiveness if only a psychological sentiment? Forgiveness cannot undo what has been done, and if it is only a sentimental or psychological experience, then we cannot claim it to be a universal good at the core of human nature and experience. In such a scenario, each person would have to decide whether forgiveness is valuable on the basis of what will benefit her psychology. This applies to both the trespasser and the trespassed-against. Both would have to determine the condition and value of forgiveness before deciding what actions are deemed offensive or not, relative to each. And each may choose to support or reject this exchange on the basis of personal preferences at the time. This means that the question of actual existential culpability would not be central to the issue of forgiveness! Instead, the issue would be whether our giving or receiving pardon—for whatever offense, whether or not it is an offense at all—benefits us emotionally at that particular time and place. In a sentimentalizing view of forgiveness, demanding or proffering forgiveness is indifferent to whether or not such an act can remit sins. Instead, what becomes meaningful is whether the linguistic eloquence of the pardoned or pardoner accomplishes superiority among competing psychological perspectives.

But what becomes of a world where forgiveness is reductively conditioned upon a psychological mindset? More still, what would be the point of forgiveness, why all of the rigamarole of it when there are a penumbra of easier ways to experience euphoria or pleasure or release? Why deal with it? The quest to understand forgiveness must be more than a sentimentalizing *accoutrement*, otherwise, "thy will be done" becomes the motto not only of the atheist, but of the one who sees no reason to forgive or to be forgiven. And "forgive us our trespasses as we forgive those who trespass against us," becomes something to tweak based on the conditions of each historical era. The entirety of Medea's person and being is enveloped in anger, through it she descends into wells of sin, but what drives her is objective justice, not mere personal offense. The question of atonement is far more serious than one of competing affective stances. Medea misses the mark in devastating fashion, but still she recognizes the mark must be somewhere, the line that divides good and evil, heaven and hell, is at stake for her, as it is for all of us. Anger is uneasily but fundamentally at the core of the human experience, which stands somewhere between mortal and immortal, with a foot simultaneously in both camps yet a stranger/alienated from full admission to both. Earth is neither heaven nor hell but is formed of both camps, and we travelers must find the clues to our home within its unified womb and tomb.

When one act of violence occurs, it threatens to set off a chain reaction of endless mimetic retaliatory violence and interminable rectifying vengeance.[21] Sacrifice is essential and instituted by each civilization to break the eternal historical cycle of reciprocal violence associated with the concept of endless revenge. Revenge here is not solely retaliatory but also seeks to reform/teach the offender justice through a sheer experience of how original offense was unjust. Vengeance is viewed as the punishment designed to express how much human beings abhor violence, but once within vengeance the cycle cannot be broken without sacrifice, which unites enemies in a common cause, in a common enemy to be sacrificed, which in turn alleviates their anger, tensions, and desires for vengeance. Just as Jason's slight prompted Medea's revenge, her acts of vengeance occasion his threat of violence. There is no stopping this cyclical pattern of anger exorcized in revenge, re-inflamed by the offender now offended exorcizing his own anger in revenge.[22] This view of violence can never be local: Thebes will go against Athens, gods against gods within a competing cyclical exigency. When violence is at the point of threatening the existence of the city, town, country, a rather unnerving psychological and sociological mechanism arises, which is the scapegoat mechanism. This inexhaustible and annihilating communal violence is suddenly and inexplicably projected upon a single innocent individual or separated and earmarked group. Thus, persons and tribes that were formerly fighting and exacting vengeance on the other, now unite in an effort against a chosen individual or group as scapegoat. These enemies become alliances and even friends, as they communally and ritually participate in the execution of violence against a common enemy. And this violence temporarily, but often for a number of generations, stops. This cessation of the cyclical avenging and violence, culminating in the powerful enjoining of enemies who become allies, allows that civilization to flourish.

---

21. See Girard, "The Beheading of St. John the Baptist," *The Scapegoat*, 125–48. Rene Girard in his landmark book *The Scapegoat* argues that in all of us, as essential to the formation/growth of all civilizations, is a subterranean "scapegoat mechanism." In reference to Medea, we are going to take this theme loosely and apply it to the question of forgiveness.

22. See Tacitus, "Agricola," 42, 2 in *Bartlett's*, 275: "*Proprium humani ingenii est odisse quem laeseris.*" ("*It belongs to human nature to hate those you have injured.*")

In such a cycle, what then would be forgiveness but a companion to mimetic violence helping to govern and purge its baser instincts. In this regard, we do not have any sense of forgiveness above a sociological framework, and it would not be in the image and likeness of the God-man who seeks in his *kenosis* the total transformation of each human person, and the cleaning of the slate that condemned us to death. This scapegoat mechanism views anger and revenge as terminating in a violence that is "redemptive." But only temporarily and loosely redemptive; redemptive solely as ideologically conforming and coercive. The scapegoat cycle must be played out, again and again, in all of existence. Any sense of forgiveness is thereby conflated with a notion of redemption, which is really another term for the temporary alleviation of violence by way of a covert Hobbesian conformity. This view of forgiveness is not truly emancipatory, transcendent, and grace-filled, as forgiveness is when offered by Christ on Good Friday. This is not the type of forgiveness that can separate the wheat from the chaff,[23] the sheep from the goats,[24] the heavenly from the hellish. Such a diminished notion of forgiveness is nothing other than mimetic violence recovering unity. The initiation of violence, separation, and revolt at one end of the pendulum, climaxes in its artificial opposite—this sociological forgiveness, as time needed to remold society to its will. Sociological violence and forgiveness both serve the same purpose—the remolding of culture and values—and are only a difference of affectivity, and not in nature.[25]

Medea's oppressive "redemptive" violence cannot emancipate itself from the scapegoat cycle, it functions only from within its bondage. She attempts to place Jason within the sheer experience of his offense, to make him undergo the injustice he caused with exacting precision. Forgiveness within this cycle has no power to transform, only to manage protracted tensions until the next rapture of this constructed imitation of unity. If justice means having the offender experience the evils of the injustice as a way of remaking action, Medea views the murder of her

---

23. Matt 3:12.

24. Matt 25:31–46.

25. Girard, *The One by Whom Scandal Comes*, 31: "The most recent phase of the alternation between Occidentalism and primitivism has therefore concealed the essential thing, the universality of violence. A selective blindness in one of two forms has obscured the fact that all cultures, and all individuals without exception, participate in violence; that violence is what structures our collective sense of belonging and our personal identities."

children as the regrettable but necessary scapegoat. This is the act of sheer incalculable violence that alone is capable of breaking Jason, uniting her with the gods, and halting temporarily, by way of despair and trembling, the violence. But this so-called cyclical redemptive violence can never truly redeem. This is why she hesitates briefly before dispatching the lives of her children, calling her actions a "terrible but necessary wrong."[26] All things are bound up in fallenness, so that notions of goodness, redemption, and justice are wedded to evil, violence, and deceit; bonded in such a way that none of these attributes is really the opposite of any other. In such a view, there can be no forgiveness beyond sociological tactic. There can be no heaven either for, in the end, it is indistinguishable from hell.

Does the Gospel reflect the pinnacle of this cycle of anger and violence as finally, once and for all, giving humans a way to avoid redemptive violence with redemptive suffering? Christ as spotless victim, wholly innocent, as fully man and fully God, is the highest victim of redemptive violence, and also the only being who can overcome this cycle. His life, death, and resurrection break the cycle of redemptive violence with redemptive suffering. In the Gospel, the church (Caiaphas) and state (Pilate) subversively unite and conspire to condemn Jesus; two enemies become allies. Christ becomes the ideal scapegoat to exorcise the church and the state's guilt, to impart pseudo-redemption, and sociologically rooted variations of forgiveness and harmony. But Jesus is no ordinary scapegoat: "Father, forgive them, for they do not know what they do."[27] Christ knows *exactly* why he is the supreme scapegoat, and to what depths he must descend in order to break this non-emancipatory cycle that ends in death for all. When he offers us the gift of heaven within his flesh and

26. Euripides, "Medea," *The Greek Plays*, §1241–50
Come then, my heart, and arm yourself. Why wait
to do this terrible but necessary wrong?
Take hold of the sword, you, my wretched hand,
take it. Move to the start of a life of misery.
Don't turn coward, don't think of the children.
Don't remember that you bore them, that they're
most loved. Forget for this short day they are
your children, and then
grieve. Though you'll kill them,
they're your dear flesh and blood. I'm a luckless woman.

27. Luke 23:34. The scapegoat mechanism is mostly an unconscious operation. Scapegoaters do not recognize that they are scapegoating, instead they often think their actions are just or essential, or necessary evils in order to issue justice (i.e., Medea's "terrible but necessary wrong").

blood, he offers us forgiveness in a manner immeasurably greater than any sense of sociological modelling, which only qualifies and condition-alizes the good via the historicism befitting its epoch. Christ's death com-pletes the highest act of redemptive violence, his resurrection overcomes that violence, which hasn't the power to redeem, only condemn, with the gift of redemptive suffering, known and loved before the foundation of the world:

> For you know that it was not with perishable things such as sil-ver or gold that you were redeemed from the empty way of life you inherited from your forefathers, but with the precious blood of Christ, a lamb without blemish or spot. He was known before the foundation of the world, but was revealed in the last times for your sake. Through Him you believe in God, who raised Him from the dead and glorified Him; and so your faith and hope are in God.[28]

Christ transforms that redemptive violence, which temporarily sets things "straight" but inevitably returns us to nihilistic suffering, with re-demptive suffering as a truer form of forgiveness, as passage to eternal life. Christ taught us how to transform ourselves, to be our own scapegoat,[29] "to put off the old self" in ourselves.[30] If any person has a right to hold a grudge, it is Christ. He is wholly innocent, offers only Goodness, Truth, and Beauty, and offers it with unending love to those unworthy and incapable of recovering it on their own. Indeed, we see genuine anger in Christ,[31] there is no unproductive vulgar tolerance within him, noth-ing to muddy the water of his suffering and redemption, nothing that would undervalue his offering of forgiveness as no longer the unqualified

28. 1 Pet 1:18–22.

29. Cf. 1 Pet 4:12–13: "Beloved, do not think it strange concerning the fiery trial which is to try you, as though some strange thing happened to you; but rejoice to the extent that you partake of Christ's sufferings, that when His glory is revealed, you may also be glad with exceeding joy."

30. Cf. Eph 4:22–24: "to put off your old self, which belongs to your former man-ner of life and is corrupt through deceitful desires, and to be renewed in the spirit of your minds, and to put on the new self, created after the likeness of God in true righteousness and holiness."

31. Cf. Matt 21:12–13: "Jesus entered the temple courts and drove out all who were buying and selling there. He overturned the tables of the money changers and the benches of those selling doves. 'It is written,' he said to them, 'My house will be called a house of prayer,' but you are making it 'a den of robbers.'"

good.[32] If Christ were to hold a grudge, if God, his Father, were to retain a justifiable vengeance[33] towards us, then there would be no salvation, no heaven, no love that outwits death. What then is the appropriate balance between anger as purgative, and forgiveness as release, that does not undervalue the delicate relationality of self and other? What type of forgiveness, genuinely, heartrendingly mindful of trespasses both enacted and underwent, leads us to heaven?

1. *Why should I request that persons not resent me to whom I committed injustice?*

> But when I say to you: Think rather of the morrow I do not
> mean: Calculate about the morrow.
> Think of it as a day which will come; and that is all that you
> know about it.
> Do not be like the wretch who tosses and burns in his bed
> In order to grasp the morrow's day.
> Do not put your hand
> On the fruit which is not ripe.
> Know only that the morrow

32. Cf. Nietzsche, *The Antichrist*, §7: "Christianity is called the religion of pity. Pity stands in opposition to all the tonic passions that augment the energy of the feeling of aliveness: it is a depressant. A man loses power when he pities. Through pity that drain upon strength which suffering works is multiplied a thousandfold. Suffering is made contagious by pity; under certain circumstances it may lead to a total sacrifice of life and living energy—a loss out of all proportion to the magnitude of the cause (the case of the death of the Nazarene). This is the first view of it; there is, however, a still more important one. If one measures the effects of pity by the gravity of the reactions it sets up, its character as a menace to life appears in a much clearer light. Pity thwarts the whole law of evolution, which is the law of natural selection. It preserves whatever is ripe for destruction; it fights on the side of those disinherited and condemned by life; by maintaining life in so many of the botched of all kinds, it gives life itself a gloomy and dubious aspect. Mankind has ventured to call pity a virtue (in every superior moral system it appears as a weakness); going still further, it has been called the virtue, the source and foundation of all other virtues—but let us always bear in mind that this was from the standpoint of a philosophy that was nihilistic, and upon whose shield the denial of life was inscribed."

33. God's anger towards mankind is justifiable. He could genuinely have left us unsaved and not sent his only Son. This is not the potentially disastrous anger Nussbaum describes as "status-injury." See Nussbaum, *Anger and Forgiveness*, 21: "Anger is not always, but very often, about status-injury. And status-injury has a narcissistic flavor: rather than focusing on the wrongfulness of the act as such, a focus that might lead to concern for wrongful acts of the same type more generally, the status-angry person focuses obsessively on herself and her standing vis-à-vis others."

Which is always being discussed
Is the day which is to come,
And that it will be in my governance
Like the others.
That is all you need. For everything else, wait.
As for me, God, I have to wait. You make me wait long enough.
You make me wait long enough for repentance after a fault
And contrition after a sin,
And since the beginning of Time I await
Judgement until the Day of Judgement.[34]

What right do I have to request, let alone demand, forgiveness? What gives my faith the power to presume so much over another person, and enable that presumption to go so far as to have God himself wash our feet?[35] If I have trespassed in a such way that what is lost cannot easily be recovered, or recovered at all, then is it not a form of injustice in asking to receive the very forgiveness of which I am wholly unworthy? By accepting forgiveness, am I shortening the experience of punishment and guilt needed to come to terms with my culpability? But then, is it not the purview of forgiveness to inhabit the lives of those unworthy to receive it? The relationship between justice and forgiveness seems to reflect one

---

34. Péguy, *The Mystery of the Holy Innocents*, 85.

35. Cf. Balthasar, *Love Alone is Credible*, 102: "The first thing that must strike a non-Christian about the Christian's faith is that it obviously presumes far too much. It is too good to be true: the mystery of being, revealed as absolute love, condescending to wash his creatures' feet, and even their souls, taking upon himself all the confusion of guilt, all the God-directed hatred, all the accusations showered upon him with cudgels, all the disbelief that arrogantly covers up what he has revealed, all the mocking hostility that once and for all nailed down his inconceivable moment of self-abasement—in order to pardon his creature, before himself and the world. . . . Once a person learns to read the signs of love and thus to believe it, love leads him into the open field wherein he himself can love. If the prodigal son had not believed that the father's love was already there waiting for him, he would not have been able to make the journey home—even if his father's love welcomes him in a way he never would have dreamed of. The decisive thing is that the sinner has heard of a love that could be, and really is, there for him; he is not the one who has to bring himself in line with God; God has always already seen in him, the loveless sinner, the loveless sinner, a beloved child and has looked upon him and conferred dignity upon him in the light of this love. . . . No one can resolve this mystery into dry concepts and explain how it is that God no longer sees my guilt in me, but only in his beloved Son, who bears it for me; or how God sees this guilt transformed through the suffering of love and loves me because I am the one for whom his Son has suffered in love. But the way God, the lover, sees us is in fact the way we are in reality—for God, this is the absolute and irrevocable truth."

of the most pressing human situations: the notion of divine punishment in the afterlife.[36] If we have, in our freely chosen actions, rendered ourselves unworthy, then it be fitting that the hand of justice deal with us, as responsible party. But by rendering ourselves unworthy, we are in the very state that necessarily *precedes* forgiveness, giving forgiveness its very subject matter. What is forgiveness without those unworthy to receive it, who, through grace, are able to ask to be healed: Lord, I am not worthy that you should enter under my roof, but only say the word and my soul shall be healed.[37] It appears that genuine forgiveness works from a different angle than authentic justice while, at the same time, never incompatible in terms of their goals for cultivating goodness, happiness, and redemption. Justice seeks to balance those precarious scales amid innocence and culpability, and on earth, this must be ceaselessly fine-tuned to be as good and fitting as possible. We can never quite find the right calibration, that right earthly justice that becomes for us a "ray of beauty that strikes us to the quick, that almost 'wounds' us, and that invites us to rise toward God."[38] We are always just east of Eden, and west of heaven. There is no time spent in jail that recovers the death of the other, that pays one's dues, and dues must be paid in order to secure that foundation of order that enables love to become commensurate with life and truth, not its enemy.[39] Forgiveness, on the other hand, recognizes the divine incongruity at root in all things, and tries to balance the scales of loss and gain by way of a superabundance of love. All are sinners and all are wholly in need of love as spiritual fecundity. One cannot expect the grieved not to experience resentment for the other who committed the injustice, but both, within the terribly painful netting of original sin, have an obligation to restore the love, trust, goodness that was vitiated. The trespasser audaciously reveals the universal obligation to experience our situatedness as a world of fallen forms. Through our incarnational intentionality, we have a responsibility to counteract every single sin, both our own and those of others, with the desire to recover the love and good nature squandered at its

36. Cf Isa 43:25: "I, even I, am he who blots out your transgressions, for my own sake, and remembers your sins no more."

37. Matt 8:8.

38. Pope Benedict XVI, "General Audience," (08/31/11) §1. See also Plato, *Symposium* 210a–211d.

39. See Balthasar, "Justice and Mercy," *Dare We Hope*, 116–23, for a striking meditation on how God's justice relates to his love.

root.[40] No sin is in isolation, every act is within the fabric of intentionality, where the self needs the other and the other needs the self, where every I is the other given in otherness, and every other is the I given in selfhood. What justice is served in resentment except an all-too-worldly attempt to balance the scales via the abandonment of love? One may be able to balance those scales, to flatten out the world into lovelessness, but this surrenders the very ecstasy of our human yearning, and places us in the earthly hell of self-abandonment from God. The very enactment of love, love that is salvific, cannot co-exist with resentment. All grief demands the impossible; in it resides, in spite *and* because of itself, the possibility of beauty too magnificent to contain.

> Filled with rapture, his soul yearned for freedom, space, vastness. Over him the heavenly dome, full of quiet, shining stars, hung boundlessly. From the zenith to the horizon the still-dim Milky Way stretched its double strand. Night, fresh and quiet, almost unstirring, enveloped the Earth. The white towers and golden domes of the church gleamed in the sapphire sky. The luxuriant autumn flowers in the flowerbeds near the house had fallen asleep until morning. The silence of the Earth seemed to merge with the silence of the heavens, the mystery of the Earth to be touched by the mystery of the stars. . . . Alyosha stood gazing and suddenly, as if he had been cut down, he threw himself to the Earth. . . . It was as if threads from all those innumerable worlds of God all came together in his soul, and it was trembling all over, "touching other worlds." He wanted to forgive everyone for everything, and to ask forgiveness, oh, not for himself! but for all and for everything, "as others are asking for me," rang again in his soul.[41]

2. *If a person is culpable, what is the point of forgiving that other; that person's guilt needs to be settled through his/her own actions not mine. Furthermore, is not my absolution unjust? Am I prematurely extinguishing the just experience of guilt in the one who is culpable?*

---

40. Cf. Stein, *Essays on Woman*, 66: "The direct consequence of original sin gives a clue as to what they may be held accountable for; the consequence was that man and woman saw each other with different eyes than they had previously; they had lost innocence of interchange with one another. So, the first sin may not only be considered as a purely formal one of disobedience of God. Rather it implied a definitive act. . . . Indeed, the act committed could well have been a manner of union that was at variance with the natural order."

41. Dostoevsky, *Brothers Karamazov*, 362.

The Iliad begins as a conflict between Agamemnon and Achilles over justice, and continues so throughout most of the plot. The opening plague is a punishment sent by Apollo for the violation of his priest; the opening quarrel of the leaders concerns the justice of taking prizes from heroes; the subsequent duels and battles lead to an unrelenting bloodletting. However, at the beginning of Book VI, one Trojan, Adrestus, pleads with Menelaos for mercy: "Take me alive, Atrides, take a ransom worth my life!" Although this plea begins to touch the heart of Menelaus, his brother Agamemnon blocks him from carrying out his feelings of compassion by mocking his "tender loving care" and calling for "rough justice, fitting too" against the Trojans, even children in their mothers' wombs.[42]

For the ancient Greek tragedians, there is not a sense of forgiveness and mercy in the way they are dramatically crystallized in Christianity, changing forever the face of human relatedness. With Nietzsche, we may question whether that change benefits us, or whether it promotes the putrefaction of all those tonic passions that reflect genuine tactile embodied living. What level of commitment does the trespassed-against have in the question of forgiveness, and is the role too centralized, too overburdened and distracting? Should not the guilty party be left to her own devices as a more instrumental form of educating the offender? Perhaps the pardoner diminishes the obligations of extolling justice on a societal level when his forgiveness is handed over to the guilty party distinct from the number of other parties also affected by the trespasser's actions.[43] Is one singular

---

42. Leigh, "Forgiveness," 154. See also Leigh, "Forgiveness," 152: "Any study of the origins of 'forgiveness' in Western thought must consider the paradox of Greek culture. A study of the earliest Greek literature and philosophy indicates that the Greeks developed a strong sense of justice and law as related to both gods and humans, but did not develop a concept of forgiveness or mercy. The closest they came to the latter concept was the practice of legal leniency and the notion of 'pity.' But pity was a later development, especially in Greek epics and drama, as a human response to the strict notions of justice and law that dominated their mythology and early philosophy."

43. Cf. Kant, "The Philosophy of Law, *The Philosophy of Law*, 198: "Even if a civil society resolved to dissolve itself with the consent of all its members—as might be supposed in the case of a people inhabiting an island resolving to separate and scatter themselves throughout the whole world—the last murderer lying in prison ought to be executed before the resolution was carried out. This ought to be done in order that everyone may realize the desert of his deeds, and that blood guiltiness may not remain upon the people; for otherwise they will all be regarded as participators in the murder as a public violation of justice." See also Sterba, "Retributive Justice," *Political Theory*, 349–62.

act of forgiveness fair, or does it sidestep the chasms of unrecovered time and life, by undervaluing the incalculable difference between actions and words? Are we alleviating the guilt that alone has the power to chasten and transform? Dostoevsky was intimately acquainted with the armory of torments within the act of forgiveness:

> Listen! I took the case of children only to make my case clearer. Of the other tears of humanity with which the Earth is soaked from its crust to its centre, I will say nothing. I have narrowed my subject on purpose. I am a bug, and I recognise in all humility that I cannot understand why the world is arranged as it is. . . . I want to see with my own eyes the hind lie down with the lion and the victim rise up and embrace his murderer. I want to be there when everyone suddenly understands what it has all been for. All the religions of the world are built on this longing, and I am a believer. But then there are the children, and what am I to do about them? . . . I understand solidarity in sin among men. I understand solidarity in retribution, too; but there can be no such solidarity with children. And if it is really true that they must share responsibility for all their fathers' crimes, such a truth is not of this world and is beyond my comprehension. Some jester will say, perhaps, that the child would have grown up and have sinned, but you see he didn't grow up, he was torn to pieces by the dogs, at eight years old. Oh, Alyosha, I am not blaspheming! I understand, of course, what an upheaval of the universe it will be when everything in Heaven and Earth blends in one hymn of praise and everything that lives and has lived cries aloud: "Thou art just, O Lord, for Thy ways are revealed." When the mother embraces the fiend who threw her child to the dogs, and all three cry aloud with tears, "Thou art just, O Lord!" then, of course, the crown of knowledge will be reached and all will be made clear.[44]

Does forgiveness place an undue societal burden on the victim? And does it, in turn, not place nearly enough on the one who is culpable, whereas leaving that person unforgiven may be more just since it recognizes the un-removability of the trespass, the heartrending everlasting consequences of freely chosen actions:

> But what pulls me up here is that I can't accept that harmony. And while I am on Earth, I make haste to take my own measures. You see, Alyosha, perhaps it really may happen that if I

---

44. Dostoevsky, *Brothers Karamazov*, 243–44.

live to that moment, or rise again to see it, I, too, perhaps, may cry aloud with the rest, looking at the mother embracing the child's torturer, "Thou art just, O Lord!" but I don't want to cry aloud then. While there is still time, I hasten to protect myself, and so I renounce the higher harmony altogether. It's not worth the tears of that one tortured child who beat itself on the breast with its little fist and prayed in its stinking outhouse, with its unexpiated tears to "dear, kind God!" It's not worth it, because those tears are unatoned for. They must be atoned for, or there can be no harmony. But how? How are you going to atone for them? Is it possible? By their being avenged? But what do I care for avenging them? What do I care for a Hell for oppressors? What good can Hell do, since those children have already been tortured? And what becomes of harmony, if there is Hell? I want to forgive. I want to embrace. I don't want more suffering. And if the sufferings of children go to swell the sum of sufferings which was necessary to pay for truth, then I protest that the truth is not worth such a price.[45]

Forgiveness places an extra torment and burden on the victim by demanding the trespassed-against complete the impossible and forgive the unforgivable. For let us remember that the things most in need of forgiveness are as such unforgivable, unremittable, impossible. Let us not delude ourselves: such an act of love, surrender and pardon, one that can go the distance and not terminate in failed love, necessitates the God-man. And he, in and through his "*Eli Eli Lama Sabachthani*," more truly recognized the blinding abandonment and forsakenness within the total risk of forgiveness and redemption. Christ knew our failed loves far better than we do, he knows how little we can bear, and he bears the incongruity, the failed returns, the vitiated hopes, the many pseudo-harmonies that all live within the difficulty of forgiveness.

"Tell me yourself, I challenge your answer. Imagine that you are creating a fabric of human destiny with the object of making men happy in the end, giving them peace and rest at last, but that it was essential and inevitable to torture to death only one tiny creature—that baby beating its breast with its fist, for instance—and to found that edifice on its unavenged tears, would you consent to be the architect on those conditions? Tell me, and tell the truth." "No, I wouldn't consent," said Alyosha softly. "And can you admit the idea that the people for whom you are

45. Dostoevsky, *Brothers Karamazov*, 244–45.

building would agree to accept their happiness on the unjusti-
fied blood of a tortured child, and having accepted it, to remain
forever happy?" "No, I cannot admit it, Brother."[46]

If society demands that I forgive, as if it is an unqualified and universal good, perhaps this will only promote inner resentment, that I must
absolve an injustice that cannot be undone—the rape has happened, the
theft has occurred, the assault cannot be undone.[47] We are always under
threat in the act of pardoning. We may place ourselves in an inauthentic
position as God-usurpers, thinking that we can offer transcendence, offer
something beyond mere words uttered by one fallen being to another.

> Then one of the seraphim flew to me, having in his hand a burn-
> ing coal that he had taken with tongs from the altar. And he
> touched my mouth and said: "Behold, this has touched your
> lips; your guilt is taken away, and your sin atoned for."[48]

There is something to forgiveness that is unseemly, or rather right
down to its quick made to be unseemly. Forgiveness is proffered like water, donned as the ideal frock in situations of nakedness, handed out as
one would disperse party tricks. It is not so simple for beings of the flesh
to touch the lips of the other and take the guilt away, or to be touched with
such burning fire that our own guilt is not only extinguished, but the cav-
ern that remains is filled with a superabundance of goodness. *This* is what
the Greeks caution against, *this* very impotence within us meaningfully
to transact such a rare and holy remission. The grace of forgiveness is repeatedly and illegitimately dressed up as a human power. When our true
powerlessness is misconceived as *dynamis* (δύναμις) it absconds from us

46. Dostoevsky, *Brothers Karamazov*, 245–46.

47. Cf. Mill, *Utilitarianism*, 27: "It is a misapprehension of the utilitarian mode of
thought, to conceive it as implying that people should fix their minds upon so wide
a generality as the world, or society at large. The great majority of good actions are
intended, not for the benefit of the world, but for that of individuals, of which the good
of the world is made up; and the thoughts of the most virtuous man need not on these
occasions travel beyond the particular persons concerned, except so far as is necessary
to assure himself that in benefiting them he is not violating the rights—that is, the
legitimate and authorized expectations—of any one else. The multiplication of happiness is, according to the utilitarian ethics, the object of virtue: the occasions on which
any person (except one in a thousand) has it in his power to do this on an extended
scale, in other words, to be a public benefactor, are but exceptional; and on these occasions alone is he called on to consider public utility; in every other case, private utility,
the interest or happiness of some few persons, is all he has to attend to."

48. Isa 6:6–8.

the undertaking of the cardinal virtues—prudence, temperance,[49] justice, and fortitude[50]—by collapsing the time, and disembodying us to the process by which the virtues must incarnate themselves within our *habitus*. Cardinal virtues are directing and orienting excellences. Let us examine briefly the implicit temporality within each:

a. *Sapiential prudence* is gaining the ability to ascertain the fitting course of action, the appropriate timeliness for each situation. Such gauging balances the incarnational *longior via* where the universal must be accessed through the particular. The sophianic are like painters who have grafted within their beings the right timing: "then the lover of wisdom associated with the divine order will himself become orderly and divine in the measure permitted to man. But calumny is plentiful everywhere."[51]

b. *Sophyrosyne*: What is historically translated as temperance misses the vigor and exigency of such a virtue. This is the humming, translucent, inviting soundness that can permanently enjoin the mind and body. Its effects are moderation, restraint, self-control, but its root is *eros* itself carved in its interplay with *agape*. This most important of the virtues recognizes that no earthly perfection is to be found, and that the appetite for perfection is salvific. It is the learned balancing—gained over lengths of time, which point to heaven, and through the body's aging process, which returns us to the earth—acting between *eros* and *agape*, between the hunt for perfection, opposed to all its substitutes, and the necessity to surrender to the truth, opposed to all its substitutes.

c. *Immemorial Justice*: When Plato in the *Republic* points out that evidence of a corrupted society is its incessant alteration of law,[52]

49. Temperance as a translation of *sophrosyne* does seem to miss its erotic and excelling quality, which enables one to have self-control not out of mediocrity or apathy but out of a ravishing brilliance for the Good.

50. St. Augustine, *Morals of the Catholic Church*, XV, 25: "For these four virtues (would that all felt their influence in their minds as they have their names in their mouths!), I should have no hesitation in defining them: that temperance is love giving itself entirely to that which is loved; fortitude is love readily bearing all things for the sake of the loved object; justice is love serving only the loved object, and therefore ruling rightly; prudence is love distinguishing with sagacity between what hinders it and what helps it."

51. Plato, *Republic*, 500d.

52. Plato, *Republic*, 462a-b.

he is illustrating that lack of foundational justice that must secure itself in each of us, where each person should become the noble *polis* at large. The society of a *doxic* mindset[53] can never rise to the communal because it is not unified by what truly unifies human nature as a shared transcendency. The liar and the corrupt create the "ideal" state, conjuring a dream, a fantasy, the construction of a social contract over and against nature to enable each to act out his lowest common denominator of pleasures and whims. The language of the so-called ideal state is disembodied justice, injustice itself. It is an effort to immanentize transcendent categories, such as truth, happiness, perfection, fulfillment, goodness, beauty. Justice demands fairness and never confuses that with pseudo-equality or a forced uniformity of values. It is hierarchical, exhaustive, and places us in our existential relationship with the divine, as immemorial and uncreated. Such a justice falls neither into the trappings of immanentized relativisms or absolutized historicisms; it discovers fairness and truth through its intrinsic association with human nature as naturally supernatural and therefore *viatoric*.[54]

---

53. Cf. Voegelin, *Order and History Vol. 3*, 125–41. See also Webb, *Eric Voegelin: The Philosopher of History*, 11: "It is this immanentizing pattern of gnostic thought that Voegelin refers to as 'doxic,' because of the emphasis it places on the perfect truth of the *doxa* or speculative idea. Doxic thinking focuses on the interpretive model and tends to assume that this is not merely a representation but a direct view of the real as it is in itself. The result is that model, which should remain subsidiary and retain its transparency for the reality beyond it becomes focal and thereby opaque. The proper cognitive relation of reflection to experience is consequently broken and the structure of inquiry distorted."

54. Cf. Jaspers, "The Tragic," *Tragedy*, 19–20: "Transition is the zone of tragedy. According to Hegel, the great heroes of history are tragic figures in this sense. They embody the new idea, purely and uncompromisingly. They arise in sunlike splendor. Their real significance goes unnoticed at first, until the old way of life senses its danger and gathers all its forces to destroy the new in the form of its outstanding representative. Whether Socrates or Julius Caesar, the first victorious protagonist of the new principle becomes, at the same time, the victim at the border of two eras. The old is justified in asserting itself, for it still functions; it is still alive and proves itself through rich and elaborate traditional patterns of life, even though the seed of decay has already begun its fatal germination. The new is justified also, but it is not yet protected by an established social order and culture. For the time being it is still functioning in a vacuum. But it is only the hero, the first great figure of the new way of life, whom the old, in a last frantic rally of all its forces, can destroy. Subsequent breakthroughs, now untragic, will succeed. Plato and Augustus Caesar are brilliantly triumphant; they realize the vision; they mold men through their works; they shape the future. But they live with their gaze fixed upon the first hero who was the victim."

d. Fortitude as Cross and Liberation: Fortitude is what, in unison with the other three directing virtues, gets us through the uneasy business of life, ever skirting the edge of annihilation. This is the virtue that wears armor and bears a sword. It is in the image of the crucifixion which shows the wounds, the sweat, the protruding rib cage, the beginnings of putrefaction. This is the virtue that endures death, the quickening, in every single moment of life, and it does so without denial, dismissal, cheap wish-fulfilling hope, nihilism, or scientized disengagement. Through fortitude we are freed to confront endurance and its limits, to distinguish just from unjust fear and act according to the demands of immortal souls which find their perfection through bodies, and bodies that age and die but that find their perfection through souls that do not. Fortitude bears the agonizing incongruity of human life.

If forgiveness is going to be authentic it must be done within, and guided by, these virtues, which set out the proper timeliness for every action, for every word and deed, a forgiveness that reveals in us the yearning in all times for heaven. Through these directing virtues—directing us towards paradise—forgiveness becomes stretched across our bodies inhabiting even our fingertips. Such an act of pardon and of being pardoned is perhaps the most serious affair in all of existence for it foreshadows what it means to be forgiven by our Father through Christ on the cross. Every failure of love resides within acts of forgiveness. Every forged essence, every dead end, every unresolved hope and dream and demand of character exists either to be exorcised or materialized within this most impossible of acts. The cardinal virtues show us the true type of time that befits human beings, and what persons are to undergo via a lifetime of transcendent incarnated meaning. The danger of forgiveness is that it more often than not seeks to outwit this time-consuming process, to settle and suppress the *agon* at root in the dark business of sacred living. In doing so, often well-meaning but empty forgiveness becomes the stumbling block for the virtues, becomes the quick word and passing phrase in which we set aside the demands of our human nature in favor of caricatures of smug tolerance and artificial kindness. Forgiveness, the highest of all goods, has a more popular doppelganger, which is the porter at the gates of hell. Thus, as much as there is a temptation not to forgive, we may also and counterintuitively say that there is a temptation to forgive, and even to become complicit in guilt through premature forgiveness. And while we can more easily recognize the dangers of the former, the refusal to forgive, and conceive it to be the far worse action, let us not confuse the murky waters of the temptation to a thoughtless and premature forgiveness as no less a vice. While forgiveness is the chiefest of blessings, the false and superimposed achievement of dispensation and pardon is actually far graver than the honest recognition that one has failed to find harmony, failed to figure a way of being in the image and likeness of Christ, has failed to conceive what remission actually looks like and how it inhabits a body and soul. To act as if the word conjures the deed is the tyranny of the fool:

> Like a thorn that falls into the hand of a drunkard is a proverb in the mouth of a fool. Like an archer who wounds at random is he who hires a fool or passerby. As a dog returns to its vomit, as a fool repeats his folly.[55]

When we misplace forgiveness, when we misuse it in situations that need more time, that place us in the many odd predicaments of remission—such as how we can forgive or be forgiven for actions done out of ignorance, how forgiveness is even possible if one party refuses this demanding relationality—we are in danger of being unable to call to mind the genuine dimensions of forgiveness, of being simply unaccustomed to its presence. How do I forgive if the person does not want to be forgiven, or if the person is dead? How do I receive forgiveness if it is denied to me, or if the person is dead? Can we legitimately say forgiveness can somehow occur in both of these accounts? Isn't forgiveness relational, and don't these accounts demonstrate that the relationship that would enable forgiveness has been removed? How do I forgive the one who killed the child, when I am not the child, not the one who died? Do I have that right? And the child now dead has been stripped of that right. Do I have the right to take that victim's choice? In the thicket of these difficulties, we may even, as we did with Christ, condemn forgiveness to death, and do so in the name of the many emotivist substitutes for forgiveness such as anti-intelligent tolerance, and a hostile demand for peace at all costs. Accept all or die, forgive all or perish, replace forgiveness with the denial of sin, and from there find nothing in need of forgiveness but the death of those still seeking forgiveness. Such a situation lines the very halls of institutions of higher (but more often lower) learning.

55. Prov 26:9–11.

Finally, it is no longer completely fantastic to think that a day may come when not the executioners alone will deny the inalienable rights of men, but when even the victims will not be able to say why it is that they are suffering injustice.[56]

3. *Shouldn't forgiveness be utterly gratuitous, but then what does it add to the situation, if utterly gratuitous? Perhaps, instead, forgiveness as utilitarian is the essence of the situation.*

The general object which all laws have, or ought to have, in common, is to augment the total happiness of the community; and therefore, in the first place, to exclude, as far as may be, every thing that tends to subtract from that happiness: in other words, to exclude mischief. But all punishment is mischief: all punishment in itself is evil. Upon the principle of utility, if it ought at all to be admitted, it ought only to be admitted in as far as it promises to exclude some greater evil.[57]

What calculable gain do we get from forgiveness? Often we "feel" better, we gain a sense of goodwill, an elation in overcoming such hurdles as anger and resentment. Perhaps being the pardoner evokes a sense of superiority towards which we gravitate a little too frequently; a heady intoxicant we are too polite to admit stirs the more lasting motivations for forgiveness. Perhaps even within us is a recognition that such forgiveness provides a social advantage in future relations with the one whom we pardon. Through forgiveness we can do the very opposite of what it intends, we do not wash away the debt[58] but make the pardoned the type of debtor in which no repayment is sufficient. In such a view, "you are forgiven and now you owe me" is the prevailing demand. And what is owed is an ever flexible and mercenary bounty, trading in vitiated spirits and emotional enslavement, often strung out over years and decades. And while we recognize that these emotional structures, inhabiting various power plays ever more intimate and deceitful, cannot be the true essence of forgiveness, we seem to be at a loss figuring out its genuine nature. Or more specifically, we have difficulty understanding how to utilize

56. Pieper, *The Four Cardinal Virtues*, 52.

57. Bentham, *Principles of Morals and Legislation*, 170.

58. Cf. Ezek 36:25–26; "I will sprinkle clean water on you, and you will be clean; I will cleanse you from all your impurities and from all your idols. I will give you a new heart and put a new spirit in you; I will remove from you your heart of stone and give you a heart of flesh."

forgiveness authentically, as essential companion to the sanctifying and rigorous timing of the cardinal virtues. The forgery, the emotive panto-mime of forgiveness, appears to function quite effectively in the absence of understanding what exactly forgiveness embodies. It functions so well and so ubiquitously that we slip into its netting more easily each time we evoke it.

If we look at forgiveness within the sphere of emotions and the large realm of socio-political advantage, then we are presented with two main outlooks:

a. *Contractual Forgiveness*: forgiveness as a kind of contractual peace-maker, a checks-and-balances to absolve another in order to quell social unrest. I forgive you, you forgive me, we do not look towards some perfect state, we solely keep keeping each other in line by what we "owe" each other through giving and receiving pardon.

In this type of forgiveness, we are viewing the act as one that involves the most minimal amount of moral and spiritual intentionality. Forgiveness (within reason) should be given as quickly as possible, deftly avoiding the minutiae that will lead nowhere but to dead-ends and anxiety, and prompt those pesky questions of a spiritual nature that cannot be easily answered within the natural attitude. The world is merely "out there" and any sense of the experience of wonder, our *experience of experiences* is best to be ignored, sublimated, suppressed in favor of the pre-set, ready-made data we gather about the world, which especially includes how to navigate social situations via acceptable forms of clemency. This social contract of forgiveness should therefore change its values reflective of particular situations in view of the cost-benefit ratio.[59] Forgiveness can never stretch one beyond reason and calculable gain. If pardoning is more worthwhile a public vantage than requesting pardon, then such a path should be traversed. If, on the other hand, life is more robustly lived enjoying oneself and requesting forgiveness for offenses along the way—well after the way is done—then this is the only sensible path.[60] To

59. Cf. Lowry, "The Humiliating Art of the Woke Apology": "There is one factor that undergirds every aspect of these apologies—it is fear, fear of the cultural power of the accusers, of their ability to ruin careers, reputations, and lives. These kinds of confessions aren't wrung from the accused under threat of torture or exile. But they are in some real sense coerced, which is why they ring so false and are so alarming in a free society."

60. Nietzsche, *Aphorisms on Love and Hate*, 37–38: "*To offend and be offended*: It is much more agreeable to offend and later ask forgiveness than to be offended and

do more would be absurd, out of character, and utterly out of bounds. Forgiveness cannot stretch us beyond ourselves, it must not demand too much, it cannot expect that our debtors should be released. This kind of forgiveness is unable to aim at a genuine resolution, or rectify an injustice, or make the culpable—to whom the pardoner may be closer in kind—any less culpable. Its refusal of any incarnational tending prevents in advance any authentic existential resolution. In fact, it does not want these resolutions for, at its core, contractual forgiveness functions within sophistic and predatory consciences. But in spite of all the efforts to manage and subdue or indoctrinate reality, the world is full of surprise, chance, contingency, error, deficit, loss, and inexplicable evil. It is also filled with a "forgiveness" that places a moratorium on becoming the other as other, setting one up for the background humming nihilism that comes to roost at the inevitable moments of weakness, old age, and decline.

> It's obvious that the happy man feels contented only because the unhappy ones bear their burden without saying a word: if it weren't for their silence, happiness would be quite impossible. It's a kind of mass hypnosis. Someone ought to stand with a hammer at the door of every happy contented man, continually banging on it to remind him that there are unhappy people around and that however happy he may be at the time, sooner or later life will show him its claws and disaster will overtake him in the form of illness, poverty, bereavement and there will be no one to hear or see him.[61]

Contractual forgiveness fails to direct us to heaven. A contract presupposes each can offer goods the other needs. We need the eternal life that Christ alone can offer us, but there is nothing we can give him that he needs. He did not need the death, the suffering, the godforsakeness that we offered him when he underwent the passion, the last contract that broke all contracts, and replaced it with the covenant of superabundant love, of love that forgives those unworthy to receive it. Christ gave himself needfulness to break us from the cycle of our trespasses and earthly remissions. They are but a series of failed transcendences immanentizing the death to come in the forms of power and delusion that are but preludes to the dust and ashes.

---

grant forgiveness. The one who does the former demonstrates his power and then his goodness. The other, if he does not want to be thought inhuman, must forgive; because of this coercion, pleasure in the other's humiliation is slight."

61. Chekhov, "Gooseberries," *The Lady with the Little Dog*, 82.

b. *Impertinent Forgiveness*: In this type of anti-forgiving, we ask our-selves why should we be beholden to another, either by the need to forgive or to be forgiven? This an attitude in revolt against the artificiality of contractual forgiveness, but in its own way, may be susceptible to form a new social contract of its own.

Impertinent forgiveness sees the moral extortion: "I forgive you, now you owe me, (now I have something on you), now you must forgive me, you hypocrite." Forgiveness needs to be a fully gratuitous act, which the position of pardoned and pardoner repeatedly violate through their exchange of goods as selling off pieces of the soul. The impertinent and anarchic see the folly of it all.

> Say, "I am sorry, forgive me," and a shower of reproaches will follow! Nothing will make her forgive you simply and directly, she'll humble you to the dust, bring forward things that have never happened, recall everything, forget nothing, add some-thing of her own, and only then forgive you. And even the best, the best of them do it. She'll scrape up all the scrapings and load them on your head.[62]

The impertinent one rebels at the spiritual bondage and enslavement of wills by the very act of forgiveness, which claims to offer liberation. Why am I taking the *other* so seriously that I am binding everything up in that viewpoint, action, or non-action? With Rand in *Atlas Shrugged*: "It is against the sin of forgiveness that I wanted to warn you. You had the greatest chance in life. What have you done with it?"[63] You've wasted your life bound in a cycle of forgiveness, which destroys the tonic pas-sions and replaces them with enfeebled and infantilizing ineptitude. Such a view sees that we are stronger and healthier in love-of-life if we have the strength to shrug off all the little iniquities.[64] Why be bound up in an oth-

---

62. Dostoevsky, *The Brothers Karamazov*, 678.

63. Rand, *Atlas Shrugged*, 149.

64. Cf. Nietzsche, "Genealogy of Morals," *Basic Writings*, 475: "To be incapable of taking one's enemies, one's accidents, even one's misdeeds seriously for very long—that is the sign of strong, full natures in whom there is an excess of the power to form, to mold, to recuperate and to forget (a good example of this in modem times is Mirabeau, who had no memory for insults and vile actions done him and was unable to forgive simply because he—forgot). Such a man shakes off with a single shrug many vermin that eat deep into others; here alone genuine 'love of one's enemies' is possible—sup-posing it to be possible at all on Earth. How much reverence has a noble man for his enemies!—and such reverence is a bridge to love.—For he desires his enemy for

erness that preoccupies time? Only the idiot, the insane, or the religious choose the road of turmoil and protracted forgiveness.

In such a stance, forgiveness is viewed as indifference, and this is where its own bondage may take effect. The instinct of the impertinent is certainly correct: much of forgiveness is a forgery, a bondage rather than an intentional linking. A great deal of the former involves egos being "wounded" and the incessant and whining resurrection of anger and resentment. But an attitude that thinks it can stand above the fray only re-envisions intentionality among spiritual homunculi. There are debts, and debtors, and one cannot place himself outside of his own debt or the debt of others that are indelibly bonded to him. Impertinent forgiveness as indifference may recognize the hypocrisy, but itself is impotent to act, or meaningfully to explore the difficulty of forgiveness. It is all too familiar with persons infused with anger and vengeance, with very little of the opposing *élan vital* infusing souls. When was the last time we let our souls be infused with trust, friendship, and fidelity with the same amount of intense devotion? Forgiveness should be an exercise in cultivating magnanimity through justice with the same force with which we cultivate anger and the lust for vengeance.[65] But aloofness to our situatedness within existential debt contracts itself to the debt by way of its false disposition. It surrenders itself to ignorance through a titanomachy of self-enclosed egos, each unable to get outside the loop: we know ourselves only in the face of otherness, an epiphanic face that necessitates shared joy, suffering, and forgiveness.

Difficulties thus far: it seems that for forgiveness to be meaningful something must truly benefit both parties, or all parties involved. It also seems that for forgiveness to be central to human meaning and existence

himself, as his mark of distinction; he can endure no other enemy than one in whom there is nothing to despise and very much to honor! In contrast to this, picture 'the enemy' as the man of *ressentiment* conceives him—and here precisely is his deed, his creation: he has conceived 'the evil enemy,' 'the Evil One,' and this in fact is his basic concept, from which he then evolves, as an afterthought and pendant, a 'good one'—himself!"

65. Hume, *Principles of Morals*, 145: "Who sees not that vengeance, from the force alone of passion, may be so eagerly pursued, as to make us knowingly neglect every consideration of ease, interest, or safety; and, like some vindictive animals, infuse our very souls into the wounds of the enemy; and what malignant philosophy must it be, that will not allow to humanity and friendship the same privileges which are indisputably granted to the darker passions of enmity and resentment?"

it must be *more* than a psychological changing of sentiment, which would remain conditional and not a universal good. It also appears that forgiveness actually has to change what looks to be set in stone and unable to be changed, which renders genuine forgiveness salvific but exotic and rare. Forgiveness that is transformative, and thus more than changing emotive sentiments, necessitates that something divine must be intermingled with human life, that heaven has dwelt on earth and we cannot escape its promise. We recognize our powerlessness to undo or change the past, we cannot slow aging, we cannot stop death, we cannot undo a choice we made. Where then shall we find forgiveness? How and where are the unforgiven redeemed?

7

The Unknowing Heart of Forgiveness

I N THIS, THE UNKNOWING heart of forgiveness, the love needed to conquer all, requires the remission of the irremissible past and, through it all, we do *and* do not know what we have done. Here forgiveness appears too high a price to pay, too good a gift to receive, and yet if it were possible it would grant entrance into our natures exorcized, canonized, and fulfilled in paradise.

> Does not forgiveness require the remission of the irremissible past? Do we not, in forgiving, reach back into the past in order to remedy what has been done, in order to undo the harm done? . . . Yet the real is irremissible and, much as God would like to help, what is done is done.[1]

Ivan's Grand Inquisitor speech in *The Brothers Karamazov* already raised the painful unrelenting difficulty of the impossible harmony offered within forgiveness, and he gave back his ticket. Von Balthasar in his much-debated *Dare We Hope That All Men be Saved* wrestled with another facet of the problem: how does God's justice and mercy unify intrinsically and not haphazardly? On one end of the Balthasarian tension, we must say with certainty that God sending his only Son reaffirms that the works of salvation desire that all persons be saved, and that God seeks to save all. God wills only salvation for us, he does not will it in itself that we should go to hell, which is wholly contrary to salvation and divine

---

1. Caputo, *The Weakness of God*, 185.

love, as permanent abandonment from God. On the other end, hell evokes the worst pain and suffering beyond all imagining, to be forever alienated from creation, Creator, and love. Such a sentence is an ever-diminishing return wholly at odds with Christ's desire to save all sinners. It seems wholly opposed to God's mercy and thus realizes a state wherein the work of mortal man can undo the work of divine salvation. Yes, God does not send us to hell *per se,* instead we freely refuse the call, we are presented with the promise of infinite love and mercy, and for reasons strange and heartbreaking, we can freely dismiss, through the power of creation, that eternally beautiful courtship. Yet does God truly surrender his uncreated will by allowing creaturely wills to forfeit his power *against* their own good, beyond their own knowledge, of its devastating results? Does this not present more than a conundrum in terms of his pure *Actus,* as abiding, unchanging, and necessary for life itself, presenting instead an existential reckoning itself?

To deny universal salvation and affirm that some persons indeed are irredeemably separated from God may devalue Christ's total desire for the salvation of all persons, as well as diminish his supreme power to save, in threat of undermining the worthiness of Christ's *kenosis.* It also seems to place too heavy a price to pay on finite creatures, who "know not what they have done." To affirm universal salvation may devalue the unique *imago dei,* which we co-substantiate through God's grace as open and free natures. This is the prime gift needed for love and redemption in the first place. Our *imago dei* means that we are creatively responsible for our choices and for the good and evil they bring. We must accept that we live or die by those consequences, otherwise we forfeit our very nature as incarnated spiritual substance, far closer to the angels than the animals.[2] If we make hell for ourselves by repeatedly refusing the call, if we demonstrate that we do not want God and show this refusal again and again—which is what hell is, the place for those who do not want God's love—why would it be just for God to force those persons into salvation? Even if salvation is the only good for us, does not a forced nuptial invalidate that good? As if to continue within the vein of Ivan and Alyosha and the Grand Inquisitor we may permit ourselves to put forth the following difficulties regarding the harmony encircling forgiveness and heaven:

2. Cf. Gilson, *The Spirit of Thomism,* 34: "From the intellectual substances to the spiritual substances the distance is considerable, yet it is a small one compared with the distance there is from man to brute, . . . man is much farther removed from beasts than from angels."

With Aloysha in all of us: Do we not pray for all persons to be saved? Shouldn't we trust in God's will over our own powers? Shouldn't we believe that God's desire for our salvation is stronger than the power of death, and of all human evils put together? Isn't this the inner dynamite of Easter Sunday? Does not Christ descend into hell to break us free and save all mankind? Christ died for all sinners, broke open the gates of hell, and now, at the same time, we are also to accept that his salvific love cannot save all sinners, that the power of hell, as our own impoverishing self-debasement is stronger than he is? Such a structure of belief is incredulous not by the astonishing power of the *credo quia absurdum* but by competing platitudes that herd civilization into social conformity. We are no longer in the salvific *absurdum* of the God-man, the impossible but necessary redemption realized within our flesh, but in the worthless sophism that keeps religion present by way of incongruous sentiments that appeal to mediocrity as sufficient. Still, would God really let the sinful works of mankind thwart his divine salvation, which seeks the salvation of all persons? "Father, forgive them; for they know not what they do": truly the more we enter into sin, the less we are able to *see* and *experience* the horror of our sinfulness. That is precisely why Christ, the spotless lamb and wholly innocent victim, suffers more than any other human being. He knows what we have done. The more we enter the sin, in a way the less free we are to be able to excise ourselves from its annihilation of wisdom. Isn't there something just and merciful about an avenue for universal salvation given how sin itself cripples us? Isn't Christ's justice supremely merciful? For Christ, whoever is without sin throws the first stone. He alone is capable of throwing that decisive stone, and he declines. If we are finite beings with finite actions, then commensurate to that finitude are finite sins. How is *eternal* damnation just for those who function from within finite and limited knowledge? How is it the proportionate response to human finitude? "They regard it as unjust that anyone should be 'doomed to an eternal punishment for sins which were perpetuated in a brief space of time.'"[3] Wouldn't it make more sense that the fires of hell are a sort of self-induced punishment we place upon ourselves by our choices that extends into the fires of the afterlife? And what is experienced as burn and turmoil, warms and draws the person desirous of God. The difference between fire as hell, and fire as beckoning salvific warmth is the human co-substantiating response to heaven and

---

3. Balthasar, *Dare We Hope*, 48.

hell. These fires are in themselves cleansing—for they are wholly identical with God's infinitely loving *To Be*—not obstinate, and by being the former, even the most wicked sinner will recover the good that was once his and enter into the light of salvation. Von Balthasar reminds us, again, that Christ suffers most particularly for the un-pardoned, and we were all, through our shared original sin, in a state of durationally failed love:

> The seriousness that we are confronted with is the seriousness of a love that goes beyond all justice. God's love for every man is absolute, it is ineffable. Who can "by rights," claim adequacy before it? No saint would presume "I can." No one has loved God with his whole heart, with his whole soul, with all his strength. Everyone, without exception, has to say: "Lord, I am not worthy." . . . Nothing is more serious than love, precisely because it is "abundance that goes farther than justice": one must surrender oneself to it for better or for worse.[4]

With Ivan in all of us: It may not be unjust to pray for all to be saved, but isn't it unjust to believe all are saved? Then what is the point of confession, of forgiveness for our sins, of avoiding temptation and sin, of the whole theo-drama of ritual, which demands that the anonymous Christian is not enough? Perhaps the hedonist is the best utilitarian and taking the only sensible line—pleasure here on earth, and the certain expectation of pleasure in the afterlife. Why then cover the tabernacles on Good Friday? Why claim that Christ truly dies every Good Friday, of every year, of every century, if sins by our own obstinate choices do not have the power to "uncrown a hope in God,"[5] to be irremediable and irredeemable? Is restoration to the origin and recovery of what is lost truly possible, is it actually a just act, a good act, if it violates our free will, the very free will that enables us to have, to choose, to experience, and to refuse the relation of divine love in the first place. There has never been 100 percent clarity in knowing what will happen to us and others by the choices we make, both good and bad. But we are responsible to follow the good whatever the results. In our sinful actions, we are never in a position fully to know the panorama of outcomes of what would happen if we lie, or cheat, or steal, or murder, but we know they are wrong, that they are shortcuts. We recognize these errors in our conscience. It is not necessary, and never has been necessary, to know completely what results

---

4. Balthasar, *Dare We Hope*, 140.
5. Péguy, *The Portal of the Mystery of Hope*, 83.

occur as a result of our actions in order to decide whether or not to act. No human has ever been given this amount of knowledge. We are not Prometheus, but we are still responsible. Even Prometheus' foreknowledge did not give him fore-experience.[6] Even he did not conquer the full panoply of consequences, but this does not invalidate his responsibility. It is not ours to decide who goes to heaven and who goes to hell, nor is it ours to say that God's mercy wipes away hell. Nor is it ours to say that hope for the salvation of all is off the table. Least of all, it is not ours to claim that our sins are finite. Do we not commit murders that mean that the victim has lost his earthly life eternally? Do we not kill the proto-innocent in the womb, infinitely extinguishing the long and meandering realm of possibilities only rightfully belonging to the unborn? Do we not irrevocably alter the lives of many beyond the immediate victims of our transgressions? But "'must the criminal be confined only for so long a time as he spent on the offence for which he is committed?' Are there not punishments lasting a lifetime here on Earth, and is there not the death penalty, which can be justly imposed? Why not also, then 'the punishment of the second death?'"[7] Isn't there a problem confusing the fires of hell with those of purgatory, one that does not point to a mere error in judgment, but which unfastens the very connective tissue of human responsibility?[8] If God extends his freeing image to humans, we may use

6. Cf. Yu, "The New Gods and Old Order," 28: "After his crucifixion, Prometheus is left alone to lament his suffering. Stressing its unjust but unavoidable nature, his soliloquy gives voice to a paradoxical idea constantly heard in the play. By his very name, Pro-metheus is supposed to foreknow what will befall him. Yet, despite having this advantage, he still cannot resist the force of necessity. He does not deny that his punishment is self-induced; at the same time, however, it is a penalty harsh beyond his expectation (269–270), an arbitrary blow that greatly affronts his divine status. As the *epanodos* in line 92 has it, his hurt is the god's but wrought by gods. Because his suffering is both foreknown and yet beyond anticipation, Prometheus is caught in a dilemma. He has little reason to complain because, as he puts the matter, no new affliction may come to him unforeseen. On the other hand, the deep sense of outrage compounded with the gnawing presence of pain makes it impossible for him to be silent."

7. Balthasar, *Dare We Hope*, 48.

8. Cf. St. Teresa of Ávila, *The Life of St. Teresa of Ávila*, xxxii, §1–9: "The entrance seemed to be by a long narrow pass, like a furnace, very low, dark, and close. The ground seemed to be saturated with water, mere mud, exceedingly foul, sending forth pestilential odors, and covered with loathsome vermin. At the end was a hollow place in the wall, like a closet, and in that I saw myself confined. . . . I felt a fire in my soul. . . . My bodily sufferings were unendurable. I have undergone most painful sufferings in this life . . . yet all these were as nothing in comparison with what I felt then, especially

it for *this* or *that* choice, but these choices do over time reflect *how* we desire to be judged in light of the ultimacy of meaning. God as eternal and infinite makes the eternal choice to give humans free will, which can only act itself out within situations within the frame of ultimacy. Why then would he suddenly treat that decision as conditional, finite, and limited, by conflating the fires of hell with the cleansing fires of purgatory? No situation is finite because it exists within a vacuum of pure environment; the finite indelibly points to the infinite, as human yearning pants for the divine.

> Without an "end" you might have environment, but you could not have a situation which all moral quandaries are: what shall I do and why shall I do it, here & now? It is true that all ethical acts and decisions are, so to speak, situational, but this is so precisely because and insofar as they involve a relation to an end, for it is exactly this that defines a situation as what it is: a particular complex or matrix of actuality and possibilities the order and meaning of which can only be determined (i.e., in decision) in relation to the end willed or recognized. By its very nature, a situation refers beyond itself to a possible end: in other words, there is no such thing as an absolute situation (except in relation to an absolute end): the "human condition" taken as a universal situation would be such an absolute situation. Also, the very idea of an absolute or supreme or final or perfect or complete end already involves the notion of situation in order that it may be realized or approximated or actualized in ethical action. Thus, there are no absolute rules (as there are in speculative knowledge) that can be invoked to determine a

---

when I saw that there would be no intermission, nor any end to them. . . . I did not see who it was that tormented me, but I felt myself on fire, and torn to pieces, as it seemed to me; and, I repeat it, this inward fire and despair are the greatest torments of all. . . . I could neither sit nor lie down: there was no room. I was placed as it were in a hole in the wall; and those walls, terrible to look on of themselves, hemmed me in on every side. I could not breathe. There was no light, but all was thick darkness. . . . I was so terrified by that vision—and that terror is on me even now while I am writing—that though it took place nearly six years ago, the natural warmth of my body is chilled by fear even now when I think of it. . . . It was that vision that filled me with the very great distress which I feel at the sight of so many lost souls, . . . for they were once members of the Church by baptism—and also gave me the most vehement desires for the Salvation of souls; for certainly I believe that, to save even one from those overwhelming torments, I would most willingly endure many deaths."

priori the relation of a situation to its end; this role is performed
by prudence.[9]

It is essential to show that the relationship of mercy and justice is
not evidence of a disjointed caricature of God, a being unworthy of belief,
a balancing juggler tossing too many unwieldy plates in the air. God is
identical with love and offers only heaven,[10] but thumb a few pages down
in the Gospels and it is better for Judas and those like him—the many
who are left outside the banquet—never to have been born, not even to
be recognized by Christ when they knock feverishly at the door.[11] Perhaps we reconcile these difficulties of forgiveness and harmony by putting God in the same boat as ourselves. Because God is intrinsic to our
incarnational intentionality, the consequences of our original sin inflict
a weakness on God, which, like us, he cannot overcome in its irremediable consequences. Or to overcome it would be to commit a theological
oxymoron—a merciful injustice. He cannot forgive without undermining
justice, rendering forgiveness unworthy *because* unjust, and yet he must
offer forgiveness, for without it, justice has no *telos*, no transcendency,
nothing to place our actions within his divine contextuality. What is to
be done? Forgiveness without justice is meaningless, and justice without
forgiveness annihilates relationality. And God, who is Justice and Love,
does nothing to contradict himself. Our goodness is enacted in freedom,
for any of God's acts to oppose that freedom is to oppose the very Good
of his creation as one in Being with him. But, on the other hand, how
can God, whose essence is identical with his own *To Be*, oppose himself.
How can he fail in Goodness by not saving us and leaving us annihilated
from his own *To Be*? But how does God avoid opposing his Goodness
if his salvific actions parcel out goodness from our freedom in order to
save us? God's saving us against our will requires the violation of our created nature, and thus necessitates an impossible violation of God's *Actus*.
Once again, have the consequences of our sin affected God's relationality

9. Gilson, *Subordinated Ethics*, 241.

10. Cf John 16:33.

11. Matt 7:21–23. See Sophocles, "Oedipus at Colonus," *The Greek Plays*, §1224–35:
"Never to have been born is best. Everyone knows that, and a close second, once you
have appeared in this life, is a quick return, as soon as you can, to where you came
from. In our light-headed youth we carry blithe ideas, not knowing what blows await,
what hardships are bearing down, closer and closer. Murder, hatred, strife, resentment,
and envy are lurking, and then, behind them, bitter old age, powerless, friendless, with
evils our only neighbors."

to us? And while it is fitting to extend the rescue mission through his only Son, who does overcome the world, this doesn't mean the participants in the world choose that *kenotic* overcoming.

Perhaps God remains Love *now love*, and Justice *now justice*, through a metaphysical weakness of Being. This weakness gives his *Actus* the inactive watchfulness of the referee. God, the contradiction, is better than God the non-existent. Or not: God, the non-existent, does not give us false hope, and nothing is quite as vicious as hope that has no redeeming entelechy. Such a God would be the weakening of heaven to fable, and then sheer irrelevance, and then finally to non-existence, with God himself tagging along in all the reductions. And perhaps this is the reality of the situation we are in, for it appears almost impossible to conceive of heaven as anything other than the naive celebration. Our difficulty may be a symptom of our very weak God, so weak there is no whit of difference between his existence and non-existence. Faced with the death of the other, heaven is the hopeful color and texture and richness transforming the vacant lot of futurity made unbearable by the richness of memory. But we cannot quite envision the color or the texture or the richness, only the vacant lot stares blankly back. We brush it aside, saying with half terror and half denial "never mind, it is the better place I do not yet know," not knowing whether that is an act of faith or an act of resignation from a congestive and failing faith. Besides, we will never be able to tell the difference, for God, in such a view, is far too weak to guide us.

If God is going to intercede in raising our forgiveness from good intention, which is powerless to transform, to genuine transformative reality, everything discussed above are stumbling blocks to be encountered along the road to Emmaus, and further on to our home in heaven. God does not violate our free will. We know this from the very theo-drama of his death and resurrection. Faith is not magic, and God's actions do not sidestep our free choice. And we have to wonder about the perilous vortex of onticity that resides in the longer way of flesh, when the freedom that God will not violate becomes the freedom for eternal death. What can overcome all of this, what can authentically enable this impossible harmony, what can make it not only possible but inviting and the perfecting quality of human existence? We turn to the Gospel, to what may be the resolution, but itself is enigmatic and often eludes conceptual capture: "Father, forgive them, for they know not what they do."

Can the expectation of forgiveness be reasonably sought if we do not know what we do? Christ intercedes on our behalf, for we do not know what we do. Does this mean that we are less culpable and, strangely enough, less in need of forgiveness? This does not seem to strike us quite right. But let us follow the path into its painful bewilderment.

> Whether or not we are able to forgive: How can one forgive them at all, if they know not what they do! One has nothing whatever to forgive. But does a man ever know completely what he does? And if this must at least remain questionable, then men never do have anything to forgive one another and pardoning is to the most rational man a thing impossible. Finally: if the ill-doers really did know what they did—we would have the right to forgive them only if we had the right to accuse and punish them. But this we do not have.[12]

Don't all sinful and evil acts revolve around ignorance and involve acting against our own best interest?[13] And this reality of ignorance seems naturally to follow a reality in which we do not grasp all the potential consequences of our choices. Unlike the angels, human beings appear handicapped from the start. We are responsible, though unable to know all the outcomes when deliberating potential choices. This natural un-knowingness is sometimes dispelled in repeated actions, and in the cultivation of virtues, but just as much, and perhaps more, it is magnified and transformed, becomes the occasion for a thorough steeping in pride and sinfulness. There is no expectation, given our finitude, that this blindness is overcome within the natural world full of contingency, risk, and non-sequiturs. If culpability requires truly knowing that we did wrong, and knowing why we acted against our true self-interest, why would anyone do wrong? That is part of the mystery of Satan's fall,[14] and this is why Nietzsche's understanding of forgiveness is a theoretical postulate and not a lived experience. Forgiveness in his view necessitates a more completed

---

12. Nietzsche, *Human, All Too Human*, 326.

13. Cf. Plato, *Protagoras*, 358b-c: "No one who either knows or believes that there is another course of action better than the one he is following will ever continue on his present course when he might choose the better."

14. Cf. Balthasar, *Dare We Hope*, 112: "God can create no creature that is free yet, at the same time, 'congealed in goodness' and that, instead, it is of essence of the gift of freedom to be able to choose one's own highest value, thereby realizing oneself for the first time. Even if an angel were, in what pertains to his nature, created as perfect and as possessed of insight into all values, he would still have retained his freedom of choice with respect to the supernatural God. From this perspective, the doctrine of the Fall of the angels, which is deeply rooted in the whole of the Tradition, becomes not only plausible but even, if the satanic is accepted as existent, inescapable."

understanding of actions, events, situatedness, a self-knowledge above
and beyond what humans actually possess. Christianity is parasitical
because it expects too much and too little of persons within the same
sweeping judgment.[15] In terms of the former, it demands that we enact
cycles of morbid pity and grotesque humility to place ourselves into the
orbit of forgiveness, which has always been existentially inaccessible to
us. And in terms of the latter, what Christianity claims to be the wheat is
instead the chaff.

The pardoned/pardoner structure, the subordinated need for
the other, is vampiric for Nietzsche, and creates the pessimistic world
that is a cult against life, an enemy against vitality, fortitude, strength,
and magnanimity. The pardoned and the pardoner cannot exist as two
separate persons each playing a vitiating interiorization and exteriorization of the other. To pardon and be pardoned exist as powers of the self,
strong enough to understand the joy of nothing other than the force of
one's own time and presence: "the desire to bear the entire and ultimate
responsibility for one's actions oneself, and to absolve God, the world,
ancestors, chance, and society, involves nothing less than to be precisely
this *causa sui* and . . . to pull oneself up into existence by the hair, out of
a swamp of nothingness."[16] The higher, stronger person, full of the will to
power, is magnanimous, fair, generous, benevolent. When the pardoner
and the pardoned are realized as the same person, those tonic passions
are the natural reality. They are not insipidly forced upon others through
shame, pity, fallenness, the weapons of choice within forgiveness. What

15. Nietzsche, *The Antichrist,* §62: "With this I come to a conclusion and pro-
nounce my judgment. I condemn Christianity; I bring against the Christian church
the most terrible of all the accusations that an accuser has ever had in his mouth. It is,
to me, the greatest of all imaginable corruptions; it seeks to work the ultimate corruption, the worst possible corruption. The Christian church has left nothing untouched
by its depravity; it has turned every value into worthlessness, and every truth into a lie,
and every integrity into baseness of soul. . . . All this, to me, is the 'humanitarianism'
of Christianity!—Parasitism as the only practice of the church; with its anemic and
'holy' ideals, sucking all the blood, all the love, all the hope out of life; the beyond as
the will to deny all reality; the cross as the distinguishing mark of the most subterranean conspiracy ever heard of,—against health, beauty, well-being, intellect, kindness
of soul—against life itself. . . . This eternal accusation against Christianity I shall write
upon all walls, wherever walls are to be found—I have letters that even the blind will be
able to see. . . . I call Christianity the one great curse, the one great intrinsic depravity,
the one great instinct of revenge, for which no means are venomous enough, or secret,
subterranean and small enough,—I call it the one immortal blemish upon the human
race."

16. Nietzsche, *Beyond Good and Evil,* §21.

Nietzsche rejects specifically is our numbing effort to raise up what is nebulous, such as forgiveness, allowing it to become the standard and champion of the Good of nature and society. For Nietzsche, we must not allow the ill-constituted to define what is beautiful and healthy. Through the incessant and eroding cycle of forgiveness, we place ourselves at the mercy of the other. This is how we have become infected with their pallid spiritual outlook. Then the belief that "life is denied, and made worthy of denial" becomes central.[17] In Christianity, the search for heaven, for paradise, for a world of irrational and impossible perfection, as empty and meaningless a category error as "side-less square," is a result of such pity, which inverts the natural order and denies the *élan vital* of life. We do not know what forgiveness is because there is nothing deeper to know about it than that it is most assuredly a power-play, a maneuvering, the most egregious of the Christian deceits. The only way to conquer it is not to be held hostage to its unknown status as threshold to the divine, when it is the context of disease and nihilism. "Father forgive them, they know not what they do," is the primal contradiction that has malformed two thousand years of human progress. If we do not know what we do, if we do not have this complete knowledge, we are not in need of forgiveness, we are only in need of ridding ourselves of its yoke. Then, and only then, can we return to the powers that we do know, and to the goods that are their natural vital effects.

Yet, on the other hand, why would anyone want to subscribe to the end results of Nietzsche's eerily prophetic teaching? How is life capable of any transcendency if forgiveness is only an unexperienced presupposition, or rather a theoretical postulate experienced only by way of defection and bondage? In such a view, forgiveness that seeks, in any way, intentionally to extend and become the other as other, to need the other to forgive the self, has no choice but to degrade itself into cheap sentiment at best, and petty nauseating power-plays at worst. But at least Nietzsche's view recognizes the sheer *difficulty* of forgiveness. He acknowledges the obscurity we should force ourselves to encounter when confronted with the mystery of what it means to wipe away sin, and what it entails to give and receive pardon.

As a young man on pilgrimage in Mount Athos, the playwright Eugene Ionesco experienced the galling, unremitting mystery face to face.

17. Nietzsche, *The Antichrist* §7.

This event profoundly affected him and remained a cornerstone of Christian meaning and purpose for the rest of his life.

> I was born in an Orthodox family, and I lived in Paris. At twenty-five years, I was a genuine young man of the secular culture of the then Paris. I got the idea to visit Mount Athos because of its position as—and indeed was—a place of asceticism in the Orthodox Church. And there I had another thought in mind: to confess. So, I went and found a hieromonk, a spiritual father. What did I say to him? The usual sins of a secular young man who lives without knowing God. The hieromonk, after hearing me, said: "Do you believe in Christ my child?" "Yes, yes, I believe Father. Besides, I am baptized Orthodox Christian." "Well, my child, do you believe and accept fully that Christ is God and Creator of the world and us?" I lost it, because this was the first time a person put forward this question to me, and which I had to answer honestly and take a position. Not just if I believe someone made the world, but that this God, the Creator of the world, has to do with me. And that I have a personal relationship with him! I replied: "Father, I believe, but help me understand this fact well." "If you really believe, then all corrects itself."[18]

"If you really believe, then all corrects itself": this is the astonishing foundation in which Word and Act unite in the image of Christ. This is where our always failing and unknowing words—to forgive and to be forgiven—do not dissipate in the weight of language unfit to cover the silence, but co-substantiate heaven's incarnation within our flesh, revealing the immemorial in memory. "The utter incomprehensibility of the *existence* of a divine Being Who is Love, and the total incomprehensibility that this Being *might not exist*, live as one in the memory of the lover."[19] It is as inconceivable that Being becomes a Who that exists *for us* as that it does not.[20] Our forgiveness seeks always to infinitize, to hold the infinitesimal and the grand, *to be* the gatekeeper of every nuance that can possibly undo the unremitted. Forgiveness has always lived in the impossible and unknowing territory of that which cannot be undone. It is always before us, and after us, in our midst as we walk, and into us in the grave, growing into our flesh and taking away its shape, ever eliding and

18. Eugene Ionesco in an interview with French magazine *Paris-Match*, in Jacobse, "Eugene Ionesco and the Elder on Mount Athos."

19. Gilson, *Immediacy and Meaning*, xxviii. See also St. Augustine, *Confessions*, X, xvii.

20. Pascal, *Pensees*, §434.

eluding our grasp. Our forgiveness yearns for heaven because heaven as the infinite memorial act already became us in the immemorial love that existed "before the foundation of the world."[21] Our forgiveness cannot be all these things, it cannot know fully what we have lost and gained in the giving, receiving, and refusal to give and to receive forgiveness. And yet it is and retains these things, it is the apex in which we extinguish and resurrect all life and hope within us. It is the altar at which we fumble, attempting to make ourselves an offering for the other and receiving more than we are in return. "Father, forgive them they know not what they do" is identical with "the unique offering of the incarnate Word, and from the substitution, which he alone could bring about, in which he took our place in death, so that we might become free. It is in him and by him alone that the world is gathered and unified so as to be offered to the Father."[22] Christ completes the sacrifice required in forgiveness, which we know but do not know, which we know by way of silence, which we know by our failure to move the summit,[23] which we know in every recited prayer[24] that contains within it the eternal Word united with deed. We repeat the prayers our Father gave us without efficacy, with little belief, and yet still, through the centuries, it is plenitude. We know the power of forgiveness in the failure of our words and deeds.[25] Forgiveness is the prayer that contains the whole power of the uncreated as Person whose *kenotic* love became sacrificial, offering us the form of remittance that is more than scratching against the dust and emptiness, infinitely more

21. 1 Pet 1:20; Eph 1:4.

22. Chrétien, *The Ark of Speech*, 148

23. Cf. Matt 17:20: "If you have faith as small as a mustard seed, you can say to this mountain, 'Move from here to there,' and it will move. Nothing will be impossible for you."

24. Cf. Debout, *My Sins of Omission*, 20–21: "I accuse myself of having no profound belief in the efficacy of prayer—of having believed in prayer only with my nerves, under the pressure of anguish and as a means in despair. . . . I accuse myself of not having realized that by prayer I might have rendered audible to certain hearts words which no tongue can utter—the only words that do not betray my secret soul because they are themselves betrayed by their poverty of expression and accent—because the sound does not pervert the sense. I accuse myself of not having given God time to act when I prayed and of having hastened immediately to His rescue with a prodigious fuss. I accuse myself, finally, of not having realized that prayer must obey laws of a supernatural nature and be able to wait, without exasperation or passivity, for the bursting forth of the seed sown in the eternal heart of God."

25. Job 14:12: "He cometh forth like a flower, and is cut down: he fleeth also as a shadow, and continueth not."

than those partial resurrections of beauty that cannot complete.[26] Within the wounds of Christ, we reveal the one Word who can offer and receive forgiveness as sins remitted, as salvific and everlasting.

26. Dostoevsky, *Demons,* 601: "There are seconds—they come five or six at a time—when you suddenly feel the presence of the eternal harmony perfectly attained. It's something not earthly—I don't mean in the sense that it's heavenly—but in that sense that man cannot endure it in his earthly aspect. He must be physically changed or die. This feeling is clear and unmistakable; it's as though you apprehend all nature and suddenly say, 'Yes, that's right.' God, when He created the world, said at the end of each day of creation, 'Yes, it's right, it's good.' It . . . it's not being deeply moved, but simply joy. You don't forgive anything because there is no more need of forgiveness. It's not that you love—oh, there's something in it higher than love—what's most awful is that it's terribly clear and such joy. If it lasted more than five seconds, the soul could not endure it and must perish. In those five seconds I live through a lifetime, and I'd give my whole life for them, because they are worth it. To endure ten seconds one must be physically changed."

8

Three Mistaken Views on the
Impossibility of Forgiveness

WE ARE BORN AND often die unhappy, and the most essential things in existence are often impossible. To shortchange this reality, to place the transformative lengths of forgiveness within our own natural capacity, is a particularly cruel *hubris* that expeditiously renders forgiveness too possible for its own good. When forgiveness is too easily won, too much a given, the very netting of neediness, beauty, and the transcendent experience of our own unworthiness, necessarily at root in grace, is squandered almost to its core. This choice is the all-too-common view that makes heaven the scrap heap for any uneasy views of forgiveness that do not fit the equation and must avoid serious reflection at all costs. Here, the desire for heaven is dramatically undercut, marginalized, and infantilized, firstly because earthly norms have sufficiently psychologized and sociologized forgiveness, and secondly, what is left over, those set-aside existential grumblings, those quiet dissatisfactions, have been stripped of any guiding *telos*; they are merely non-conformities, insignificant blips with no power to challenge the progressive therapeutic culture that now ensures the self-with-others.[1]

> Our Father, Who art in heaven, hallowed be Thy name; Thy kingdom come; Thy will be done on Earth as it is in heaven. Give us this day our daily bread; and forgive us our trespasses

1. Cf. Rieff, *The Triumph of the Therapeutic: Uses of Faith after Freud.*

as we forgive those who trespass against us; and lead us not into temptation, but deliver us from evil. For the kingdom and the power and the glory are yours forever.[2]

When forgiveness is viewed as achievable, utterly separate from the will of the uncreated, we make ourselves foolish God-usurpers, tin-pot dictators. When we lose the Godhead's "thy will be done" we ignorantly separate forgiveness from the necessity for the remittance of sins, reducing it to endless artifices of hurt, competing personal perspectives, and therapeutic remedies that are covertly earthly reactions when faced with the impossibility of forgiveness. But none of these has the power to approach the demands of human-and-divine forgiveness.

On the other hand, those who recognize and resignedly accept the genuine impossibility of forgiveness are also susceptible to misunderstanding its purgative power. When the impossibility of the remittance of sins is disengaged from the blood of the Lamb,[3] who washes white our baptismal robes with the most crimson of blood,[4] this carries such existential risk, and its own unique forms of lostness and sin. This heartaching impossibility to achieve genuine forgiveness within our own natural powers finds itself devolved into the following three existential alternatives, each failing fully to encounter the role of Christ's *kenotic* self-emptying. Each emphasizing the impossibility of forgiveness but to the neglect of its equally commanding necessity: "with man this is impossible, but with God all things are possible."[5]

I. *The Promethean Heart*

> Behold with what indignities mangled I shall have to wrestle through time of years innumerable. Such an ignominious bondage hath the new ruler of the immortals devised against me. Alas! alas! I sigh over the present suffering, and that which is coming on. How, where must a termination of these toils arise? And yet what is it I am saying? I know beforehand all futurity exactly, and no suffering will come upon me unlooked-for. But I

2. Cf. Matt 6:9–13.

3. Rev 7:14: "And I said unto him, Sir, thou knowest. And he said to me, These are they which came out of great tribulation, and have washed their robes, and made them white in the blood of the Lamb."

4. Isa 1:18: "Come now, and let us reason together, saith the LORD: though your sins be as scarlet, they shall be as white as snow; though they be red like crimson, they shall be as wool."

5. Matt 19:26.

needs must bear my doom as easily as may be, knowing as I do, that the might of Necessity cannot be resisted. But yet it is not possible for me either to hold my peace, or not to hold my peace touching these my fortunes. For having bestowed boons upon mortals, I am enthralled unhappy in these hardships.[6]

Here belong the hearts who have collapsed theory and practice, fore-knowledge and fore-experience, knowledge and wisdom. They have the words but not the way, and in losing the way they find themselves startled, dismayed and crestfallen, by the unseemly reality that something always exceeds knowledge, and that this truth may not be fully understood by us until so much more is revealed to us. If ever even revealed, forgiveness takes far more than knowledge as it takes far more than feeling. These hearts recognize that we know what we do not know, and need what we do not know how to grasp. They have discovered the gaping chasm that separates knowledge and wisdom but know not how to traverse it so as to encounter forgiveness as truly remittance of sins, as finally an overcoming of the world. The Promethean Heart sees far ahead, but never sees far enough, for it refuses to surrender that sight to Christ's self-emptying, which alone gives us vision when he enters under our roof.

> O world of spring and autumn, birth and dying
> The endless cycle of idea and action,
> Endless invention, endless experiment,
> Brings knowledge of motion, but not of stillness;
> Knowledge of speech, but not of silence;
> Knowledge of words, and ignorance of the Word.
> All our knowledge brings us nearer to our ignorance,
> All our ignorance brings us nearer to death,
> But nearness to death no nearer to GOD.
> Where is the Life we have lost in living?
> Where is the wisdom we have lost in knowledge?
> Where is the knowledge we have lost in information?
> The cycles of Heaven in twenty centuries
> Bring us farther from GOD and nearer to the Dust.[7]

II. The Tragic Heart

The person who recognizes the tension between fate and free will and knows that—even with many things taken away, and so much beyond his

---

6. Aeschylus, "Prometheus Bound," *The Greek Plays*, §77–109.

7. Eliot, "Choruses from the Rock," *Collected Poems 1909–1962*, 147.

control—nothing interiorly alleviates human responsibility. Thus, nothing can emancipate us from the ever-present inescapable need to forgive and to be forgiven. We are faced with our choices, our responsibility, and then faced with the impossibility to make forgiveness what it needs to be—something more than a shifting of psychological perspective, more even than the sinner suffering in grief and repentance.[8] For the tragic heart, the whole of existence is often experienced in one event, as if universal time is caught up in one particular event, as if one is freed into a harmony, and a forgiveness that can liberate us beyond the cyclical return of competing fates. But the experience of the universal in the particular as the immediacy of the divine in the *longer* way of the flesh becomes like the tablecloth pulled quickly beneath the plates, leaving everything intact, everything still as it was, and nothing ultimately transformed. We glimpse in forgiveness what could be, but more still we experience the tragedy of our failure to undo what has been done. We are each particular beings, each having to experience life by way of finitude, where the All must be distilled in more palatable experiences. The tragic essence of human forgiveness both liberates us into that knowledge of the All and then traps us in its fate. We cannot complete the task at hand, we are left stranded as nomads, fully responsible and yet unable to break free from the web of fate. We have experienced the All but cannot act upon it, this is the recognition of the impossibility of forgiveness as one in being with the tragic essence of existence.

> A man who has thus, so to speak, put his ear to the heart-chamber of the cosmic will, who feels the furious desire for existence issuing therefrom as a thundering stream or most gently dispersed brook, into all the veins of the world, would he not collapse all at once? Could he endure, in the wretched fragile tenement of the human individual, to hear the re-echo of countless cries of joy and sorrow from the "vast void of cosmic night," without flying irresistibly towards his primitive home at the sound of this pastoral dance-song of metaphysics? But if, nevertheless, such a work can be heard as a whole, without a renunciation of individual existence, if such a creation could be

8. Cf. Shakespeare, "Two Men from Verona," *The Complete Works*, Act V, Scene IV.
   My shame and guilt confounds me.
   Forgive me, Valentine: if hearty sorrow
   Be a sufficient ransom for offence,
   I tender 't here; I do as truly suffer
   As e'er I did commit.

created without demolishing its creator—where are we to get the solution of this contradiction?[9]

The Tragic Heart reductively views that *kenotic* self-emptying as his own action, rather than a co-substantiating of heaven through Christ, who alone fills us up, and fills us with the body of forgiveness.

III. *The Heart (In)Justice*

This is the heart that recognizes the strange paradox of justifiable anger having little justifiable outlet. A parent's pure inconsolable anger in response to the murder of her child is justifiable, but then, the anger cannot act, it must exorcise itself into other forms in the name of a measured justice. The parent must accept that the killer's legal punishment is, more often than not, *not* commensurate with the magnitude of the crime, since a more commensurate retribution is paradoxically viewed as injustice. And even if the life of the killer is to be taken in return, this still is not commensurate, for it fails to recover what is lost and buried, only adding another lost soul to the process. How odd it is that something such as justifiable anger—which as natural designates a fitting completion of itself and not frustrated in incompletion—cannot be acted upon easily. Where is the end that appropriately fulfills that anger, that authentically transforms it? We must take more than a moment to wrap our minds around earthly law, as essential structure of society, perpetuating an imperfect sense of justice in order to enable civilization to function. This heart recognizes how forgiveness attempts to fill the gap, to rectify the incommensurate relationship between justifiable anger and earthly justice. Earthly forgiveness tries and fails to resuscitate justifiable anger beyond the reach of frustrated ends and within the orbit of an end that can make sense of all the good and evil within the world. But like Ivan in *Brothers Karamazov*, such a heart is repeatedly wounded with the impossibility to achieve such a forgiveness that could square the circle, and make up the difference between what appears irrevocably lost and what is owed.

> The greatest temptation: In Dostoevsky's Grand Inquisitor lurks a dreadful idea. Who can be sure, he says—metaphorically, of course—that when the crucified Christ uttered His cry: "Lord, why hast thou forsaken me?" He did not call to mind the temptation of Satan, who for one word had offered Him dominion over the world? And, if Jesus recollected this offer, how can we

9. Nietzsche, *The Birth of Tragedy*, 162.

be sure that He did not repent not having taken it? . . . One had better not be told about such temptations.[10]

The Heart (In)Justice has confused self-emptying with impotence, and surrender with powerlessness. In doing so it sees our participation in Christ's *kenosis* as a covering over of trespasses, a facile harmony with little to offer but trading forms of resignation and rage. It views Christ's forgiveness on the cross in all too human conceptions of forgiveness, while actually neglecting what human beings are called to do via incarnational intentionality. It is quite true that no future enjoyment on earth can make up for the evil that destroys a life, but heaven does not work in primarily this respect. Our earthly intentionality already gives us glimpses of the directionality at work, we exteriorize the self which already had interiorized the other, and we interiorize the other which has already, again and again, exteriorized the self. Intentionality is our greatest earthly clue to divine justice. Christ has loved us before the foundation of the world as the primordial incarnational self-as-other by which intentionality was first made possible. This means that heaven is not only a union of selves-as-others fulfilling the anticipation of supreme joy and love, but that it accomplishes this love by way of a spiraling reversal which works through time, history, memory, into the very immemoriality of Being itself. Every loss is shown debrided as gain, every failure is consumed within his flesh, every earthly incompletion nailed to the tree. And more paradoxically, not only are failures overcome but achievements are stripped bare. All achievements are revealed as failures to achieve, every saint revealed as a sinner, every gain revealed as loss and every loss revealed as gain, all together becoming a chorus unearthing our transcendent neediness and the power of Christ to overcome the world, to turn everything upside down, so that it can be made anew. *Kenotic* justice is not a mere "the action has been done, now let's scramble to figure out how to make it better" as is the case in earthly justice. But, instead, "the action has been done but always occurred on the body of Being itself. Being as Christ empties himself so completely and in turn empties each of us—our sins, our failures—within him as his co-substantiating otherness.[11] Our emp-

10. Shestov, *All Things are Possible*, 108.

11. Cf. Balthasar, "The Fathers, The Scholastics, and Ourselves," 353: "Thus, one finds in one's human nature a place—perhaps only a point, but this point suffices—where one can, as it were, traffic with God 'religiously' on the same footing, where a mystical identity obtains between Creator and creature. Now to reach this mysterious identity-point requires all kinds of strenuous effort: The earthly atemporal now seem

tying is simultaneously the plentitude that overflows in his renunciation. Through this supreme interpenetration we finally, through grace, have a chance not only for commensurate justice but a justice that is erotically merciful, and a mercy that is agapetically just, so that we are remade in love, wholly born anew:

> "Truly, truly, I say to you, unless one is born again he cannot see the kingdom of God." Nicodemus said to him, "How can a man be born when he is old? Can he enter a second time into his mother's womb and be born?" Jesus answered, "Truly, truly, I say to you, unless one is born of water and the Spirit, he cannot enter the kingdom of God. That which is born of the flesh is flesh, and that which is born of the Spirit is spirit. Do not marvel that I said to you, 'You must be born again.' The wind blows where it wishes, and you hear its sound, but you do not know where it comes from or where it goes. So it is with everyone who is born of the Spirit." Nicodemus said to him, "How can these things be?" Jesus answered him, "Are you the teacher of Israel and yet you do not understand these things? Truly, truly, I say to you, we speak of what we know, and bear witness to what we have seen, but you do not receive our testimony. If I have told you earthly things and you do not believe, how can you believe if I tell you heavenly things? No one has ascended into Heaven except he who descended from heaven, the Son of Man. And as Moses lifted up the serpent in the wilderness, so must the Son of Man be lifted up, that whoever believes in him may have eternal life."[12]

---

in this regard to be only an external husk that envelopes and hides the inner kernel which must be shattered ascetically, 'denied,' and made transparent. The perfected and knowing exercitant looks through all this as mere appearance, for all non-identity with the divine is basically a non-being; and this applies as well therefore to the constricted ego and to one's unique individuality."

12. John 3:3–15.

9

Guilt and the Mystery of Forgiveness

The question of guilt, however, is not limited to the actions and lives of individual men. Rather, it refers to humanity as a whole, of which every one of us is a part. Where are we to look for the guilt that is responsible for all this undeserved disaster? Where is the power that makes the innocent miserable? Whenever men saw these questions clearly, they conceived of the idea of complicity in guilt. All men are jointly committed and jointly liable. Their common origin and their common goal account for this. A token of this, though not an explanation, is that we feel shaken and perplexed at the following thought, which seems absurd to our limited understanding: I am responsible for all the evil that is perpetrated in the world, unless I have done what I could to prevent it, even to the extent of sacrificing my life. I am guilty because I am alive and can continue to live while this is happening. Thus, criminal complicity takes hold of everyone for everything that happens. We must therefore speak of guilt in the wider sense of a guilt of human existence as such, and of guilt in the narrower sense of responsibility for a particular action. Where our own guilt is not limited to certain specific wrongdoings but, in a deeper sense, is found in the very nature of human existence, there the idea of guilt becomes truly inclusive.[1]

THE HEART OF INTENTIONALITY lives out the interdependence in which no sin is done in isolation, and no goodness is done without

1. Jaspers, "The Tragic," *Tragedy*, 22.

communion. We are each the other *as* other, revealing through our flesh the self for others within every other. Once this sinks in and lingers for a good while, such a heart comes to realize its total responsibility for all actions, where each choice becomes co-extensive with eternal judgment. We are to understand in being that if my brother has sinned then, in a way sacred and profound, I have sinned with him. If I have not done everything I can, then I am complicit in all sins of the world. But this structure of intentionality as intrinsic and impossible obligation renders forgiveness too difficult to achieve, too painful to undertake. Forgiveness becomes too global and too intimate in one stroke of the brush. If all are complicit, who among us is capable of offering forgiveness? If we are permitted to offer forgiveness, in the image and likeness of Christ, how can we if we are unable to put ourselves in contact with all the sins that surround us, or place ourselves completely within the will of another? Every *alter Christus* knows the literal preposterousness of the term. Intentionality places us squarely within the impossibility to complete forgiveness.

Camus' *Caligula* is one such a tragic figure who recognized the cosmogonic incongruity of existence, that lives are lost, and little adds up, and what is gained is like quicksand, escaping and consuming us before it is ever really ours. Rather than enter the dishonesty of a world of too easily won harmony, of too quickly achieved remittance of sins, ceaselessly bartered and traded in order to maintain the *toujours la politesse* of superficial polite society, he chose the madness, which is really the calculating sanity, when faced with a world of dead ends. Caligula opts for the path of impossibility as impossible, unapproachable, yet devastatingly present—indeed, the only source that could give genuine meaning, but as impossible, no longer a source of anything whatsoever. From there, he lives out its capriciousness, where the only rule is the arbitrary concatenation of events. And if he and others can endure this impossibility sufficiently, perhaps the impossible will transfigure them and give them happiness:

> And I'm resolved to change them. . . . I shall make this age of ours a kingly gift—the gift of equality. And when all is leveled out, when the impossible has come to Earth and the moon is in my hands—then, perhaps, I shall be transfigured and the world renewed; then men will die no more and at last be happy.[2]

---

2. Camus, *Caligula*, 17.

Caligula has recognized the impossibility of forgiveness and embodies the three main existential alternatives (Promethean, Tragic, Injustice), which honestly acknowledge the incongruity at work in every second of life, and the impossible harmony heaven appears to offer. He then commits his sufferings to others, causing his subjects relentless and absurd degradation and humiliation. Caligula demands the reality of the impossible be present in every spontaneous action, calculated whim, and cruel command, in all the secret places of his heart and the hearts of others. Caligula never uses escapism, he confronts the abyss, and knows that ineluctable impossibility guards the gate to everything meaningful and worthy of belief. Through reason and logic, Caligula takes the only path before him: what is impossible, *as* impossibility, *is* impossible to achieve. There is nothing to be done but to endure or not to endure. This is the end of achievement, but not the end of heartache. Nearing his warranted betrayal and assassination, he has neither expected nor achieved any of that impossibility, though he still hoped for it, as he hoped for the moon in his hands. All that remained in him was that wild unforgiving hope—or is that despair?—that can exist even when certitude shows only its contradiction. He knowingly desires what he knows to be impossible. Still, Caligula calls out moments before his assassination that he has taken the wrong path:

> And I'm afraid. That's cruelest of all, after despising others, to find oneself as cowardly as they. Still, no matter. Fear, too, has an end. Soon I shall attain that emptiness beyond all understanding, in which the heart has rest. Yet, really, it's quite simple. If I'd had the moon, if love were enough, all might have been different. But where could I quench this thirst? What human heart, what god, would have for me the depth of a great lake? [Kneeling, weeping] There's nothing in this world, or in the other, made to my stature. And yet I know, and you, too, know [still weeping, he stretches out his arms toward the mirror] that all I need is for the impossible to be. The impossible! I've searched for it at the confines of the world, in the secret places of my heart. I've stretched out my hands [his voice rises to a scream]; see, I stretch out my hands, but it's always you I find, you only, confronting me, and I've come to hate you. I have chosen a wrong path, a path that leads to nothing. My freedom isn't the right one.[3]

---

3. Camus, *Caligula*, 73.

How can the path, which is impossible, not only be a path, but be the *right* one? Our best intentions are always met with failure, failure to transform, failure to forgive into the bones. For again, and with Caligula, we are searching for something so much more than the Aristotelian virtue of magnanimity. For Aristotle, one of the chief signs of a magnanimous or high-minded person would be the way forgiveness is handled. This person is too wrapped up in his own transcendent likeness to the wisdom of the divine mind[4] that it would be a contradiction to hold a grudge, to obsess on retribution. The tangential trespasses of the inferior man are too trifling a project to consume one's time and energies. Forgiveness, for Aristotle, becomes more a one-way affair. The high-minded person prefers to offer forgiveness and seeks never to be in a position to receive it. Forgiveness of a debt is a virtuous act, providing goodness, but the receiving of forgiveness only illustrates one's inferiority:

> He who received a good is inferior to the man who conferred it, and a high-minded man wishes to be superior. And he hears of the former [i.e., conferring benefits] with pleasure, but of the latter [i.e., receiving benefits] with displeasure. . . . It is the mark of the high-minded man, too, never, or hardly ever, to ask for help but to be of help to others readily. . . . Nor will he bear grudges; for it is the mark of a high-minded man not to bring up the past, especially what was bad, but rather to overlook this.[5]

The Aristotelian rationale for not seeking retribution is not incompatible with the Christian understanding of forgiveness, but neither does it even come close to what is needed, desired, and made possible through Christ's donative self-emptying. In this one-way affair, there could never be friendship between the superior and inferior man, between the pardoner and the debtor, as Christ extends to us. Such a forgiveness terminates in a more solipsistic conclusion, where the act ensures the maintenance of one's own so-called magnanimity, but does not seek the better of the debtor except perhaps in the most peripheral way that a degree of release or accord has been granted. The pardoning does not intend directly to promote the cultivation of the debtor's happiness and virtue. Again, we return to the interior solipsism of such a notion of forgiveness that does not necessitate incarnational intentionality: "the forgiveness [given by

---

4. Cf. Aristotle, *Nicomachean Ethics*, 1123b: "A high-minded man is thought to be one who, being worthy of great things, requires of himself that he be worthy of them."

5. Aristotle, *Nicomachean Ethics*, 1124b.

the] magnanimous person is in the image of divine forgiveness—more a forgetfulness or an indifference than an active engagement with the one forgiven for his or her good."[6]

Forgiveness is redemptive only because it is simultaneously impossible. If this impossibility is not held central in all discussions, we have nowhere to direct ourselves except perpetual self-annihilation, hell. "Whoever reckons with the possibility of even only one person's being eternally lost besides himself is unable to love unreservedly."[7] Mustn't we take Ivan's statement gravely to heart that forgiveness and harmony are too high a price to pay? Perhaps we are gambling not only with eternal life but also the only meaningful gift in the world—love. How can we make sense of its mystery by an all too easy pardoning/harmonizing of evils? Forgiveness has *always* been about forgiving the unpardonable, the impossible, otherwise it is not the arduous act that Christ alone completed, in which all the glory and folly of humanity resides.

All the evils Caligula has done are far weightier than those final single lines that are only the inklings of repentance: "I have chosen a wrong path, a path that leads to nothing. My freedom isn't the right one." Are we not taught, and rightly so, that actions speak louder than words? But here, with Caligula, we are presented with a predicament: the loss of the ability to love unreservedly. If Caligula is unforgiven, thus unredeemed, thus eternally lost, isn't that loss far weightier, does not it include each of us? It must and does, if we take seriously the demands of incarnational intentionality dramatically en-fleshed in the God-man. No sin is done in isolation: if we have not done all we can—and we never achieve all that the day demands[8]—then we are complicit in each other's sins. To fail to forgive or to be forgiven means that we have lost the ability to love and be loved unreservedly. And should Christ refuse to forgive us, being one

6. Brown, "St. Thomas Aquinas on Human and Divine Forgiveness," 2.

7. Cf. Verweyen, "The Life of All as the Outermost Horizon of Christology," in Balthasar, *Dare We Hope*, 58: "Whoever reckons with the possibility of even only one person's being eternally lost besides himself is unable to love unreservedly."

8. Cf. Romano Guardini in Balthasar, *Dare We Hope*, 67: "Being genuinely good would mean that we would accomplish in every hour what that hour required, and thus life would ascend to the fullness of its achievement and perfection as called for by God. What is not done now cannot, however, be made good later on, because every hour comes but once, and the next has, once again, its own demands. What becomes of the gaps and voids in this continually passing life? And how do things stand with what has been done wrong? . . . What has been done rests in being. What will become of that when time has run out and man can do nothing more?"

with us, then all would amount to nothing in the end. How do we manage this forgiveness genuinely, a forgiveness that appears to violate all logic and common sense? It appears that a true remission of sins may be the most beautiful act, and yet the most incommensurate in all existence. Life does not add up, it never has . . . .

10

Christ's Kenotic Intentionality
in His Seven Last Words

Is our claim that forgiveness is impossible except through Christ one that emaciates forgiveness? In Christ, the impossibility is both overcome and maintained in its worldly aspect, revealing the Word to be inescapable: only say the word and my soul shall be healed. One may look at this argument and contend that forgiveness is now too rare, restricted, and removed from any natural context and placed instead within the realm of theological belief, and that such sequestering injures acknowledgment of the universality in which all persons are called. But we argue to the contrary. Without Christ's *kenosis* which en-fleshes the uncreated, revealing the infinite in the finite, the universality of forgiveness would be a non-redemptive ideological postulate. But the forgiveness we seek is the ubiquitous and erotic presence that enables us to co-substantiate paradise. Christ's *kenosis* alone universalizes forgiveness within the intimacy of the particular. Forgiveness hinges entirely on his *kenotic* justice as martyrological intentionality, and it is revealed to us in the seven sayings of Christ on the cross:

1. *"Father, forgive them; for they know not what they do."*[1]

The God-man's *homoousias* unifies itself with entire self-emptying as restraining the glory of his Godhead. His totalizing tension allows our

---

1. Luke 23:24.

most confused desires for the remission, indeed disintegration, of sins to enter the depths of the impossible and the failed, and for Christ to subsume that ignorance, impossibility, and failure within human language in its pure form spoken by God as Word.[2] Christ as the Word is able to speak the Word that can overcome the world and recover what is lost. This is meant on every level of existence. "We do not know what we do," not only signifies the moral level[3] of ignorance or limited understanding of the injustice caused against another. Christ's first saying on the cross has a two-fold significance within the economy of salvation. It also evokes the metaphysics of our union of body and soul. As intellectual substances, our souls act from eternity when they act in time. And because it is our nature to be unified to a body, to be a dual unity, we are connaturally *in* and *not in* time in every act of intentionality.[4] Human persons act from eternity as united to their incorporeal intellectual substance, which, as the form of the body, protracts that eternity into the moving image of their own selves. This is why embodied existence, as existentially dependent on God, is our individuating principle. This longer way is the moving image of eternity discovered in the experience of time. We are able to be the moving image of eternity because our aeviternal nature directs us to one *aeviternity*[5] by which all—man and angels—are measured, thereby reaffirming that we act from eternity when we act in time. But what happens when, through sin, we sever the intentional relationship

---

2. Cf. Balthasar, *Theo-Logic II*, 78: "That the incarnating Word 'came into his own' (John 1:11), thus he does not simply (as Karl Barth says) go somewhere foreign, rather into a land whose language he knows: not only the Galilean variety of Aramaic that the child learned in Nazareth, but more deeply the speech of creaturely being as such. The logic of the creature is not foreign to the logic of God; it could be likened to a dialect of the standard language spoken in pure form by God."

3. Cf. Pope Benedict XVI, *Jesus of Nazareth II*, 208: "It remains a source of comfort for all times and for all people that both in the case of those who genuinely did not know (his executioners) and in the case of those who did know (the people who condemned him), the Lord makes ignorance the motive for his plea for forgiveness: he sees it as a door that can open us to conversion."

4. Cf. Pegis, *At the Origins of the Thomistic Notion of Man*, 14: "Like other thinkers of their age, William of Saint-Thierry and Godfrey of Saint-Victor . . . had great difficulty in understanding how a simple and immaterial soul was present to the body and yet not in a spatial way. But this problem, which is at least as old as Plotinus and St. Augustine, not to mention Nemesius, is witness to the metaphysical innocence of the twelfth century."

5. ST I, 10, 6, ad. 2.

with the eternal, and thwart that grace[6] that allows us to take in ourselves as the moving image of the eternal? We are looking through the glass darkly,[7] and unable to know what we yearn to know but had already chosen to forsake to such finality as death that we are unable to recover it. With Aquinas: "The first cause of the defect of grace is on our part; but the first cause of the bestowal of grace is on God's according to Hosea 13:9: 'Destruction is thy own, O Israel; thy help is only in Me.'"[8]

2. *"Today you will be with me in paradise."*[9]

Christ suffered for all with an arduous, personal, and sacrificial love.[10] His martyrological intentionality enabled us, his body, the other, to become united with him, and to receive our personhood through his godforsakeness. United to him in the passion we enter the homelessness where all unremitted sins reside, where the impossibility to undo our trespasses devours everything it caresses. Through him, we are forgiven because we know not, nor could we conceive, what we have done, and now accomplished through him who has unraveled sin to its core. He took us in and became Death itself, making what was once impossible the threshold to the heaven that he is.

3. *"Woman, behold, thy son! Behold, thy mother!"*[11]

Christ's self-emptying left himself stranded within partial knowledge, incomplete understandings, unfinished actions, and godforsakenness. Christ took on the history of our post-fall intentionality of failed loves,

6. Cf. St. Thomas, *Commentary on the Sent.*, I, dist. 40, q. 4, a. 2: " It is . . . evident that the first cause of the absence of grace is purely and simply on the side of man to whom grace is lacking—because he had not been willing to receive it—on the side of God, there is no cause of the absence of grace, except once admitted that which is the cause on the side of man."

7. 1 Cor 13:12.

8. ST I-II, 112, 3, ad. 2.

9. Luke 23:43.

10. Cf. Stein, *The Science of the Cross*, 121: "We already know from the *Night of the Senses* that a time arrives at which all taste for spiritual exercises as well as for all terrestrial things is taken away from the soul. She is put into total darkness and emptiness. Absolutely nothing that might give her a hold is left to her anymore except faith. Faith sets Christ before her eyes: the poor, humiliated, crucified one, who is abandoned on the cross even by his heavenly Father. In his poverty and abandonment she rediscovers herself."

11. John 19:26–27.

and recovered them within his body. He transformed our neediness of dead-ends into a unity, where each may *kenotically* participate in the *theotokos* or bearer of Christ for the other.

4. *"My God, my God, why hast thou forsaken me?"*[12]

Christ's *kenotic* justice surrendered his omnipotence to the Father, prefiguring the lengths and total risk of forgiveness within the rescue mission. He placed himself completely at the will of the supreme Other, and experienced the profound unnaturalness of bodies subjected to death through sin, and souls that can persist but do so far outside the good of their natures. The piercing of the nails, the lancing of the flesh, the crown of thorns, all of these violations of his once inviolate Being, experience the terrible unimaginable suffering of the torn separation, the rupture across all history and time, of the human body and soul. "Father forgive them, they know what they have done," and now he must bear the impossible weight of justice needed for forgiveness. He must complete what we have done to ourselves, to our bodies and souls in time and for all time. Only in Christ do we receive the forgiveness that recovers the unity of body and soul we hope to gain in a glorified manner in the resurrected life.

5. *"I thirst."*[13]

Our Lord's *martyrological kenosis* prefigured the riskiest and most distressing of leaps, entering into flesh, blood, and time. This is not a forgiveness for the few, it is for the many, offered for all. Every last drop of his substance flows forth and Christ is exsanguinated, he is poured out like water, and he thirsts because of it. He has entered nothing by his own self-emptying. Let us never forget how impossible forgiveness is without the God-man's donative gift. Christ thirsts for the world in its un-redeemability, which demands more and more of his water and blood: "I am poured out like water, and all my bones are out of joint: my heart is like wax; it is melted in the midst of my bowels. My strength is dried up like a potsherd; and my tongue cleaveth to my jaws; and thou hast brought me into the dust of death."[14]

12. Matt 27:46; Mark 15:34.

13. John 19:28.

14. Ps 22:14–15.

6. *"It is finished."*[15]

In his *consummatum est*, Christ's completion of his martyrological *kenosis* illuminates the invisible Trinitarian union, and most particularly grants us sight of the third person, the Holy Spirit, who is to be our Helper on earth. Christ has paid our debt, completed the architecture of salvation. In self-emptying, he breathes his last breath, and the breath of Holy Spirit is upon us. This completion enables us to be alive with the Holy Spirit. Christ's *consummatum est* fulfills the Old Testament: "And it shall come to pass afterward, that I will pour out my spirit upon all flesh; and your sons and your daughters shall prophesy, your old men shall dream dreams, your young men shall see visions."[16] And it also prefigures why, after his resurrection, Christ tells his flock: "And I will ask the Father, and he will give you another Helper, to be with you forever, even the Spirit of truth, whom the world cannot receive, because it neither sees him nor knows him. You know him, for he dwells with you and will be in you."[17]

7. *"Father, into thy hands I commend my spirit."*[18]

Heaven truly visited the earth and remains both in the earth in the body of the church, in us through the Holy Spirit permeating each of us with gifts, and in heaven with Christ seated at the right hand of the Father. In his last Word, Christ's *kenotic* splendor completes what his first saying set out to do: "Father forgive them they know not what they do." Now we know what we must do. We must commend everything we are, as Christ has already done for us, body and soul, to God the Father. Human forgiveness is an act of *kenotic*, self-emptying trust. "If you really believe, then all corrects itself." This is an impossible foundation but the impossible has occurred and died and resurrected for us. The impossible God-man is in us, through us, in every bone, flesh, blood, heart, spirit, soul, and mind that constitutes our being. We are permeated with the impossible, as we live on the dying earth and yet simultaneously possess the eternalizing portico to heaven. Christ's completion of forgiveness is the astonishing foundation in which there is finally a spoken word—"only say the word and I shall be healed"—in which forgiveness now means that that lostness, emptying, and abandoning of ourselves can become

15. John 19:30.
16. Joel 2:28.
17. John 14:16–17.
18. Luke 23:46.

the plenitude and abundance of new life. The truly transformative inten-tionality, the only one where I complete becoming the other *as other*, is in the forgiveness that is one with Christ's *kenotic* and martyrological love.

Forgiveness is both impossible and necessary: this is the heart of the God-man's ever-present *kenosis*. His blood and water flow, eternally bear-ing these tensions of Good Friday and Easter Sunday, of time and eterni-ty, of hell and heaven. Through his incarnation, heaven has visited earth and opened the door to the ultimate and astonishing remission of sins. If we are to achieve forgiveness, it works in reverse, by debriding every event of its finality, incompletion, failure, and achievement. All events are subordinated to Christ, who has emptied himself and completed within his flesh every intentionality of failed love. When we become his body and enter the heaven on earth, even with all our sinfulness, we experience the poignant beauty that cleanses the impossible of its impossibility. "If we really believe, then all corrects itself": this is the endlessly donative power Christ offers to the faithful when he gave us himself, emptied on the cross, and gloriously en-fleshed in the resurrection. We intention-ally interiorize and exteriorize the God-man within us so that if we truly believed, again, "all would be corrected." This belief must be in the image and likeness of Christ. Belief must become a co-substantiated *kenosis*, a divine self-emptying within us, transforming us, and completing what is within us as perpetually un-completed. Only then are we able to forgive and be forgiven.

> "Son," he said, "ye cannot in your present state understand eter-nity: when Anodos looked through the door of the Timeless he brought no message back. But ye can get some likeness of it if ye say that both good and evil, when they are full grown, become retrospective. Not only this valley but all their earthly past will have been Heaven to those who are saved. Not only the twilight in that town, but all their life on Earth too, will then be seen by the damned to have been Hell. That is what mortals misunder-stand. They say of some temporal suffering, 'No future bliss can make up for it,' not knowing that Heaven, once attained, will work backwards and turn even that agony into a glory. And of some sinful pleasure they say 'let me have but *this* and I'll take the consequences': little dreaming how damnation will spread back and back into their past and contaminate the pleasure of the sin. Both processes begin even before death. The good man's past begins to change so that his forgiven sins and remembered sorrows take on the quality of Heaven: the bad man's past already

conforms to his badness and is filled only with dreariness. And that is why, at the end of all things, when the sun rises here and the twilight turns to blackness down there, the Blessed will say 'We have never lived anywhere except in Heaven,' and the Lost, 'We were always in Hell.' And both will speak truly."[19]

19. Lewis, *The Great Divorce*, 69.

Part III

All This and Heaven Too:
The Resurrected State

11

The Dignity of the Senses & the
Intentionality of the Glorified Body

T O ENGAGE SUCH QUESTIONS as friendship, play, whether our animals accompany us in the resurrected state, and the status of spousal unions and intimate relationships, we must first reflect on the nature of the glorified body as essential to any meaningful encounter with paradise. Our glorified bodies exceed and elevate the very best and most virtuous dispositions of earthly embodiment.[1] And this glorification works from within grace as perfecting nature, not destroying it. Our attention must profoundly return to the lifelong elegy of the senses, to the flesh, and to how we, as beings on the horizon between time and eternity, act out our immortality. Earthly embodiment, through the senses, is always placing the person outside himself to know himself. The body's very architecture is to yearn, unite, and extend in and towards otherness. Let us pay serious attention to the Scriptural expressions of sense experience as essentially denoting an incarnated phenomenological spirituality. In the lowly senses dwell the specific hope for a resurrection befitting our en-fleshed intentionality. Their oft-overlooked magnificence for beings in the image and likeness of God, is that *through* them we unearth manifold layers of

1. Cf. Engelland, *Phenomenology*, 40: "Flesh places us in a world of present and absent things, and it places us in that world with others who can experience our flesh and thus experience our experience. Our living bodies give each of us a vantage point on the world, and, in doing so, they enable the vantage point of others to be experienced as well."

intensifying immateriality. And we do so *through* their netting or portal or shape-making kaleidoscopic richness which prefigures the incarnational power of Word made flesh and blood. Our immateriality is not meant to be abstract or disembodied, but to have shape, breadth, length, texture, sound, smell, and, more still, to enliven the ecstatic reaches of human beings who act from eternity when they act in time. We seek to avoid the anemic spiritualism that forsakes the senses as something shed along the way to enlightenment, or their reduction to a biological soft determinism whose varying degrees of physiological difference could never account for the phenomenological difference *as difference* between humans and animals.[2]

Smell as Signatory of Resurrected State

So he went to him and kissed him. When Isaac caught the smell of his clothes, he blessed him and said, "Ah, the smell of my son is like the smell of a field that the LORD has blessed. May God give you heaven's dew and Earth's richness—an abundance of grain and new wine."[3]

But I have all, and abound: I am full, having received of Epaphroditus the things *which were sent* from you, an odour of a sweet smell, a sacrifice acceptable, well pleasing to God.[4]

Smell as Signatory of Fallenness

Instead of fragrance there will be a stench; instead of a sash, a rope; instead of well-dressed hair, baldness; instead of fine clothing, sackcloth; instead of beauty, branding.[5] I hate, I despise your religious festivals; your assemblies are a stench to me. Even though you bring me burnt offerings and grain offerings, I will

2. Cf. Engelland, *Phenomenology*, 100: "Life can be perceived by life only in the mirroring of the self and other made possible by the twofoldness of flesh: we perceive ourselves perceiving and we perceive others perceiving. In this way, Edith Stein argues that a non-living observer, say, an alien robot, would be able to track mechanical movements but would be blind to life experienced in that moment."

3. Gen 27:27.

4. Phil 4:18.

5. Isa 24:25.

not accept them. Though you bring choice fellowship offerings,
I will have no regard for them.[6]

A third of the human race was killed by these three plagues—by
the fire, the smoke, and the sulfur that came from their mouths.[7]

In the sacrifice of the Mass, the incense billows into the air, wafting between the material and the immaterial. The smoke is the visible presence of our prayers commingling with the Word of God, uniting heaven and earth.[8] In the nativity of our Lord, myrrh and frankincense are gifts given by the Magi that foreshadow Christ as the only person born to die. Fragrance permeates his swaddling clothes, the winding funeral linen, and the tomb.[9] This redolence attached itself to Christ throughout his life, enshrines prayer, and rises forth in Revelation to unveil what is veiled, within the presence of judgment itself.[10] Scent is also present in the Scriptures as the antithesis to the perfume of sanctity. Instead, we are accosted with the noxious waste in which sin damages human relationality aligned with the stench of decomposition and death.[11] It becomes almost impossible to avoid inhaling that death. We have traded the breath of life for something else altogether. We can imagine the smells on Golgotha of a Christ beaten, bruised for all the sins unto death Christ must have taken into his Being:

6. Amos 5:21–22.

7. Rev 9:18.

8. Cf. Ps 14:1–2: "Let my prayer rise like incense before you. The lifting of my hands like the evening offering."

9. Cf. John 12:3–8: "Then took Mary a pound of ointment of spikenard, very costly, and anointed the feet of Jesus, and wiped his feet with her hair: and the house was filled with the odour of the ointment. Then saith one of his disciples, Judas Iscariot, Simon's son, which should betray him, Why was not this ointment sold for three hundred pence, and given to the poor? This he said, not that he cared for the poor; but because he was a thief, and had the bag, and bare what was put therein. Then said Jesus, let her alone: against the day of my burying hath she kept this. For the poor always ye have with you; but me ye have not always." See also John 19:39–49.

10. Cf. Rev 8:3–4: "Another angel came and stood at the altar, holding a gold censer. He was given a great quantity of incense to offer, along with the prayers of all the holy ones, on the gold altar that was before the throne. The smoke of the incense along with the prayers of the holy ones went up before God from the hand of the angel."

11. Cf. Deut 29:23: "All its soil will be a burning waste of sulfur and salt, unsown, producing nothing, with no plant growing on it, just like the fall of Sodom and Gomorrah, Admah and Zeboiim, which the LORD demolished in His fierce anger."

Dislocated, almost ripped out of their sockets, the arms of the Christ seemed trammelled by the knotty cords of the straining muscles. The laboured tendons of the armpits seemed ready to snap. The fingers, wide apart, were contorted in an arrested gesture in which were supplication and reproach but also benediction. The trembling thighs were greasy with sweat. The ribs were like staves, or like the bars of a cage, the flesh swollen, blue, mottled with flea-bites, specked as with pin-pricks by spines broken off from the rods of the scourging and now festering beneath the skin where they had penetrated. Purulence was at hand. The fluvial wound in the side dripped thickly, inundating the thigh with blood that was like congealing mulberry juice. . . . [T]he knees had been forced together, twisting the shins outwardly over the feet which stapled one on top of the other, [and] had begun to putrefy and turn green beneath the seeping blood. . . . Above this eruptive cadaver, the head, tumultuous, enormous, encircled by a disordered crown of thorns, hung down lifeless. One lacklustre eye half opened as a shudder of terror or of sorrow traversed the expiring figure. . . . The torture had been unendurable, and the agony had frightened the mocking executioners into flight.[12]

But Christ had also been a child, "a tender milky child,"[13] he is always for us the nativity and the passion. And the perfume of each is within and among us: the sweet scent of life carrying the surprise expectation of death, and the terrible scent of death as impossible but truly given promise of life. The mother takes the newborn child in her arms and closes her eyes, places her face, buries her nose into the crown of the child's head. She breathes in the sweetness of the holy innocent who smells of manna, honey, and of spirit. Every mother at that moment of time and breath is a Marian figure, breathing in Our Lady and Our Lord:

> Their new souls, their fresh souls.
> Fresh in the morning, fresh at noon, fresh in the evening.
> Fresh like the roses of France.[14]

---

12. Deut 8–9.

13. Péguy, *The Mystery of the Holy Innocents*, 72: "The most hardened warrior has been a tender infant nourished with milk; and the toughest martyr, the strongest martyr tortured on the iron horse, the martyr with the roughest bark, the most wrinkled skin, the strongest martyr on the rack and in the thumbscrew has been a tender, milky child."

14. Péguy, *The Portal of the Mystery of Hope*, 117.

Here we come to the primal intentionality that most immediately responds to God's breath of life. Our in-spiration/inhalation of the child's new life phenomenologically corresponds to Our Lord's expiration/exhalation of his spirit in the forming of the world.[15] And it is there in the haunting, lingering perfume of grief, where clothes are pulled into one's arms and smelled, taken deeply into the lungs, placing presence within the absence. In this valley of dry and deadened bones[16] our inhalation, even in all its shallow breaths punctuated by weeping, is synonymous with hope. The scent of the transcendence of the other, our breath that takes the other in, is intentionality acted out in the longer way of our spiritual carnality. In breathing, our bodies physically yearn for the resurrection, we are relentlessly seeking the breath that not only prolongs life but returns us to eternality. The desire for the glorified state is not a mere sociological idea put on for this time or that, but rhythmically present in every historical being. It is as foundational as our sense of smell, in the taking in of another through the air, the fragrance brought into the center of our beings, to be commingled with our own vital essence and exhaled in image and likeness of the divine breath.

Touch as Signatory of Resurrected State

And he arose and came to his father. But while he was still a long way off, his father saw him and felt compassion, and ran and embraced him and kissed him.[17]

Then he poured water into a basin and began to wash the disciples' feet and to wipe them with the towel that was wrapped around him.[18]

15. Gen 2:7: "And the LORD God formed man *of* the dust of the ground, and breathed into his nostrils the breath of life; and man became a living soul."

16. Cf. Ezek 37:4–6: "Again He said to me, Prophesy over these bones and say to them, 'O dry bones, hear the word of the LORD.' Thus says the LORD God to these bones, 'Behold, I will cause breath to enter you that you may come to life. I will put sinews on you, make flesh grow back on you, cover you with skin and put breath in you that you may come alive; and you will know that I am the LORD.'"

17. Luke 15:20.

18. John 13:5.

Then the LORD put out his hand and touched my mouth. And the LORD said to me, "Behold, I have put my words in your mouth."[19]

And taking him aside from the crowd privately, he put his fingers into his ears, and after spitting touched his tongue.[20]

Touch as Signatory of Fallenness

But God said, "You shall not eat of the fruit of the tree that is in the midst of the garden, neither shall you touch it, lest you die."[21]

And if anyone touches an unclean thing, whether human uncleanness or an unclean beast or any unclean detestable creature, and then eats some flesh from the sacrifice of the LORD's peace offerings, that person shall be cut off from his people.[22]

Touch is the fundamental sense that chiefly alludes to our non-mediated union with the uncreated. In our incarnated intentionality, we tend exteriorly and interiorly and do so repeatedly throughout life. This tending is enacted on the body of God's *To Be*,[23] which means we also have an intense immediacy of union, irreducible to concept, with the uncreated *Actus* enabling existence. Our reflexive actions attempt to mediate what cannot be reduced and assimilated. Even the other senses, which dialogue with this immediate and binding unity, do not do so with the same efficacy as touch. Each carries within it greater and varying degrees of eidetic distance, most noticeable in sight as vantage point, as an achievement over a length or space. But touch reminds us of this irreducibility, of this sheerness of power and presence that precedes so as to ground all reflection and knowledge.[24] We become in touch as close

19. Jer 1:9.

20. Mark 7:33.

21. Gen 3:3.

22. Lev 7:21.

23. Cf. Balthasar, *The Christian and Anxiety*, 124–25.

24. Cf. Guardini, *Pascal for Our Time*, 144: "For the distanced cognitive experience, the concrete accomplishment of understanding falls basically out of the realm of the essential. It is experienced merely as the necessary way in which the noetic vis-à-vis of subject and object is brought about. Here, on the contrary, the living process belongs absolutely to the core of knowledge. Its realization is experienced not only in the vis-à-vis of the correct view of the object, but just as much, if not even more, in the special nature of this touching of the object, of this living fusion with the substantially existant."

as physically possible to becoming identical with the object being tacti-
cally held and consumed by hands, pressed directly against our lips and
cheeks. The tangible features of an object's warmth, texture, size, shape,
and weight are experienced in an immediacy of union.[25]

When the self and other are no longer objects but the lover and
beloved, touch carries with it the greatest intoxicant, the tragic sense that
we can raise the dead; as if the most furious and nearest of touch, the
touch with the most ecstatic love, could cross the divide, dive through the
flesh into the uncreated, and recover our lost incarnated immortality.[26] In
touch, no matter how much love and gentleness abound, we each enact
the hereditary kiss of Judas on Christ. We furiously seek the everlasting
bond but instead hand goodness, along with ourselves, over to death.[27]
Touch places us squarely within the humbling reality that we cannot
complete transcendence, cannot recover what is lost. We are pressing
our fingers to a mirror image of what is lost, we can feel its contours
gnawing at our fingertips. In the embrace of the prodigal son touch offers
only a temporary union, it claims only a transient spiritual enjoining,
and we hold and hold the other longer than customary time allows. But
this embrace must end, and each of us is parted by death. Touch, most
particularly in marriage vows, is the audacious and central promise, that
through endlessly loving grace, we can overcome the kiss of existential
betrayal,[28] and become truly one. How dearly we hope that we can grasp
the glory that left us long ago, and remains only by a touch that caresses
everything but holds on to nothing. In touch we seek its truer form that
can hold on through every age, through time, memory, recollection, and
forgetfulness. "So they are no longer two but one flesh. What therefore

25. Cf. Fulkerson, *The First Sense*, 40: "[There] does not seem, at least to introspec-
tion, to involve association between separate experiences. . . . There does not seem to
be a separate kinesthetic experience independent and distinguishable from one pressure experience, both of which are different again from the thermal experience, and
so forth. Instead, one has a unified experience with different constituent elements."

26. Cf. Unamuno, *Treatise on the Love of God*, 7–8.

27. Luke 22:48: "Jesus asked him, 'Judas, are you betraying the Son of Man with a
kiss?'"

28. Huysmans, *The Oblate*, 242: "Only on the God-Man did she lavish all that
was most exquisite in her armoury. His capacity for suffering exceeded all that she
had known. She crept towards Him on that awful night, when, alone, forsaken in a
cave, He took upon Himself the sins of the world, and, having embraced Him, she
gained a grandeur that was never hers till then. So terrible was she that at her touch He
swooned. His Agony was His Betrothal to her."

God has joined together, let not man separate."[29] Every act of touch in existence is simultaneously a reminder of the uncreated and paradisal, and of our failure to complete the task, to find our way back to our permanent home. "If only I may touch his clothes, I shall be made well."[30]

Hearing as Signatory of Resurrected State

> To him the gatekeeper opens. The sheep hear his voice, and he calls his own sheep by name and leads them out. When he has brought out all his own, he goes before them, and the sheep follow him, for they know his voice.[31]

> Behold, I stand at the door and knock. If anyone hears my voice and opens the door, I will come in to him and eat with him, and he with me.[32]

Hearing as Signatory of Fallenness

> And they heard the sound of the LORD God walking in the garden in the cool of the day, and the man and his wife hid themselves from the presence of the LORD God among the trees of the garden.[33]

> We know that God does not listen to sinners, but if anyone is a worshiper of God and does his will, God listens to him.[34]

"In the beginning was the Word, and the Word was with God, and the Word was God. The same was in the beginning with God."[35] Our existence, life, meaning, the root of all action begins in responsiveness, in a listening to the Word that brings us into life itself, as in the image of the Word.[36] Our lives evoke the reception of God into our hearts and minds,

---

29. Matt 19:6.

30. Mark 5:28.

31. John 10:3–4.

32. Rev 3:20.

33. Gen 3:8.

34. John 9:31.

35. John 1–2.

36. Cf. Gen 26–27: "And God said, 'Let us make man in our image, after our

most originally experienced in hearing as the *ab-origine* foundation for intentionality. Our existence is identically responsive to the Word, it intimately necessitates listening to the divine creative call, one that blesses and gives our unique *entelechy*. In Genesis 1 God creates existence, dividing the night from the light, the firmament from the waters, the stars and sun, the winged creatures and all the other animals. We learn that the creation of these glorious things in his likeness but not his image evokes an "it was so" and "it is good." But as God turns to created human beings in his image and likeness, he initiates the call and response of intentionality so constitutional to our lives on earth and as signatory of heaven. The *arche* of our existence begins in hearing God's Word as blessing:

> God blessed them and said to them, "Be fruitful and increase in number; fill the Earth and subdue it. Rule over the fish in the sea and the birds in the sky and over every living creature that moves on the ground."[37]

Our image necessitates that we are not only created in the likeness of that call *as* Word *as* blessing, but that our natures, in the image of the Word, are fulfilled only when we hear and obey (*ob-audire*) that call. For the Angelic Doctor, our nature, whose intentionality is most primordially designated to hear and respond to God's call, necessitates that our creaturely likeness is also elevated in the process.[38] Not only do we have the more static and general likeness that pertains to all created things as the *unknowing* and good result of the image of God, but because human beings are freed to hear God's call, our likeness also has another sense, a likening power. We knowingly act in ways that "signify the expression and perfection of the image."[39] This unique effulgence correlates most intimately with the cultivation of the virtues through the union of human and divine love.[40] A cultivation dependent upon hearing the Word

---

likeness: and let them have dominion over the fish of the sea, and over the fowl of the air, and over the cattle, and over all the Earth, and over every creeping thing that creepeth upon the Earth.' So God created man in his own image, in the image of God created he him; male and female created he them."

37. Gen 28.

38. Cf. ST I, 93, 2, *sed contra*: "Man's excellence consists in the fact that God made him to His own image by giving him an intellectual soul, which raises him above the beasts of the field. Therefore, things without intellect are not made to God's image."

39. ST I 93, 9, *resp.*

40. ST I 93, 9, *resp*: "In the same sense 'likeness' is said to belong to 'the love of virtue': for there is no virtue without love of virtue."

is intrinsic to our beings. For Aquinas, this likening power even places us *relatively* higher than the angels in terms of how we engage that hearing of God's call. Listening is the primal incarnational act of intentionality, it grounds how we become the other *as other*, how the soul in a way becomes all things,[41] and how—while the image of God is far more perfect in the angel than in the human person due to their intellectual powers—we have a dignity, a likening power, within the *entirety* of our flesh that can raise us above the angels:

> The fact that man proceeds from man, as God from God; and also in the fact that the whole human soul is in the whole body, as God from God; and also in the fact that the whole human soul is in the whole body, and again, in every part, as God is in regard to the whole world. In these and the like things the image of God is more perfect in man than it is in the angels.[42]

We were made to hear the Word who in his donative power "was made flesh, and dwelt among us, (and we beheld his glory, the glory as of the only begotten of the Father,) full of grace and truth."[43] Hearing is not a mere collating of random unrelated sounds, when we hear we are phenomenologically obeying the ground of Being in which *if* there are things, there is a *way* for things to be.[44] Only if there is a *way* for things to be is there meaning, otherwise one has, at best, indecipherable noise. In hearing, our senses are triggered beyond themselves through the act of intentionality, which assimilates within us that way for things to be. This is why a foreign language for a good while sounds too quick, run together, indistinct. This remains the case until the sound hides, and the event of being, pattern, action, meaning comes to the forefront through gained understanding. Just as in learning a new language, all genuine hearing intrinsically involves a turning of one's whole being to the words, an *obedience* to assimilating oneself to the reality of the otherness that enables one to know the self. Only when the foreign language ceases to be heard as sound and finally heard as meaning, do we arrive at the depth of hearing as obedience.[45] In hearing, we turn our whole being to the other to assimilate what is offered by that other.

41. Aristotle, *De Anima*, in *Basic Works*, 431b21.

42. ST I 93, 3, *resp.*

43. John 1:14.

44. Cf. Parmenides, "Poem of Parmenides," *Parmenides of Elea*, 12–43.

45. Cf. Huey, "Obedience—A Neglected Doctrine," 6: "Hearing the word of God

Note that if I think of what I am going to say, the word already
exists in my heart. But if I want to speak to you, I am concerned
to render present to your heart what is already present in mine.
Then, seeking a way to let the word that exists in me reach you
and dwell with you, I have recourse to my voice. Its sound communicates my word and its meaning to you. When it is finished
it vanishes. But my word is now in you, without ever having
left me. (Sermon 293, 3) I ask you God, to reveal me to myself.
(*Confessions*, 10, 1)[46]

In God's divine call, our hearing is completed through obedience,
so that true hearing is identical with obedience to the truth. Through the
totalizing reception of the other, our souls become in a way all things. The
sound communicates the Word which dwells in us, the sound fades but
the reception remains. We receive so that we may act; we are obedient so
we may be free; we hear so that Christ will make his home in us. Through
obedience, Christ intentionally makes his home in us:

Do not let your hearts be troubled. You believe in God; believe
also in me. My Father's house has many rooms; if that were not
so, would I have told you that I am going there to prepare a place
for you? And if I go and prepare a place for you, I will come back
and take you to be with me that you also may be where I am. You
know the way to the place where I am going. . . . Anyone who
loves me will obey my teaching. My Father will love them, and
we will come to them and make our home with them. Anyone
who does not love me will not obey my teaching. These words
you hear are not my own; they belong to the Father who sent
me.[47]

Our originary intentional hearing of God's Word as blessing evokes
obedience to the ground of truth, which enables that separation of noise
from meaning, the unreal from reality, untruth from truth. Noise is
the foreign and unable-to-be-received anti-language, it is the looking

---

is the basis for obedience in the Old Testament. In fact, hearing and obeying were so
closely related that the Hebrew language uses the same word to convey both ideas.
James Smart has observed that the verb 'to hear' in Hebrew 'significantly denotes not
any passive receiving of words into the mind but the response of a man's whole being' (*The Old Testament in Dialogue with Modern Man*, Westminster, 1964, p. 11).
The Israelite needed no psychological or philosophical explanation for the doctrine of
obedience; for him, hearing the word of God was tantamount to obeying it."

46. St. Augustine, *Augustine Day by Day*, 103.

47. John 14:1–4; 23–24.

through a glass darkly. But our hearing, as one with obedience, was designated by God's call to be revelatory. The Word made flesh beckoned us at the moment of our creation to hear and to take-in meaning, truth, goodness, beauty, and action.

In hearing, we experience the heaven on earth, because we have heard and taken-in the call of creation as Word and blessing. Through this originary intentionality, we become in a way all things, most essentially permeating us with the yearning for paradise. That primal hearing of God's Word saturates us with the intentional presence of the divine.[48] Our excellence consists in the dramatic gift of hearing and responding to our image and likeness. This indelibly reveals our end as only realized in heaven, most particularly in the resurrected state. The hope for the resurrection of the bodies is justified within the senses, and especially within hearing as first enactment of creational intentionality. The glorified body properly reflects and fulfills the dignity of the senses as co-extensive with our likeness to God as likening power, which relatively raises us in our carnality above the angels.

Sight as Signatory of Resurrected State

Now the appearance of the glory of the LORD was like a devouring fire on the top of the mountain in the sight of the people of Israel.[49]

Again, Jesus spoke to them, saying, "I am the light of the world. Whoever follows me will not walk in darkness, but will have the light of life."[50]

48. Cf. SCG III, 18–20: "All created things are some sort of image of the prime agent, God: for every agent acts to the production of its own likeness: now the perfection of an image consists in representing its original by likeness thereto: the image in fact is made on purpose. All things then exist for the attainment of the divine likeness; and that is their last end."

49. Exod 24:17.

50. John 8:12.

Sight as Signatory of Fallenness

The LORD will smite you with madness and with blindness and
with bewilderment of heart.[51]

And why do you see the speck that is in your brother's eye, but
do not notice the beam of wood in your own eye?[52]

Let them alone: they are blind, and leaders of the blind. And if
the blind lead the blind, both will fall into the pit.[53]

Sight is the privileged sense that gives us access into our *longer way*,
the spectatorial status of intellectual beings united in flesh and spirit. Sight
enables us to understand our distance, our own otherness, the difference
as difference between ourselves and the existents that also participate in
the world of Being.[54] While our hands in their immediacy cannot touch,
or smell in its inspiration cannot as of yet inhale or take-in, or hearing
cannot assimilate in its receptivity, sight alone is able to gaze upon that
difference that the soul has not as of yet, by way of immateriality, become
the other *as other*. Sight renders us historical beings by stretching us into
the presence of experiences, beings, objects, artifacts that necessitate a
story, an order, a cause-and-effect relationship by which these things can
be assimilated in their interplay of meanings. Every experience of sight
stretches us back into memorial otherness and into the immemorial root.
One enters an antique curio shop, scans the room, taking in generational
layers of existence. The dented guitar, a porcelain figurine, a tea set from
India, the travel case from another century, a Madonna with its paint
chipped: each enables us to envision the interrelatedness of historical engagement. In sight, we connect the world of things, we uncover aspects of

51. Deut 28:28.

52. Matt 7:3.

53. Matt 15:14.

54. See St. Augustine when he refers to 1 John 2:16 "the lust of the eyes" as an apt
analogy for this priority of the senses. *Confessions*, xxxv, 54: "Seeing is the property of
our eyes. But we also use this word in other senses, when we apply the power of vision
to knowledge generally. We do not say 'Hear how that flashes,' or 'Smell how bright
that is,' or 'Taste how that shines' or 'Touch how that gleams.' Of all these things we say
'see.' But we say not only 'See how that light shines,' which only the eyes can perceive,
but also 'see how that sounds, see what smells, see what tastes, see how hard that is.' So
the general experience of the senses is the lust, as scripture says, of the eyes, because
seeing is a function in which eyes hold the first place but other senses claim the word
for themselves by analogy when they are exploring any department of knowledge."

an invisible string from one to another forming a netting of unity, which we then co-substantiate when we assimilate their otherness. This is only heightened when the other that we see is another person who sees us, and whose sight is also one long, ever-connected engagement stretching from eternity into time.

> In the household where a new child is born, all objects change their sense, they begin to anticipate from this child some still indeterminate treatment, someone new and someone additional is there, a new history, whether it be brief or long, has just been established, and a new register is open. My first perception, along with the horizons that surround it, is an ever-present event, an unforgettable tradition; even as a thinking subject I am still this first perception, I am the continuation of the same life that it inaugurated. In a sense, there are no more distinct acts of consciousness or of *Erlebnisse* [experiences] in a life than there are isolated things in the world.[55]

Time and space are given within sight, in seeing-the-other we experience ourselves as the center or nucleus where we can engage presences that contain, protracted within them, the past and future. Things are held at a distance; even as they are brought forward for closer inspection, we experience in sight the alterity of the being in question.[56] The past and future, unveiled within the sight of the other, dilates alongside our own recollective and futural experiences. In sight, we begin to encounter the magnitude of the soul as the form of the body and how human persons, as aeviternal, enjoy the union of time and eternity within their shared flesh. In the *De Potentia* III, Question 10, objections 8–10, we see the mystery of which sight reminds us. The nature of the soul as an intellectual substance is measured by aeviternal duration, as are the angels, and thus the objectors make the reasonable claims that: a) souls must have been created at the beginning of the world prior to bodies; b) the aeviternity that human beings possess is experienced in something other than "before" and "after," otherwise it would not differentiate itself from temporality; and c) human persons, being far closer to the angels than

---

55. Merleau-Ponty, *Phenomenology of Perception*, 429–30.

56. Jonas, "The Nobility of Sight," 519: "It would not be correct to say that in sight the distant is brought near. Rather it is left in its distance, and if this is great enough it can put the observed object outside the sphere of possible intercourse and of environmental relevance. In that case, perceptual distance many turn into mental distance, and the phenomenon of disinterested beholding may emerge, this essential ingredient in what we call 'objectivity.'"

the animals, attest to a unity of place as a unity of nature, signifying their soul, not their bodies, were derived with the angels in heaven.[57] St. Thomas responds to the objectors in the following manner:

> The soul is measured by time with respect to the being in accordance with which it is united to the body, although when it is considered as a spiritual substance it is measured by eviternity. Nevertheless, it need not be that it began to be measured by eviternity when the angels did. Although the things measured by eviternity have no before and after, nothing prevents one thing from partaking in eviternity before another. Although the soul and angel agree in intellectual nature, they differ in that the angel is a nature complete in itself, whence it could be created in itself. But since the soul's nature is perfected in its union with the body, it must be created not in Heaven but in the body whose perfection it is.[58]

The Thomistic objectors rightly emphasize our aeviternal status, but wrongly do so at the cost of embodiment, unable to reconcile how the senses are signatories of our glorified state. Their misstep, we contend, costs them a robust understanding of the promise of paradise befitting human nature. The human person resides on the borderline between time and eternity.[59] The objectors are absolutely correct to stress that our aeviternity is marked by a duration other than "before" and "after." Without this essential interior non-mediated duration that unites us with the angels—in participation in the divine image—we would be natural beings to natural ends, utterly inscribed and defined by our environments.

57. St. Thomas, *De Potentia*, III, 10, Obj. 8–10. Obj. 8: "The substance of rational souls is not measured by time because, as is said in the *Book of Causes*, it is above time. Neither again is it measured by eternity, since this belongs to God alone. Indeed, in the *Book of Causes* the soul is said to be beneath eternity. Therefore, it is measured by eviternity, as angels are, and thus angels and souls have the same measure of duration. Therefore, since angels were created at the beginning of the world, it seems that souls also were created then and not in bodies. Obj. 9: There is no before and after in eviternity; otherwise it would not differ from time, as some think. But if angels were created before souls or if one soul is created after another, then before and after would be in eviternity, since the measure of the soul is eviternity, as has been shown. Therefore, all souls must be created at the same time as the angels. Obj. 10: Unity of place attests to unity of nature, and so bodies of different natures are in different places. But the angel and the soul agree in nature, since they are spiritual and intellectual substances. Therefore souls are created in the empyrean Heaven just as the angels were and not in bodies."

58. St. Thomas, *De Potentia*, III, ad. 8–10.

59. SCG III, 61.

We are the unity of the uncreated and created, of the eternal and the temporal, and the universal within the particular. Human temporality differs from the animals, and it is sight, especially, that provides recognition of that dramatic difference. We are participants in the immediate presence of the *imago Dei* befitting our aeviternal status. That *imago Dei* as exemplified in Christ's incarnation is unified with our bodies which elongate that immediate eternal image through the incarnating experience of before and after. Our flesh, through our senses, enacts this dramatic range where we are fully immersed in each, with each being a fundamental sign of our glorified state. Sight, which stands distinct and is achieved over distance, is the privileged sense that reminds us of our difference from the animals, and of our nearness to the angels. We are more than an accidental difference on the scale of animal sensory powers.[60] If this were the case, our sight would be unremarkable and a mediocre tool for processing the world. We cannot see clearly in the dark like the birds of prey, who accurately track and capture their meals, nor swivel our eyes like chameleons, each in opposite directions to process two different sensory experiences. But our sight is far more remarkable than any other animal's because it signifies our co-substantiating of heaven.[61] Our senses are not passively bound to our environment. As open-natures, we transcend that

60. Cf. Engelland, *Phenomenology*, 101–2: "Dogs, dolphins, and chimpanzees don't philosophize, and they don't do science. They don't ask such questions. It is strange but true that human beings find themselves alone in the world of theoretical investigation. What sort of difference is this one between humans and animals? A difference in degree is accidental, just a matter of tweaking what is already there. Is this a difference in degree. If so, humans would not be that much different from dogs and dolphins. A difference in kind, however, is essential; we need new principles to explain it. Is this a difference in kind? If so, humans would be significantly different from dogs and dolphins, and we would have to appeal to new principles to make sense of the human."

61. Cf. Engelland, *Phenomenology*, 102–3: "Heidegger states the environments of animals are not as such poor; they are poor only when those various environments are compared with the human world of linguistic experience and truth. The point is the richness of the human world rather than the poverty of the animal. Bees navigate and forage by living out a range of relevance specified by the good of the hive. They notice sources of nectar but they don't contemplate the intelligibility of the flower or the beauty of the blossom; there are no bee botanists or bee poets. Now, this might seem like a trivial point. But phenomenologists are not calling attention to random differences between bees and humans. They are highlighting the character of the fundamental difference that makes the observation of this differences possible. The bee or any other animal is inscribed within the domain of an environment. Humans, by contrast, can transcend their environment and dwell within world. As a result, they can compare one environment with another."

passivity and actively substantiate worlds within worlds. Human sight, which calls to mind the historicity of every vantage point, of the objects within its view, calls us also to their immemorial givenness. Sight cannot help but connect all, reveal to us glimmers of the invisible thread that connects all moments, underscoring all reality. This is why the blind man who asks for sight in the Gospels, paradoxically sees more than many with physical sight.[62] Human sight is not lost with the loss of physical sight, the latter is a portal into the former, as time is a portal to eternity, and flesh to the resurrected state: "we look not to the things that are seen but to the things that are unseen. For the things that are seen are transient, but the things that are unseen are eternal."[63] Human sight is only ever fully realized when it sees that it desires the vision of the unseen,[64] the illumination of that invisible thread connecting and transfiguring all things in the radiant vision of sanctified love.[65]

> [The Son] is the image of the invisible God, the firstborn over all creation. For in him all things were created: things in heaven and on earth, visible and invisible, whether thrones or powers or rulers or authorities; all things have been created through him and for him. He is before all things, and in him all things hold together. And he is the head of the body, the church; he is the beginning and the firstborn from among the dead, so that in everything he might have the supremacy. For God was pleased to have all his fullness dwell in him, and through him to reconcile to himself all things, whether things on earth or things in heaven, by making peace through his blood, shed on the cross.[66]

62. Cf. Luke 18:3–43.

63. 2 Cor 4:18.

64. Cf. 1 Tim 1:17: "Now unto the King eternal, immortal, invisible, the only wise God, be honour and glory for ever and ever. Amen." 1 Tim 6: 16: "Who only hath immortality, dwelling in the light which no man can approach unto; whom no man hath seen, nor can see: to whom be honour and power everlasting. Amen." John 1:18; 4:12: "No one has ever seen God." Heb 11:27: "By faith he left Egypt, not fearing the king's anger; he persevered because he saw him who is invisible."

65. Cf. 1 Cor 13:12: "For now we see in a mirror dimly, but then face to face." Heb 12:14: "Follow peace with all men, and holiness, without which no man shall see the Lord."

66. Col 1:15–20.

Taste as Signatory of Resurrected State

The house of Israel named it manna, and it was like coriander seed, white, and its taste was like wafers with honey.[67]

My son, eat honey, for it is good, yes, the honey from the comb is sweet to your taste; know that wisdom is thus for your soul; if you find it, then there will be a future, and your hope will not be cut off.[68]

Taste and see that the LORD is good; blessed is the one who takes refuge in him. Fear the LORD, you his holy people, for those who fear him lack nothing. The lions may grow weak and hungry, but those who seek the LORD lack no good thing.[69]

But we see Jesus, who was made a little lower than the angels for the suffering of death, crowned with glory and honour; that he by the grace of God should taste death for every man.[70]

Taste as Signatory of Fallenness

And the woman said to the serpent, "We may eat the fruit of the trees of the garden; but of the fruit of the tree which is in the midst of the garden, God has said, 'You shall not eat it, nor shall you touch it, lest you die.'" Then the serpent said to the woman, "You will not surely die."[71]

Can something tasteless be eaten without salt, or is there any taste in the white of an egg? My soul refuses to touch them; they are like loathsome food to me.[72]

I tell you, not one of those who were invited will get a taste of my banquet.[73]

67. Exod 16:31.

68. Prov 24:13–14.

69. Ps 34:8–10.

70. Heb 2:9.

71. Gen 3:2–4.

72. Job 6:6–7. See also St. Jerome's version in the Vulgate: "can anyone taste that which being tasted produces death?"

73. Luke 14:24.

They came to the chief priests and the elders and said, "We have bound ourselves under a solemn oath to taste nothing until we have killed Paul."[74]

Through taste we consume and assimilate within ourselves the foods that will sustain our being. Taste is violent, visceral, *and* one of the most pleasurable exercises of intentionality. In taste, we move beyond the contemplative gaze of sight and hearing. We are also far past an ethereal imbibing or inhaling of the spirit that comes with smell. The closest, touch, even as it dominantly grips and grasps, cannot devour the other the way in which taste initiates such power within us. This unique sense positions us in a direct placing of the other on our lips and in our mouths. It goes even further than direct placement, it forcibly breaks down the elements of the other with our teeth and tongues. We reshape, dissolve, texturize the substance, then swallow, ingest, and digest it. We make it a plaything that becomes one with our bodies, feeding our flesh and blood and vital organs. We deconstruct its structure and order and accost its lifeforce, we empty its being to nourish our own. The tongue itself also capitalizes on another sense, touch. It presses and rolls the sustenance around the mouth and against the back of the teeth, taking also the world of sight, smell, and hearing within its presence. The wine tastes of the straw we hear crushed underfoot, it tastes of the inhaled fragrance of honeysuckle, fire, tobacco, nuts, oak, the crispness of Autumn, and through them we find ourselves in a clearing in a forest where such tastes inhabit and intermingle. The honeysuckle and the oak remind of backyard play in the lateness of warm days. The straw and the tobacco bring us elsewhere into the past, of grandfathers, farms, and where cool sunsets each arrives earlier than the day before. Taste does not solely contemplate these memories but grafts them into our flesh, breaking each piece down into the minutest of forms so that the entirety of their substances can be assimilated into us, so that we concretely, viscerally, violently, become the other as other. Taste reminds us that, compared to the angels, we take the longer way to spiritual contemplation, a way that never sheds the richness of embodiment. We may become the other as other immaterially, but we do so *through* the body, for the soul orients itself as one in being with the senses. The transcendency of spirit, much like prayer and grace, must be consumed and ravished within our being.

74. Acts 23:14.

While they were eating, Jesus took bread, said the blessing, broke it, and giving it to his disciples said, "Take and eat; this is my body." Then he took a cup, gave thanks, and gave it to them, saying, "Drink from it, all of you, for this is my blood of the covenant, which will be shed on behalf of many for the forgiveness of sins. I tell you, I will not drink from this fruit of the vine from now on until that day when I drink it new with you in my Father's kingdom."[75]

Christ alone fulfills our need to consume the spirit, to understand sanctity through taste. His *kenotic* gift, his total self-emptying fulfills and marvelously exceeds what has always been signified within taste.[76] In taste, we empty the other to nourish ourselves; we consume the other to complete what is lacking in us. But no taste ever emancipates us from the cycle of need. What we have consumed is now absent, we have emptied it of its essence, and while it is within us, it is only transient fullness revealing itself as disintegrating form. This consumption as consummation of the other achieves its climax and fulfillment in the Eucharist, which involves a twofold sense of consummation: 1) the consumption of the outward appearance of the host, the accidents of bread and wine, which remains and which the senses readily perceive and 2) the consumption of the substance of the bread and wine[77] transformed into the substance of Christ's body and blood. In the consumption of food, we desire a substantial change, but never fully achieve retaining the fullness of the thing consumed. We must empty what is consumed in order to engage it, losing its substance in the process. And when we consume, our accidents change—we may become heavier, thinner, fuller—but our substance remains the same. In taste, we long for the consumption as consummation of the other that transforms our entire beings: "like newborn infants, long for the pure spiritual milk, that by it you may grow up into salvation—if

75. Matt 26:26–28.

76. Cf. Ps 42:1–3: "As the deer pants for streams of water, so my soul pants for you, my God. My soul thirsts for God, for the living God. When can I go and meet with God? My tears have been my food day and night, while people say to me all day long, 'Where is your God?'"

77. Cf. ST III, 75, 3 *sed contra*: "God is not the cause of tending to nothing. But this sacrament is wrought by Divine power. Therefore, in this sacrament the substance of the bread or wine is not annihilated." ST III, 75, 3, ad. 1: "The substance of the bread or wine, after the consecration, remains neither under the sacramental species, nor elsewhere; yet it does not follow that it is annihilated; for it is changed into the body of Christ; just as if the air, from which fire is generated, be not there or elsewhere, it does not follow that it is annihilated."

indeed you have tasted that the Lord is good."[78] We hunger to taste the substance that evokes within us that essential substantial change, the one that realizes the inklings of heaven on earth.

Christ's Eucharistic *kenosis* completes what taste has always desired but could never achieve. The texture, look, smell, the accidents of the bread and wine (taste, texture, appearance) do not change. We handle them as we did before. But the substance does change. It tastes like bread and wine, but it is Christ's body and blood. In transubstantiation, Christ turns taste upside down to fulfill what taste has always signified but could never clearly convey or capture. Christ offers us not accidental change but a taste of substantial change filling us with the hope for the resurrection of our bodies. When we consume the Eucharist, we experience a two-fold layering of tastes. In tasting the bread and wine *as bread and wine*, we are reminded of time and memory relegated to a recollection of past events. In this first form, we taste and confirm our bondage to accidental change. But like human sight which sees without physical sight, all our senses point beyond themselves to the significance of our incarnational intentionality. Taste has always pointed past itself in yearning to something that could substantially fill us, not merely accidentally and temporarily satiate. In tasting of the body and blood of Christ, time and memory are not relegated to recollection by way of accidental changes but elevated to be recovered and glorified in the substantial change that offers us the only true taste of Life itself. This taste brings us into the very body of the resurrected state. We adore the Eucharist, lower ourselves onto our knees to receive as birds do from their mothers. It dissolves on our tongue, is crushed between our teeth, subsumed into our substance, as we are subsumed into it. This second form of tasting is not a recollection or remembrance of a past event, this is the foundational re-collection of Being, this is making present what *Is*, Christ's total self-emptying re-collected, re-membered in us. The Eucharist is contemplated within the violence of *eros* colliding with *agape*, with life bleeding out agonically into death, and death resurrected joyously into life. This act of tasting re-collects the passion of our Lord. This consumption as consummation completes within us the Paschal mystery. In tasting, we are physically re-membering Christ's *kenotic* death and resurrection.

> For I received from the Lord what I also passed on to you: The Lord Jesus, on the night he was betrayed, took bread, and when

---

78. 1 Pet 2:2–3. Cf. Hütter, *Aquinas on Transubstantiation*, 27–56.

he had given thanks, he broke it and said, "This is my body, which is for you; do this in remembrance of me." In the same way, after supper he took the cup, saying, "This cup is the new covenant in my blood; do this, whenever you drink it, in remembrance of me." For whenever you eat this bread and drink this cup, you proclaim the Lord's death until he comes.[79]

79. 1 Cor 11:23–26.

12

Summary Remarks on the Senses
in and for Paradise

O God, you are my God; earnestly I seek you; my soul thirsts for
you; my flesh faints for you, as in a dry and weary land where
there is no water. So, I have looked upon you in the sanctuary,
beholding your power and glory. Because your steadfast love is
better than life, my lips will praise you. So, I will bless you as
long as I live; in your name I will lift up my hands. My soul will
be satisfied as with fat and rich food, and my mouth will praise
you with joyful lips.[1]

I F WE ARE TO hope for the resurrected state with as much persistence as
tendrils climb and turn towards the sunlight, then it is essential that we
rediscover the wealth of indications housed within our five senses. History
is an interminably long ledger of misappropriated senses. They are either
filed under forms of suppression, abandonment, subjugation—which have
their merits in only the rarest of forms—or the human person is expected
to surrender to the senses *because* what is held in view is a reduced form,
as biological drives, indifferent to, and alienated from, their incarnated
spiritual appetite. The latter is more often than not the response to a dearth
of theological efficacy; it still seeks a spiritual consummation in roundabout
ways and means, but is without the directionality to rediscover what it

1. Ps 63:1–5.

is no longer capable of desiring. The former, for all its wildly adamant gesticulations, fails to find any real home on earth because everywhere *is* the carnal, the soul is not housed in flesh, as water is contained within the glass, the flesh is permeated with soul. Bypass the senses, and one bypasses the spiritual altogether. There is no faith without the flesh.[2]

Sin has always been about senses stripped of their proper end (entelechy). And sin will forever be the denial of the incarnational status of the senses. It reduces the senses out of their *habitus* in eternity and forces them into the closed loop of biological drives.[3] Every sin of the flesh is simultaneously, or more interiorly, a sin of disembodiment, no matter how much the body is used, devoured, centralized, and manipulated. Such sins are the promise of heightened senses, when what is actually on offer are dulled and worn-down motivations approaching nothingness. But senses given space within the powerhouse of reality that a) we act from eternity when we act in time, befitting our aeviternal status, and b) in a relative manner our likeness, as likening power, is higher than the angels' likeness to God, is revealed as magnificently nuptial in nature and activity. It is crucial we recover the dignity and charge of these nuptial-bound senses within the journey to our permanent home. The senses enable us to experience the incarnational intentionality Christ offers to us as the bridegroom:[4] a transcendentally sensual and encompassing fidelity prefigured in the erotic lover and beloved union of the Song of Solomon:

> How beautiful is your love, my sister, my bride! How much better is your love than wine, and the fragrance of your oils than any spice! Your lips drip nectar, my bride; honey and milk are under your tongue; the fragrance of your garments is like the fragrance of Lebanon. A garden locked is my sister, my bride, a

2. Cf. 1 John 1–4: "That which was from the beginning, which we have heard, which we have seen with our eyes, which we looked upon and have touched with our hands, concerning the word of life—the life was made manifest, and we have seen it, and testify to it and proclaim to you the eternal life, which was with the Father and was made manifest to us—that which we have seen and heard we proclaim also to you, so that you too may have fellowship with us; and indeed our fellowship is with the Father and with his Son Jesus Christ. And we are writing these things so that our joy may be complete."

3. Cf. Ps 115:5–7: "They have mouths, but cannot speak, eyes, but cannot see. They have ears, but cannot hear, noses, but cannot smell. They have hands, but cannot feel, feet, but cannot walk, nor can they utter a sound with their throats."

4. John 3:29: "He that hath the bride is the bridegroom: but the friend of the bridegroom, which standeth and heareth him, rejoiceth greatly because of the bridegroom's voice: this my joy therefore is fulfilled."

spring locked, a fountain sealed. Your shoots are an orchard of pomegranates with all choicest fruits, henna with nard, nard and saffron, calamus and cinnamon, with all trees of frankincense, myrrh and aloes, with all choice spices—a garden fountain, a well of living water, and flowing streams from Lebanon. Awake, O north wind, and come, O south wind! Blow upon my garden, let its spices flow.[5]

Each of the five senses unveils the perfumed pattern of the bridegroom transfixing our lives, transposed with all newness, promise, peace, and sanctification.

- Smell completes itself in inspired breath that climbs into the center of our chests, into the place where the Sacred Heart resides. We who inhabit his fragrance of creation, his perfumed passion redeemed, inhale the God that happens within us repeatedly. Our physical bodies rhythmically remind us, every moment, of the breath of God that brings us to life, to our lives ever in need of the Holy Spirit.

- In touch, we seek to cross the divide that separates things, beings, objects. We look towards becoming one in being with the other and desire that touch accomplishes a nuptial level of union, where if only we could touch the cloth that our bridegroom wears, all shall be made well.

- The exquisite power of hearing as obedience to God's call, is a receptive surrender where every lover is the beloved in otherness, and every beloved is the lover in selfhood. We the bride surrender to the pillar of Truth, Goodness, and Beauty, where in hearing we must turn our whole being to distinguish the Word from the idle noise and chatter.

- Sight achieves its union with the bridegroom through the recognition of distance and nearness. Sight is the privileged sense, which unveils how much closer we are to the angels than to the animals while also acknowledging the vast unseen lengths that must be traveled before we can arrive at the wedding of the Lamb.[6] Human sight united to but exceeding physical sight immerses itself in the unseen netting that encompasses all things and desires the invisible to be

5. Song of Sol 4:10–16.
6. Cf. Col 1:15: "He is the image of the invisible God, the firstborn of all creation."

made visible.[7] This is the sight aligned with faith as "the substance of things hoped for, the certitude of unseen things."[8]

- Taste reveals to us the incarnational physical contemplation specific to human beings born to the *longior via*. Our spiritual contemplation arises through consumption and ravishment, it is to be moved along our teeth, within our mouths around our tongues. We tasted of the forbidden fruit and lost our earthly paradise. Now our taste seeks to consume and reconstitute what is lost, a new Eden. Taste unveils the desire for Christ's *kenosis*. In and through it, we desire a substantial change, but it is impossible to retain the fullness of the thing consumed. The tasted is consumed, emptied, and has nothing left to give. Only Christ restores the savor in the salt,[9] only the God-man has something left to give when tasted, consumed, utterly emptied and abandoned.[10]

The body politic as mystical body begins in heaven and is fulfilled in the resurrected state.[11] Only through our senses does Christ come home. We make home in Christ's flesh who first offers himself to us in his home identical to his flesh and blood. We *smell* and breathe in the fragrance of his Word, *hear* his call necessitating our entire bodies to turn towards him, *touch* his garment so that all manner of thing shall be well,[12] *see* the invis-

---

7. Cf. Rev 22:3–5; 16–17: "The throne of God and of the Lamb will be in the city, and his servants will serve him. They will see his face, and his name will be on their foreheads. There will be no more night. They will not need the light of a lamp or the light of the sun, for the Lord God will give them light. And they will reign for ever and ever. . . . I, Jesus, have sent my angel to give you this testimony for the churches. I am the Root and the Offspring of David, and the bright Morning Star. The Spirit and the Bride say, 'Come.' And let the one who hears say, 'Come.' And let the one who is thirsty come; let the one who desires take the water of life without price."

8. Heb 11:1.

9. Matt 5:13.

10. Cf. John 2:19: "Jesus answered them, 'Destroy this temple, and in three days I will raise it up.'"

11 Cf. 2 Cor 5:1–5: "For we know that if the tent that is our earthly home is destroyed, we have a building from God, a house not made with hands, eternal in the heavens. For in this tent we groan, longing to put on our heavenly dwelling, if indeed by putting it on we may not be found naked. For while we are still in this tent, we groan, being burdened—not that we would be unclothed, but that we would be further clothed, so that what is mortal may be swallowed up by life. He who has prepared us for this very thing is God, who has given us the Spirit as a guarantee."

12. Norwich, *Revelations of Divine Love*, 54–55.

ible with the eyes of faith, and *taste* his *kenotic* love, which alone satisfies all hunger. If we forsake or shortchange the senses, we reduce the glorified state to a recitation of empty, well-meaning but deadly, platitudes. Our flesh permeates our soul, a reality glorified in Our Lord's agony on Golgotha. And it is illuminated even further in the ecstasy wherein Didymus places his fingers in Christ's wounds, touching the spiritual crucible that clarifies the mystery of our senses transubstantiated through faith and grace.[13] Bypass the senses, and one bypasses the cross and resurrection altogether. There is no in-between state, the glorified body does not perniciously reside halfway between body and soul, but inhabiting neither. Christ, our body and our bridegroom, is no mere go-between:

> Let not your heart be troubled: ye believe in God, believe also in me. In my Father's house are many mansions: if it were not so, I would have told you. I go to prepare a place for you. And if I go and prepare a place for you, I will come again, and receive you unto myself; that where I am, there ye may be also. And whither I go ye know, and the way ye know. Thomas saith unto him, Lord, we know not whither thou goest; and how can we know the way? Jesus saith unto him, I am the way, the truth, and the life: no man cometh unto the Father, but by me.[14]

There is no faith without the flesh, only disembodied homelessness, hell itself.

13. John 20:25–29: "'Unless I see the nail marks in his hands and put my finger where the nails were, and put my hand into his side, I will not believe.' . . . 'Put your finger here; see my hands. Reach out your hand and put it into my side. Stop doubting and believe.' Thomas said to him, 'My Lord and my God!' Then Jesus told him, 'Because you have seen me, you have believed; blessed are those who have not seen and yet have believed.'"

14. John 14:1–6.

13

Stairway to Heaven

*What the God-man as viatoric and comprehensor
tells us about the resurrected state*

Blessed are the pure in heart, for they will see God.[1]

What can we now justly infer regarding the manifestation of embodiment through our senses in the resurrected state? What we surmise must be united to humility, and to the profound acknowledgment that although our inferences may have wiped away much of the easy wish-fulfilling hope and disembodied ideological speculation, it is still a looking through the glass darkly. And it will always be this way until the light that *is* Christ, that *is* the flesh of the beatific vision, illuminates in paradise *our* embodiment *through* his own.[2]

We must remember that Christ's incarnation leads us by way of a two-fold—emphatically impossible but necessary—unitive experience of his flesh as *viatoric* wayfarer and his spirit as immediate *comprehensor*. How are these two existential experiences, intrinsic to the God-man,

1. Matt 5:8.

2. Cf. John 12:46: "I have come as Light into the world, so that everyone who believes in Me will not remain in darkness."

186

authentically related within his supreme *kenosis* on the cross? If this mystery is not properly oriented, we cannot approach the God-man, we would not have a resurrection worthy of belief, and we would have no foundation upon which to glimpse our resurrected state. Everything is at risk, paradise has always been played for the highest of stakes. St. Thomas emphasizes this essential *comprehensor* status, otherwise we would not have in Christ the second person of the intra-Trinitarian union. We would have a quasi-human, quasi-divine go-between and not the true Mediator. Christ must be the *To Be* of the beatific vision in order to enact the message of salvation. Otherwise, he is not the Word made flesh.

Addressing whether in Christ there is faith, St. Thomas remarks the following:

> As was said above (II-II:1:4), the object of faith is a Divine thing not seen. Now the habit of virtue, as every other habit, takes its species from the object. Hence, if we deny that the Divine thing was not seen, we exclude the very essence of faith. Now from the first moment of His conception Christ saw God's Essence fully, as will be made clear (III:34:1). Hence there could be no faith in Him.[3]

In the following article, the Angelic Doctor addresses whether in Christ there is hope. Aquinas' remarks leave open a subtle and powerful avenue to explore the possibility that his godforsakeness, so aligned with his viatoric status and essential to his shepherding of all humanity, is not incompatible with his immediate and full *comprehensorship*:

> As it is of the nature of faith that one assents to what one sees not, so is it of the nature of hope that one expects what as yet one has not; and as faith, forasmuch as it is a theological virtue, does not regard everything unseen, but only God; so likewise hope, as a theological virtue, has God Himself for its object, the fruition of Whom man chiefly expects by the virtue of hope; yet, in consequence, whoever has the virtue of hope may expect the Divine aid in other things, even as he who has the virtue of faith believes God not only in Divine things, but even in whatsoever is divinely revealed. Now from the beginning of His conception Christ had the Divine fruition fully, as will be shown (III:34:4), and hence he had not the virtue of hope. Nevertheless, He had hope as regards such things as He did not yet possess, although He had not faith with regard to anything; because, although He

3. ST III, 7, 3, *resp.*

knew all things fully, wherefore faith was altogether wanting to Him, nevertheless He did not as yet fully possess all that pertained to His perfection, viz. immortality and glory of the body, which He could hope for.[4]

To approach our embodiment in the resurrected state we must dwell on the mystery of how Christ comes to God as *fully* man. Christ's entreating of the Father is, alone, the image to which our likening power must attach itself. He could not authentically petition God as the *most* fully human person, yearning for the vision of the unseen otherness, if his divinity renders such action play acting.[5] It must be a true wayfaring desire. Yet, he could not petition his Father, as more truly human than any human ever was, unless he *Is* the comprehensor, *Is* the image of the Word.[6] Christ on the cross is the apex and estuary of all human-and-divine desire for the invisible to be made visible and tangibly present in the flesh as one with spirit.[7] The God-man is a dual unity, not a dualism

---

4. ST III, 7, 4, *resp.*

5. Cf. ST III, 10, 1, *resp*: "I answer that, As is plain from III:2:6, the union of the two natures in the Person of Christ took place in such a way that the properties of both natures remained unconfused, i.e., 'the uncreated remained uncreated, and the created remained within the limits of the creature,' as Damascene says (De Fide Orth. iii, 3,4). Now it is impossible for any creature to comprehend the Divine Essence, as was shown in I:12:1,4,7, seeing that the infinite is not comprehended by the finite. And hence it must be said that the soul of Christ nowise comprehends the Divine Essence."

6. Cf. ST III, 10, 2, *resp*: "must be said that the soul of Christ knows all things in the Word. For every created intellect knows in the Word, not all simply, but so many more things the more perfectly it sees the Word. Yet no beatified intellect fails to know in the Word whatever pertains to itself. Now to Christ and to His dignity all things to some extent belong, inasmuch as all things are subject to Him. Moreover, He has been appointed Judge of all by God, 'because He is the Son of Man,' as is said John 5:27; and therefore the soul of Christ knows in the Word all things existing in whatever time, and the thoughts of men, of which He is the Judge, so that what is said of Him (John 2:25), 'For He knew what was in man,' can be understood not merely of the Divine knowledge, but also of His soul's knowledge, which it had in the Word."

7. Cf. Maritain, *On the Grace and Humanity*, 61: "At the moment of the Agony and of the Passion He can no longer enter there [his nest of refuge in the Father], He is barred from it by uncrossable barriers, this is why He feels himself abandoned. That has been the supreme exemplar of the night of the spirit of the mystics, the absolutely complete night. The whole world of the Vision and of the divinized supraconscious was there, but He no longer experienced it at all through His infused contemplation. And likewise, the radiance and the influx of this world on the entire soul were more powerful than ever, but were no longer seized at all by the consciousness, nor experienced. Jesus was more than ever united with the Father, but in the terror and the sweat of blood, and in the experience of dereliction."

of unrelated natures held together by forced dialogue and strained connections. There can be no dividing line cut down the middle of Christ,
no partition of the curtain, when convenient, that distinguishes his intellectual and embodied experiences, some pertaining to God and others
pertaining to man. It cannot be a managing of when his *comprehensor*
status takes dominance, as if in a perpetual competition with his *viatoric*
human nature. Either his soul is the *form* of his body, or it is not. Either
Christ is *fully* man and *fully* God or our whole desire for the resurrected
state is grounded on lamentably faulty foundations. Again, everything is
at stake.

For St. Thomas, Christ is fully united to the consummation of the
divine plan, identical to the source of all hope. He does not possess the
virtue of hope as if hope is a terminus other than himself. But, crucially,
Christ is also able to possess *and* exercise hope through the human enactment of act and potency. Quite radically, Christ experiences the under-
belly of hope in the extensive dimensions of the passion by way of the
polarity of possibilities made manifest in the depths of abandonment. His
hope materializes and is elongated through the things he did not yet possess, befitting of the human soul, which acts from potentiality to actuality.
The soul is the form of the body, and his body is deteriorating and dying
on the cross. Christ, with all men, as the supreme man, is hoping for what
he has not yet achieved—immortality and the glorified body—while he
experiences its visceral contrary, namely spiritual and physical decomposition. Christ, as the only man born to die, experiences hope through the
longest and most arduous of *longer ways*,[8] overwhelming every honest
existential metaphysics. He experiences hope only by first casting and
framing its agonic impossibility within his putrefying flesh where, let us
recall, the soul is the form of the body, and human souls are *not* made
separately from their bodies. Christ experiences the longest way to hope
through the deadly waitingness before hope is properly able to be made
manifest. Hope, as connected to the ground that has the capacity to fulfill that hope, cannot be made manifest after original sin. We may have

---

8. Cf. Balthasar, *Theo-logic II*, 348: "He is the dead 'sin-bearer' of all sins. As such,
he passes through what, looked at objectively is his victory, the sin separated from
man on the Cross, which God eternally damns as the second—man-created—chaos.
However, because he is dead, he cannot know it subjectively as what he has made it to
be. He can only 'take cognizance' of it as the fearsome agglomeration of all sins that
no longer has the slightest connection with the Father who is the good Creator. This
involves an absolute overtaxing of knowledge."

wishes, desires, fantasies, dreams, but the bridge to hope, like the bridge over the river Kwai, has been thoroughly blown apart.

Christ subsumes and is subsumed by abandonment as synonymous with the torn human essence. Christ endures the entirety of the rupture of the soul unnaturally wrestled apart from the body through death, which cannot realize hope. During the passion, the God-man underwent godforsakenness, for he did not possess fully all that pertained to his perfection: immortality and glory of the body. He made himself the hope for these things by first becoming the totality of its abandonment and lostness. He entered death and then, out of nothing, became its ontological ground. All foundations necessitate their polarity. Christ's hope proceeds from potentiality to actuality in keeping with his *viatoric* human nature, only lengthened and realized through his *comprehensor* status, which alone knows the sheer nothingness as primal root of all potentiality. Christ is the body of Being, he is *To Be* itself, his potentiality does not, like ours, act on the body of Being as other than himself. Christ acts upon himself as second person within the Trinity. To reacquaint us with the hope wholly abandoned in the ruptured human essence, as a result of original sin, Christ must experience the metaphysical primordiality of potentiality. There is simply no ground left, no potentiality on the body of Being justly to hope for the resurrected state. We removed the grace of immortality because we were unwilling to receive it. From there, there is no way to claw our way back, no ontological structure of hope within human comportment.[9] Christ must metaphysically traverse the root of potentiality as nothingness itself. Christ does not experience the virtue of hope, as he is identical with the source that makes hope directional and intelligible. If Christ in his humanity is going to give humans beings hope in the resurrected state, he must self-empty everything that he Is, as *To Be* itself, as the body of Being, from which all finite act and potency spring, in order to begin again the movement of hope from potentiality to actuality. He must abandon the framework by which the potentiality knows and orients itself housed within preceding *Actus*. All was lost in original sin. Christ's passion does not shortchange this terrible reality.

It should never be a case of attempting to manage his *viatoric* and *comprehensor* status, attempting to harmonize God and man as if covertly and uneasily two unrelated entities. His *comprehensor* status does not diminish his wayfaring status, nor is it surrendered when he experiences

9. St. Thomas, *Commentary on the Sent.*, I, dist. 40, q. 4, a. 2.

the metaphysical abandonment in becoming the primordial nothingness that precedes all potentiality and enables hope. His *comprehensor* status enabled him to experience the lengths of our ruptured essence as homelessness without hope, it allowed him to move past the safety net of finite potentialities housed within preceding sets of finite acts, all returning us to the ground of Being as the uncreated *Actus*. The God-man's *viatoric* and *comprehensor* nature together prefigure all finite leaps of faith, all hope as hopeful of a terminus that can fulfill that hope. When we leap and do so on God's *To Be*, we never leave the presence of Christ's flesh as metaphysical body of Being. Our leap is never as risky as it seems. The greatest risk, the highest stakes are always played out on the cross; on every Good Friday from the beginning till the end of time. Redemption does not work by fiat, by simply returning what we freely chose to forsake. Our hope for immortality that befits the unity of soul and body was lost. The strange and uneasy state of the separated soul attests to those heartrending consequences. If Christ is to make possible what within us is impossible, he must go by way of impossibility and death. There is no longer any potential to actualize that glorified body, for we had chosen death. There were no finite potentialities left for Christ to actualize. There was no way for Christ to save us as the fireman rescues the child from the burning building. Christ is no mere superman using the tools around him to save the day. He does not actualize our potential in the same limited manner as the superhero actualizes the potential for greater strength or speed through already existing strength and speed. Christ as *comprehensor* knew all of this. Christ as *viator wayfarer* accepts its consequences with an acceptance that goes so far beyond anything we can imagine. If there is no potential for immortality and the glorified body because we have removed our link to the image that actualizes them, Christ does not undo our choice. Metaphysically there is nothing left with which to unstick the tape, and replace it as before, there is no way to undo the misplacement. There is no situational potentiality because there is no ultimate actuality that can fulfill that hope for immortality and the glory of the body. If there is an *Is*, it was lost to us and with it the structure to actualize potentiality, and not even a situational potentiality remains to be framed as such in reference to its image as goal and completion. Christ's self-emptying is exhausting and terrifying, and the last of the metaphysicians are prophets in its wake. His *Eli Eli lama sabachthani* holds all the cards to our resurrected state *because* it holds no cards. God created out of nothing and Christ, to save us, creates once again on the cross. He too must go by way of nothingness but of a different kind altogether, one of abandonment, not the nothingness of *ex nihilo* that inaugurates endless potentiality, but the nothingness of death, which ends all life, where every option is extinguished. He must resurrect by forming out of this total abandonment the new ground of potentiality and actuality. Christ can only hope for it to be formed, for all control is abandoned, all framework is lost. Should it happen it is God's grace, and the impossible made necessary. This is why there is no heaven that exists apart from his flesh, and it is why he resurrects with his scars, and why death is now the greatest of friends.

Without Christ's martyrological and *kenotic* love, there would be only fantasy and disoriented desire for our immortality and for the glorified body. On the cross, Christ alone transforms that unfulfilled wishful yearning—which is all it would ever be without him—into genuine hope. To do so, Christ completes the deepest and darkest night of the soul, the longest of longer ways, by placing himself at the center of that ruptured essence, that violent separation of our body and soul, due to our original sin. Christ accomplishes hope by creating a new path for potentiality and actuality, making the nothingness of abandonment and death the foundation to actualize plenitude and fecundity. Christ's flesh is the prayer and plea of unanswered prayers[10] answered because they are one with his flesh and blood, wholly abandoned and unanswered on Golgotha.[11]

10. Cf. Balthasar, *Theo-logic II*, 288: "We can speak of a depositing, a dimming, a non-use of his divine vision; his prayer must spring from his having become man."

11. Cf. ST III, 10, 3, *resp*. Here with Aquinas on "Whether the Soul of Christ can know the infinite in the Word"—we witness the marvelous and loving *kenosis* of Christ's longest of longer ways: "I answer that, Knowledge regards only being, since being and truth are convertible. Now a thing is said to be a being in two ways: First, simply, i.e., whatever is a being in act; secondly, relatively, i.e., whatever is a being in potentiality. And because, as is said Metaph. ix, 20, everything is known as it is in act, and not as it is in potentiality, knowledge primarily and essentially regards being in act, and secondarily regards being in potentiality, which is not knowable of itself, but inasmuch as that in whose power it exists is known. Hence, with regard to the first mode of knowledge, the soul of Christ does not know the infinite. Because there is not an infinite number in act, even though we were to reckon all that are in act at any time whatsoever, since the state of generation and corruption will not last for ever: consequently there is a certain number not only of things lacking generation and corruption, but also of things capable of generation and corruption. But with regard to the other mode of knowing, the soul of Christ knows infinite things in the Word, for it knows, as stated above (Article 2), all that is in the power of the creature. Hence, since in the power of the creature there is an infinite number of things, it knows the infinite, as it were, by a certain knowledge of simple intelligence, and not by a knowledge of vision."

Whatever is good and excelling in us must be in Christ as foundational, as the very image to which the virtue of our likening power tends. Christ delicately, exhaustively, and mysteriously illuminates for us how we can possess the substance of things hoped for, which does not extinguish—as would earthly hope in confrontation with empirical evidence and certitude—but inflames theological hope in union with the evidence of unseen things. Christ embodies how we structurally hunger for salvation while certain of its promise through the God-man. "And He was transfigured before them; and His face shone like the sun, and His garments became as white as light."[12]

12. Matt 17:2.

14

Christ's Infixion

Speculations regarding embodiment and the senses in the resurrected state

> The gift made to me by God as he holds me in his gaze and in
> his hand while remaining inaccessible to me, the terribly dis-
> symmetrical gift of the *mysterium tremendum* only allows me
> to respond and only rouses me to the responsibility it gives by
> making a gift of death.[1]

Christ has created through his death the new realm of possibility by
which we act out our incarnated immortality. We must take a closer look
at how the senses are in relationship to death if we are to glimpse a vision of our resurrected state. Christ resurrects with his scars,[2] this signifies that death paradoxically dilates our understanding of the glorified
body. Here we encounter the Platonic paradox never to love our lives

---

1. Derrida, *The Gift of Death*, 56.

2. Cf. St. Augustine, *The City of God*, xxii: "Perhaps in that kingdom we shall see on
the bodies of the Martyrs the traces of the wounds which they bore for Christ's name:
because it will not be a deformity, but a dignity in them; and a certain kind of beauty
will shine in them, in the body, though not of the body."

so much that we render them unworthy of living.[3] The best of who and what we are is discoverable in the protracted, underlying, encompassing, sanctified dying within daily living. It is the look and touch and aspect of this dying that is not ignored but transformed in the resurrected state when Christ overcomes the world. Death is not to be viewed through the lens of morbid and obsessive fear or obsequious reverence. Instead, the strong, vital desire to engage life most vigorously and within the Beautiful always means a natural, almost unthought, but dwelt-in, readiness to die.[4] Such a person is nourished on the nectar of ecstatic Being, has drunk deeply from the wells of *eros* and *agape*, whose love of the dappled things radiates from his breathing and gestures. This person is capable of such magnanimous beauty because he is a friend to death because his existence is markedly *kenotic*.

> Let the same mind be in you that was in Christ Jesus, who, though he was in the form of God, did not regard equality with God as something to be exploited, but emptied himself, taking the form of a slave, being born in human likeness. And being in

3. Plato, *Apology*, 38e–39b: "Neither in war nor yet at law ought any man to use every way of escaping death. For often in battle there is no doubt that if a man will throw away his arms, and fall on his knees before his pursuers, he may escape death; and in other dangers there are other ways of escaping death, if a man is willing to say and do anything. The difficulty, my friends, is not in avoiding death, but in avoiding unrighteousness; for that runs faster than death."

4. Cf. Chesterton, *Orthodoxy*, 170–71: "Take the case of courage. No quality has ever so much addled the brains and tangled the definitions of merely rational sages. Courage is almost a contradiction in terms. It means a strong desire to live taking the form of a readiness to die. 'He that will lose his life, the same shall save it,' is not a piece of mysticism for saints and heroes. It is a piece of everyday advice for sailors or mountaineers. It might be printed in an Alpine guide or a drill book. This paradox is the whole principle of courage; even of quite earthly or brutal courage. A man cut off by the sea may save his life if we will risk it on the precipice. He can only get away from death by continually stepping within an inch of it. A soldier surrounded by enemies, if he is to cut his way out, needs to combine a strong desire for living with a strange carelessness about dying. He must not merely cling to life, for then he will be a coward, and will not escape. He must not merely wait for death, for then he will be a suicide, and will not escape. He must seek his life in a spirit of furious indifference to it; he must desire life like water and yet drink death like wine. No philosopher, I fancy, has ever expressed this romantic riddle with adequate lucidity, and I certainly have not done so. But Christianity has done more: it has marked the limits of it in the awful graves of the suicide and the hero, showing the distance between him who dies for the sake of living and him who dies for the sake of dying."

human form, he humbled himself and became obedient to the point of death—even death on a cross.[5]

The human body in the resurrected state would be a living art form, with the keys to understanding the manifold layers of each story illuminating from the skin, shining from the face, transmitted in the warmth of touch, and in the gaze that does not hide. Every glorified body would be brightened and clarified in contour through intimacy with the beatific vision, evoking the lover-and-beloved relationship respective to each person. The resurrected state would be the story of every soul—its scars, stretch marks, hardened palms, furrowed brow—visibly overwhelmed by grace. The elusive completion of their earthly meanings, which dying intensified and distilled but could not communicate, is saturated with the outpouring of Christ's *kenotic* ardor. His relentless limitlessness knows us better than we know ourselves or any finite other. His death remakes possibility and actuality, gifting us with a new path to glory. Through Christ's death, our experience of dying becomes the very key to express what death, once the antithesis of possibility, has shaped and distilled within us. In dying we discover the throbbing need to utter the everything and the incommunicable that has always laid at the center of our chests as made in the likeness of the Sacred Heart. The realization of our terminality brings us to this climax but then strips us existentially, leaving us mute, lifeless, unable to communicate. Our anguished, spasmodic souls gasp in impotency, unable to express what is most dear.

> When the time comes to you at which you will be forced at last to utter the speech which has lain at the center of your soul for years, which you have, all that time, idiot-like, been saying over and over, you'll not talk about the joy of words. I saw well why the gods do not speak to us openly, nor let us answer. Till that word can be dug out of us, why should they hear the babble that we think we mean? How can they meet us face to face till we have faces?[6]

Our glorified bodies dramatically unveil Christ at our left, and at our right, above us, below us, in the midst of us, inside of us,[7] radically fulfilling our co-substantiation of paradise. The armor of God that we

5. Phil 2:5–8.

6. Lewis, *Till We Have Faces*, 294.

7. Cf. St. Patrick, "Lorica," *The Life and Prayers of Saint Patrick*, 66–67.

place upon ourselves in life is not a struggle against flesh and blood,[8] but against the evils that degrade its magnificence to carry eternity in time. More still, this armor is nothing other than flesh itself, Christ's flesh and blood infixed upon us. Christ's crucifixion is also an infixion: a yielding of the flesh to the Word being placed, inlayed, infused within it. The nails and lance that scar him pour forth his vital essence and fill the Word within us. This infixion fills our scars, the lines on our faces, the cracked hands, all the signs of death, disease, decay, old age, which simultaneously evoke our personhood and our failure to transmit and communicate what lays most truly within us. The God-man's *kenosis* overflows into his infixion: heaven as Christ's body is now ours, suffused with his in the resurrected state. This filling up of our scars does not cover over our imperfections, for like Christ we too rise with our scars,[9] but perfuses them with the radiant Truth, Goodness, Beauty, and Being. This donative self-emptying communicates the greater glory[10] of our *longior via*, where the universal is discovered in the particular, where eternity is realized in flesh and blood, where our glorified wounds reveal the audacious and magnificent reality[11] that our likening power to God is greater than the angels. Through Christ, we are more perfected rising with our scars, with those signs of death now transmogrified in his. Life is a prelude to the infixion: we hide in his wounds in life preparing to experience Christ filling our own wounds in paradise. In the glorified body united in Christ's infixion, each is in the other incarnationally, enabling intentionality to transcend its immaterial *actus*—to know the real thing itself immaterially—and now to know the real thing itself *incarnationally*. What sex and procreation attempt to communicate—an incarnated permanent union

8. Cf. St. Paul in Eph 6:11–13: "Put on the full armor of God, so that you can take your stand against the devil's schemes. For our struggle is not against flesh and blood, but against the rulers, against the authorities, against the powers of this dark world and against the spiritual forces of evil in the heavenly realms. Therefore, put on the full armor of God, so that when the day of evil comes, you may be able to stand your ground, and after you have done everything, to stand."

9. Cf. ST III, 54, 4, ad. 3: "Christ willed the scars of His wounds to remain on His body, not only to confirm the faith of His disciples, but for other reasons also. From these it seems that those scars will always remain on His body."

10. Cf. ST III, 54, 4, ad. 2: "Although those openings of the wounds break the continuity of the tissue, still the greater beauty of glory compensates for all this, so that the body is not less entire, but more perfected."

11. Cf. ST III, 54, 4, ad. 1: "A special comeliness will appear in the places scarred by the wounds."

where we transmit ourselves fully into the other, and where the other achieves the same immortalizing intimacy—is fulfilled and glorified through this infixion, which grafts the heaven that Christ *Is* into our bodies. What is revealed through our bodies in the resurrected state is not something less entire, but rather finally we experience the completion as ever exceeding itself within our flesh. Every story we began and could never finish, or finish as truly as intended, is now read across our bodies in their hallowed communication of perfection. Our resurrected state is not discoverable by foolishly acting as if we can inoculate ourselves against death. It is in the breaking up of the flesh, in its rupture with time and age that we make room for this loving infixion. Our glorified bodies love life, love the holy death in our living beings that is Christ's immortalizing armor of flesh and blood. To those who cannot see, who are blind to the gift of possibility that Christ has made for us through the transfiguration of death, they see only the scars, the disease, the suffering as the nihilistic vortex of failed efficacies. For the one who can see, the joyful suffering unto death makes way for the most beautiful of bodies, filled with the perfume of Christ:

> In the Messiah, in Christ, God leads us from place to place in one perpetual victory parade. Through us, he brings knowledge of Christ. Everywhere we go, people breathe in the exquisite fragrance. Because of Christ, we give off a sweet scent rising to God, which is recognized by those on the way of salvation—an aroma redolent with life. But those on the way to destruction treat us more like the stench from a rotting corpse.[12]

Our Faces

> My heart says of you, "Seek his face!" Your face, LORD, I will seek. Do not hide your face from me.[13]

In the resurrected state our faces would take on the character of every age, even the ages we did not achieve, for God knows all future contingencies,[14] and Christ's infixion as the Head of our bodies suffuses

---

12. 2 Cor 14–16.
13. Ps 27:8–9.
14. Cf. ST I, 14, 13.

us with the radiant truth of every face.[15] We would look at our mothers with every face that we are, that we were for her, every face that had heightened her incarnational intentionality. We would gaze and be gazed upon, and we would transmit in every gaze all their loving completions because of Christ's *kenotic* infixion within them. Our eyes would take-in what alone would satisfy.[16] In our glorified bodies our countenance, through this holy infixion, would look with Christ's eyes, so that our own would beam from his face who saves.[17] Our faces would be Beauty itself since we would be infixed with the light which "makes Beauty seen," the source that establishes "due proportion," rendering us "lovers of beauty,"[18] thus becoming the very "lightsomeness of glory."[19] Colors would exceed in brightness enticing every sense to enjoin. The "lustre of grace" forfeited by sin and death[20] would be magnificently restored by the divine Artisan[21] who makes our bodies the very art *as artifice* of time as profu-

15. Cf. ST III, 12, 3 *resp*: "In every genus that which is the first mover is not moved according to the same species of movement; just as the first alterative is not itself altered. Now Christ is established by God the Head of the Church—yea, of all men, as was said above (III:8:3), so that not only all might receive grace through Him, but that all might receive the doctrine of Truth from Him. Hence He Himself says (John 18:37): 'For this was I born, and for this came I into the world; that I should give testimony to the truth.'"

16. Prov 27:19-2: "As water reflects the face, so one's life reflects the heart. Death and Destruction are never satisfied, and neither are human eyes."

17. Ps 8:8-19: "So will not we go back from thee: quicken us, and we will call upon thy name. Turn us again, O LORD God of hosts, cause thy face to shine; and we shall be saved."

18. Cf. ST, II-II,180, 2, ad 3: "Beauty, as stated above (II-II:145:2), consists in a certain clarity and due proportion. Now each of these is found radically in the reason; because both the light that makes beauty seen, and the establishing of due proportion among things belong to reason. Hence since the contemplative life consists in an act of the reason, there is beauty in it by its very nature and essence; wherefore it is written (Wisdom 8:2) of the contemplation of wisdom: 'I became a lover of her beauty.'"

19. SCG IV, 86, 2.

20. ST, I II.109.7, resp.

21. St. Thomas, *Gospel of St. John*, 8, lect. 2, 1142: "Sense perceptible light, however, is a certain image of spiritual light. . . . Just as particular light has an effect on the thing seen, inasmuch as it makes colors actually visible, as well as on the one seeing, because through it the eye is conditioned for seeing, so intellectual light makes the intellect to know because whatever light is in the rational creature is all derived from that supreme light 'which enlightens every man coming into the world.' Furthermore, it makes all things to be actually intelligible inasmuch as all forms are derived from it, forms which give things the capability of being known, just as all the forms of artifacts are derived from the art and reason on the artisan."

sion of eternity. With St. Bernard through the bride's face we encounter Christ, our bridegroom:

> "Your cheeks are beautiful as the turtle dove's." The brides modesty is a delicate thing; and I feel that at the Bridegroom's reproof a warm flush suffused her face, so heightening her beauty that she immediately was greeted with: "Your cheeks are beautiful as the turtle dove's." You must not give an earthbound meaning to this coloring of the corruptible flesh, to this gathering of blood-red liquid that spreads evenly beneath the surface of her pearly skin, quietly mingling with it to enhance her physical beauty by the pink and white loveliness of her cheeks.[22]

Our Breathing

> When you hide your face, they are terrified; when you take away their breath, they die and return to the dust. When you send your Spirit, they are created, and you renew the face of the ground.[23]

In the resurrected state, our breathing would call to mind inhalation, which occurs both in dying and in the act of creation. As we die, every breath gasps for more oxygen, the body fights to receive sufficient lifeforce. Because the beatific vision is an infinite end, an inexhaustible intensity, our breath would correspond in likeness to it. Each breath would take more, would joyously grasp for more and our exhalations would incarnationally transfix our fellowship with the Spirit particular to our flesh and blood infixed with Christ's. Each breath would be more pleasing, without the prior one lacking anything or being any less pleasing. The struggle for more oxygen would be transposed into the infinite access of the spirit as alpine and clear. Every breath would be world-forming for, like God, our exhaling would be creative, it would co-substantiate paradise, forming life and landscape, citadels carved by the rhythm of each breath.

22. St. Bernard of Clairvaux, "On the Song of Songs," *Selected Works*, serm. 40.
23. Ps 104:29–30.

Our Senses: What Mary Magdalene and Didymus
Transmit through Touch

"Don't cling to me," Jesus told her, "Since I have not yet ascended to the Father. But go to my brothers and tell them that I am ascending to my Father and your Father, to my God and your God."[24]

"Put your finger here; see my hands. Reach out your hand and put it into my side. Stop doubting and believe."[25]

These two passages appear to possess a resurrected Christ in contradiction, one who urges a shocked and ecstatic Mary Magdalene, the first to witness him alive right outside the tomb, not to hold on to him, and the other where Doubting Thomas is invited to place his fingers within the wounds. How do we authentically reconcile the *noli me tangere* with the far more intimate act of placing oneself within Christ's lanced sides? What do these two mysterious and essential passages, particularly within their tension, tell us about our senses in the resurrected state? Mary Magdalene is given the most privileged task of telling the others what she has witnessed; she must transmit to others what is unbelievable and, as a woman, she would seemingly be the least credible witness, the least wise of messengers for Christ to choose. It is for this very reason that we recognize the power of Christ's self-emptying as ingrained into our flesh and transmitted through an overwhelming unification of the senses.

Christ elevates Mary Magdalene in her task by ensuring that she knows incarnationally, tangibly, without physical clinging and touch. Her witnessing of Christ evokes presence and contact more penetrative than earthly touch, and her body is infused with that power: she will run to the other disciples and every sense will leap to proclaim that Christ has risen, because she is filled with his touch through sight. The lostness and entire body-and-spirit longing in Song of Solomon—"All night long on my bed I looked for the one my heart loves; I looked for him but did not find him"[26]—which Mary Magdalene culminates in her love of Christ, gifts her with the first sighting of our risen Lord. But her touch, which still embodied the yearning and distance of the Old Testament, must be transposed and dramatically realized in the new covenant of his flesh and

24. Christ to Mary Magdalene, John 20:17.
25. Christ to Thomas, John 20:27.
26. Song 3:1.

blood. This new touch is signified when Mary does not recognize Christ until he calls her name. His calling transforms her recognition, unifying all her distinct senses as one with her Christ as heavenly teacher.[27] Christ's *kenotic* Word self-empties into all our senses as paradigmatically realized in Mary Magdalene. His resurrected Word *Is* touched when it *Is* heard, tasted when it *Is* seen, its perfume *Is* as substantial as touch, heard because tasted, inhaled as it *Is* seen, and in touching we have tasted. There are no fragmented senses, but a unity corresponding to our body as one in being with his heavenly body.

There is urgency in Christ's *noli me tangere*: Mary Magdalene corresponds to Christ's completed *kenosis*, his definitive self-emptying corresponding to the ultimacy of what he has accomplished for us in his death and luminous resurrection.[28] Mary's sight of Christ, *as* through Christ, *Is* touch, taste, hearing, smell. Sight as the most privileged of earthly senses is privileged to experience this resurrected unity as synonymous with the urgency to spread the good news. In Christ's interaction with Mary Magdalene we realize that our senses now leap forth, all united in the sensuous new life that has been washed brilliantly white with the blood of the Lamb. Christ's pouring entirely of himself into our otherness has undone the blindness, deafness, muteness, the insensitivity to touch and dullness of taste that fragments our experience of the world and our ability to become the other *as other*.

Whereas Christ's interaction with Mary Magdalene unveils the *kenosis* within every sense, which unites them as one in Christ, Didymus, our Doubting Thomas, reflects Christ's infixion. Our Lord's infixion fills us up with the Word so that what is weak is made strong, what is our fatal flaw becomes the foundation for courage and endurance. As Christ rises

27. Cf. John 20:11–22: "Now Mary stood outside the tomb crying. As she wept, she bent over to look into the tomb and saw two angels in white, seated where Jesus' body had been, one at the head and the other at the foot. They asked her, 'Woman, why are you crying?' 'They have taken my Lord away,' she said, 'and I don't know where they have put him.' At this, she turned around and saw Jesus standing there, but she did not realize that it was Jesus. He asked her, 'Woman, why are you crying? Who is it you are looking for?' Thinking he was the gardener, she said, 'Sir, if you have carried him away, tell me where you have put him, and I will get him.' Jesus said to her, 'Mary.' She turned toward him and cried out in Aramaic, 'Rabboni!' (which means 'Teacher')."

28. Cf. St. Bernard of Clairvaux, "On the Song of Songs," *Selected Works*, serm. 58: "Why the Bride is ordered to make haste: 'Arise, make haste, my love, my dove, my beautiful one, and come.' Who says this? Doubtless the Bridegroom. And is he not the one who, shortly before, earnestly forbade that his beloved be awakened? Why therefore does he now command her not only to arise but even to hurry?"

with his scars, so do we, in a way sacred and profound. Our senses are not only dramatically unified through his self-emptying, but this *kenosis* designates an infixion, a filling up of our failings, scars, defects. They are not magically erased but permeated with the Word so that in the breaking open of our flesh, in the weakness of our senses, we discover the greater glory of Being. Thomas' doubt is, through Christ, not the vehicle to fail in belief, but the vessel that gives him the glorious impertinence to place his unworthy fingers within the flesh of God himself. Remember that we had forsaken possibility when we had chosen death. When Christ saved us, he experienced the annihilating emptiness of vacated possibility. He does not save by magic but by what remained, which was the dead-end of death. Our Lord made death impossibly the greatest possibility. He filled the death in each of us with his death *as* resurrection. His infixion reflects this death overcome, not erased, in the glorified state. This infixion means that we carry death transfigured within us as the presence that glorifies our bodies. Heaven is not a homogeneity where each person sees the same, hears the same, touches the same, looks the same. Christ offers a personalist revolution to heaven, which includes permeating our weakened senses and being so that the weakness itself is the vehicle of transcending glory:

> "My grace is sufficient for you, for my power is made perfect in weakness." Therefore, I will boast all the more gladly about my weaknesses, so that Christ's power may rest on me. That is why, for Christ's sake, I delight in weaknesses, in insults, in hardships, in persecutions, in difficulties. For when I am weak, then I am strong.[29]

Christ's *kenosis* and infixion are entirely unified, each presenting a different emphasis of the donative love that unveils our co-substantiation of paradise. Each signifies two fundamental aspects of our senses in our glorified state. The Magdalenian *kenosis* signifies the defragmentation of our senses, the power that enables each one to signify the whole. To see Christ is to taste him, to hear the lover is to embrace him. The Didymusian infixion confirms that this unity of the senses in the glorified state is not some power of supererogation placed atop our senses, not a superhuman superpower indifferent to our earthly senses or outside of our life experiences, but won *through* them, achieved *through* their weakness, filling their dying, transfiguring their failing *actus*. Christ condescends

---

29. 2 Cor 12:9–10.

to become united with my eyes, my hands, my lips and tongue: this is the greatness of his infixion. Because every glorified body is infixed with Christ's *kenotic* presence, our senses in paradise would cross every divide. In our glorified bodies we now forever touch Christ's garments, and through this permanency all has been made well. In the resurrected state, our senses are penetrative, each evoking the other, fulfilling immediacy. The touch of another's arm or face enables one to love the other with such intimacy, as old friends, because the unveiling of shared experience within the touch is not as isolated ideas, facts, or descriptions of past events, but as a total unitive experience of incarnational intentionality where all things are made one and overwhelmed with goodness and sanctity.[30] The hearing of praise in paradise would elicit the taste of nectar, the sight of every beautiful moment of one's child, both recollected and unseen, now tasted in its true sweetness. The forgiveness spoken would take on the scent of every sweetness, bread pulled apart, freshness of ocean and tide, domestic and exotic, known and unknown. Our senses in paradise fulfill what is sensed on earth when we embrace, when we kiss, when we seek furiously to touch something more than skin deep, when we inhale the garment of the lover now dead and seek to reclaim with our very smell and breathing the life of the other. The bride will grasp her bridegroom and not let go.[31]

30. This intentionality won through glorified union with Christ supremely evokes God's creative Actus which pervades all things. Cf. St. Thomas, *Gospel of St. John*, 1, lect. 5, 133: "Natural agents operate from the outside: for, since they operate only by moving and changing things, they do so by acting on others. But God is immanent in things, since his action is creative. To create is to give *esse* to creatures and as *esse* pervades everything, God who gives *esse* is immanent in all things."

31. Cf. St Bernard of Clairvaux, "On the Song of Songs," *Selected Works*, serm. 79: "The bond of love by which the bride holds the Bridegroom and will not let Him go. 'Have you seen him whom my soul loves?' O strong and burning love, O love urgent and impetuous, which does not allow me to think of anything but you, you reject all else, you spurn all else but yourself, you are contented only with yourself!"

15

Strangers in Paradise

*Questions on what becomes of friendships,
fellowships, spousal love*

From quiet homes and first beginning,
Out to the undiscovered ends,
There's nothing worth the wear of winning,
But laughter and the love of friends.[1]

THE IDEA OF GENUINE fellowships, not reduced to mere utility,[2] but those that bring out the divine in the other, would seem to be a natural fit in the resurrected state. Friendship and spousal union were ordained from the beginning—"the LORD God said, 'It is not good for the man to be alone.'"[3] Christ came as bridegroom,[4] offering the greatest of

1. Belloc, "Dedicatory Ode," *Sonnets and Verse*, 74.

2. See Aristotle's commentary on the varieties of friendship in *Nicomachean Ethics* VIII.

3. Gen 2:18.

4. John 3:29: "He who has the bride is the bridegroom; but the friend of the bridegroom, who stands and hears him, rejoices greatly because of the bridegroom's voice. So, this joy of mine has been made full." See also Rev 19:17.

friendships.[5] And the three persons of the Trinity are the prime foundation for pure donative relationality as the fellowship of perfecting communion.[6] We ask not only of the important re-uniting with the spouses, children, and friends we had on earth,[7] and the immeasurably vaster discovery of their manifold dignity within the beatific vision, but of the process of *becoming* friends, of *falling* in love, of *discovering* the other, of the joys that *spark* fellowship and nuptial union. We hear from Jesus that there will be no new marriages in heaven. He clearly relays this to Sadducees who seek to trick him with their scenario regarding the marital status of a woman having been widowed multiple times.[8] Are we to assume that discovery, invitation, union, and fellowship are past us in the resurrection?

5 See John 15:15–16: "Henceforth I call you not servants; for the servant knoweth not what his lord doeth: but I have called you friends; for all things that I have heard of my Father I have made known unto you. Ye have not chosen me, but I have chosen you, and ordained you, that ye should go and bring forth fruit, and that your fruit should remain: that whatsoever ye shall ask of the Father in my name, he may give it you."

6. Cf. David L. Schindler, "The Embodied Person as Gift," 403: "It is the very relation to God, which relation always already includes relation to all other creatures, that establishes each person in his individual substantiality. The crucial point, in a word, is that the relation to God, and to others in God, that establishes the individual substance in being is generous. The relation itself makes and lets me in my substantial being be. This 'letting be' implies a kind of primordial, ontological 'circumincession,' or 'perichoresis,' of giving and receiving between the other and myself. What I am in my original constitution as a person has always already been given to me by God and received by me in and as my response to God's gift to me of myself—indeed, has also, in some significant sense, been given to me by other creatures and received by me in and as my response to their gift to me."

7. Cf. Lönnrot, "Kalevala," *Poems for the Millennium, Vol. 3,* 451–52:
Brother dear, little brother
fair one who grew up with me
start off reciting with me
since we have got together
since we have come from two ways!
We seldom get together
and meet each other
on these poor borders
the luckless lands of the North.
Let's strike hand to hand
fingers into finger-gaps
that we may sing some good things
set some of the best things forth.

8. Matt 22:23–30.

Why, then, would Christ be the bridegroom, and we the bride of Christ,[9] if we are not called to a union of love so intimate it can only be described as nuptial?[10] What then would discovery of love-of-other look like in the resurrected state?

We wonder also about the hope of salvation for those persons, sometime friends and loved ones, who helped another along the way to salvation but in themselves turned from God,[11] and estranged themselves from the other who desired their genuine happiness? What happens to such a one who excludes himself from paradise and what would it be for those who have made it to the summit of Joy should they be able to look on such a lamentable alienated soul? Embodiment on earth, particularly within our fallen state, invokes the neediness that initiates a range of alliances and types of unions both noble and ignoble. What remains genuinely of those bonds in the resurrected state? Here we must consider those many relationships that suffered damage throughout life from sin and shortsightedness.[12] And what do we make of good relationships briefly encountered but never fulfilled due to time, change, and death? Is there a process of completion and discovery, particularly since God knows all things, including the outcome of every road not taken?[13] More still, how

9. Cf. St. Bernard of Clairvaux, "On the Song of Songs," *Selected Works*, serm. 21: "The love of the Bride, the Church, for Christ: 'Draw me after you; we shall run in the odor of your ointments.' What does this mean? Is the Bride an unwilling lover, even of her Bridegroom? Does she have to be drawn to him because she lacks freedom to follow him? But not everyone drawn is reluctant to be drawn."

10. Eph 5:22–33.

11. Cf. ST II-II, 23, 1, *resp*: "Accordingly, since there is a communication between man and God, inasmuch as He communicates His happiness to us, some kind of friendship must needs be based on this same communication, of which it is written (1 Corinthians 1:9): 'God is faithful: by Whom you are called unto the fellowship of His Son.' The love which is based on this communication, is charity: wherefore it is evident that charity is the friendship of man for God."

12. Cf. Aristotle, *Nicomachean Ethics*, 1165b14–24. "What is evil neither can nor should be loved; for it is not one's duty to be a lover of evil or to become like what is bad; and we have said that like is dear to like. Must the friendship, then, be forthwith broken off? Or is this not so in all cases, but only when one's friends are incurable in their wickedness? If they are capable of being reformed one should rather come to the assistance of their character or their property, inasmuch as this is better and more characteristic of friendship. But a man who breaks off such a friendship would seem to be doing nothing strange; for it was not to a man of this sort that he was a friend; when his friend changed, therefore, and he is unable to save him, he gives him up."

13. This, it seems, would be a particularly pressing question regarding the abortion of the unborn, and the children whose lives are tragically cut short.

does the earthy life lived as an existential letting go confirmed in death, play a part in the nature of paradisal unions? Do fellowships bridge the gaps in salvation,[14] help to recover what may be lost?[15] How are they to be envisioned or transformed? Or is the work of loving union completed at the moment of death: strangers enter into paradise *as friends*, as a community bonded in the *philia* that exudes from the beatific vision?

14. 2 Cor 13:11–14: "Finally, brothers and sisters, rejoice! Strive for full restoration, encourage one another, be of one mind, live in peace. And the God of love and peace will be with you. Greet one another with a holy kiss. All God's people here send their greetings. May the grace of the Lord Jesus Christ, and the love of God, and the fellowship of the Holy Spirit be with you all."

15. Cf. John 15–13: "Greater love has no one than this, than to lay down one's life for his friends."

16

Old and New Love
in the Resurrected State

S T. FRANCIS XAVIER, FOUNDING companion in the Society of Jesus, wrote the following letter to his dear friend St. Ignatius:

> You say in the excess of your friendship for me, that you would most ardently wish to see me once more before you die. Oh! God alone, who looks into the heart, knows how vivid and how deep an impression this dear proof of your affection has made on my soul. Each time I recall it—and that happens often—my eyes involuntarily fill with tears; and if the delightful idea that I could embrace you once more presents itself to my mind (for, however difficult it might appear at first sight, there is nothing that holy obedience cannot accomplish), I find myself for an instant surprised by a torrent of tears that no power can arrest. I pray God that if we are not to see each other again while living, we may together enjoy in a happy eternity the repose never to be found in this life. It is all over; we never shall meet again on Earth otherwise than by letters; but in Heaven—ah! We shall meet face-to-face. And then with what transport shall we not embrace one another! Who, indeed, can tell the transports which two virtuous friends will experience for each other eternally in heaven, after having here below loved each other unto perfection, and verified the saying of Holy Scripture: "A faithful

friend is the medicine of life and immortality; and they that fear
the Lord shall find such a friend."[1]

From this ever-timely letter on *philia*, eternity, transience, and embodiment, we witness the centrality of those bonds that are faithful compan-
ions on the royal road of suffering and sanctification. Let us intelligibilize
the possibility of unions in paradise as authentically reflective of the
metaphysics and phenomenology of the human person, by reflecting on
four critical indicators that support a robust discovery of friends, family,
spouses, and loved ones in the resurrected state:

- God has never been a self-referential monad. Paradise is unity with
  the image, the archetype, the uncreated *Actus* as Love, which makes
  possible and realizes all relationality.

God is not a windowless insensate monad. If this were the case, there
would be no relevant discussion of paradise. Nor are we in a one-way relationship with an unmoved mover, which we can strive towards, but itself
is encircled, enclosed, demarcated, and separated in its own finite, eternal
perfection, having no view towards us. Paradise is instead grounded on
the ever-infinitizing and overflowing foundation of God as Trinitarian,
revealing Love itself as creatively in communion with all things. Thus, it
is far more unrealistic and strained to imagine our participation in the
beatific vision to be something *other* than, or opposed to, friendship.
Friendship is understood as the dilation of the other in and towards the
fulfillment of the Good and the possession of happiness, and it must necessarily dwell in all genuine loves from fellowships to spousal love and,
particularly, intimacy with Christ in faith. In its ultimacy, friendship is
joy-filled praise of the divine in-and-for the other. It is realized when you
love others "so as to desire their happiness, with a thirst equal to the zeal

---

1. Blot, *In Heaven We'll Meet Again*, 95. See also St. Gregory Nazianzen to his
friend St. Basil, *Oratio* 43, 15–21: "We acknowledge our friendship and recognized
that our ambition was a life of true wisdom. . . . Our love for each other grew daily
and deeper[;] . . . our single object was virtue, and a life of hope in the blessings that
are to come; we wanted to withdraw from this world before we departed from it. With
this end in view, we ordered our lives and all our actions. We followed the guidance of
God's law and spurred each other on to virtue. If it is not too boastful to say, we found
in each other a standard and rule for discerning right from wrong. Different men have
different names, which they owe to their parents or to themselves, that is, to their own
pursuits and achievements. But our great pursuit, the great name we wanted, was to be
Christians, to be called Christians."

of your own,"[2] and it is consummated in Christ as the substance of the bread and wine who alone transmits eternal satiation.

- Human beings cannot access their humanity without an intentionality that is perfected in virtuous friendships.

Without intentionality, we would be extremely poor of world, blocked off from existential engagement with our historical essences. We cannot fulfill the task of human personhood without the other *as other* who assimilates and reveals the self as erotic, agapetic, and in the impossible but essential image of the infinite. Intentionality is the primordial netting that incarnates the world of Being for us, realizing the dignity of our open natures made in the image and likeness of God as relational Love itself. It would be a defecting condition that the blessed should be alienated from each other in paradise. And it would be analogous to modern neighbors, each in his own house occasionally coming outside to see what commotion has transpired on the streets, proceeding to rattle off to each other the usual forms of *toujours la politesse*. The blessed are united in the image of the divine as supremely donative.[3] They would be enveloped in divine friendship itself, becoming in that uncreated light, friends of the highest order, with each infused with the image or archetype to which all earthly virtuous friendships tend in likeness.

---

2. Traherne, *Centuries of Meditations*, 20–21: "You never enjoy the world aright, till the Sea itself floweth in your veins, till you are clothed with the heavens, and crowned with the stars: and perceive yourself to be the sole heir of the whole world, and more than so, because men are in it who are every one sole heirs as well as you. Till you can sing and rejoice and delight in God, as misers do in gold, and Kings in sceptres, you never enjoy the world. Till your spirit filleth the whole world, and the stars are your jewels; till you are as familiar with the ways of God in all Ages as with your walk and table: till you are intimately acquainted with that shady nothing out of which the world was made: till you love men so as to desire their happiness, with a thirst equal to the zeal of your own: till you delight in God for being good to all: you never enjoy the world. Till you more feel it than your private estate, and are more present in the hemisphere, considering the glories and the beauties there than in your own house: till you remember how lately you were made, and how wonderful it was when you came into it: and more rejoice in the palace of your glory, than if it had been made but to-day morning."

3. Cf. St. Augustine, *City of God*, xiv. When God is "all in all," (1 Cor 15:28) then he will be the completion of every human desire, both realized and unrealized. Our union will be an endless love, a praise that never tires, an activity which is itself intimate and shared by all.

- Christ offers not servitude but the friendship that he initiated and made possible through love as identical with his flesh and blood.

"A servant does not know his master's business,"[4] but we are each called to that audacious intimacy. Christ, whose body itself is heaven, and whose incarnation brings heaven into earth, permeating the latter with its mission and goal, offers us friendship and sublime nuptial union through his martyrological intentionality. He chose us, he gifts us through his flesh and blood with the *caritas* of immortalizing communion. Fellowship begins in the relational call and response of creation, magnified in the Holy Trinity's donative intra-unity, and exercised in Christ's *kenosis* and infixion, which fill our scars with *kenotic* love. It would be a contradiction, a paradise unworthy of our longing, if that *kenotic* ardor somehow dissipated, and was rendered inessential to the co-substantiation of the architecture of the resurrected state. Christ infixes his Word within us, and his Word is self-emptying. This means that we are never closed-off, as sin and ignorance tyrannically demand of us, but in the image and likeness of that overflowing abundance which offers friendship as Love.

- It would be the most terrible of contradictions to possess the glorified body and enact that embodiment void of friendship.

The magnitude of our hope for the resurrection of the dead is supported metaphysically in the understanding that the soul is the form of the body. The body is *for* the soul, as the soul is *for* the body; each is the perfecting agent for the other, constituting the dual unity that illuminates the human person. Embodiment even at its most shell-like existence evokes the seeds of relationality intrinsic to human beings. To have a body means to claim space, to take up a specific location within multitudinous points and features in the world. Sensory embodiment cannot help but mean a relation to other entities by virtue of existentially recognizing itself as nearer to or farther from other beings. The human body is always engaging what in its surroundings is more or less like itself.

---

4. Cf. John 15:12–17: "My command is this: Love each other as I have loved you. Greater love has no one than this: to lay down one's life for one's friends. You are my friends if you do what I command. I no longer call you servants, because a servant does not know his master's business. Instead, I have called you friends, for everything that I learned from my Father I have made known to you. You did not choose me, but I chose you and appointed you so that you might go and bear fruit—fruit that will last—and so that whatever you ask in my name the Father will give you. This is my command: Love each other."

More still, this physical engagement also evokes the relationality of intellectual substances united in transcendent meaning.[5] The human person
incarnationally tends towards otherness, towards union and fellowship,
and we experience this tending from our most basic physical states to
our transcendent desires. How would it make any sense that our corrupt-
ible bodies, "sown in dishonor,"[6] be capable of engaging the processes of
intensive relationality, which uncover the beauty of friendship and the
desire for eternal life, but that our resurrected and incorruptible bodies
are less capable of the ontological tending that enables the true friend,
the greater lover, and the most blessed of fellowships?[7] Certainly, that
does not make any sense, especially since we are *most* like Christ *and*
specifically the Godhead in our resurrected bodies[8] and, again, since God
is identical with Love. St. Thomas argues how, for the blessed, the resurrection of their bodies increases the intensity of joy in and towards God,
dilating the very mansions or degrees of beatitude. Friendship would be
vigorously intensified in the glorified state, not vitiated.

> Although finite added to infinite does not make a greater thing,
> it makes more things, since finite and infinite are two things,
> while infinite taken by itself is one. Now the greater extent of
> joy regards not a greater thing but more things. Wherefore joy is
> increased in extent, through referring to God and to the body's
> glory, in comparison with the joy which referred to God. More-
> over, the body's glory will conduce to the intensity of the joy that
> refers to God, in so far as it will conduce to the more perfect

5. Cf. Plato, *Theaetetus*, 145a-d. Socrates in the *Theaetetus* compares his physical
likeness to Theaetetus, noting that both are short, stout, and snub-nosed. The conversation moves quickly from the similarity of their bodies to the similarity of their souls.
Are they alike in intellect and wisdom as well?

6. Cf. 1 Cor 15:42–44: "So will it be with the resurrection of the dead. The body
that is sown is perishable, it is raised imperishable; it is sown in dishonor, it is raised in
glory; it is sown in weakness, it is raised in power; it is sown a natural body, it is raised
a spiritual body."

7. Cf. ST Suppl. 92, 1 *resp*: "It is manifest that the happiness of the saints will increase in extent after the resurrection, because their happiness will then be not only
in the soul but also in the body. Moreover, the soul's happiness also will increase in
extent, seeing that the soul will rejoice not only in its own good, but also in that of the
body. We may also say that the soul's happiness will increase in intensity."

8. Cf. ST Suppl. 92, 1 ad. 1: "The soul united to a glorified body is more like to God
than when separated therefrom, in so far as when united it has more perfect being. For
the more perfect a thing is the more it is like to God: even so the heart, the perfection
of whose life consists in movement, is more like to God while in movement than while
at rest, although God is never moved."

operation whereby the soul tends to God: since the more perfect
is a becoming operation, the greater the delight [Cf. I-II:32:1], as
stated in Ethic. x, 8.[9]

None of us is certain to be one of the blessed who resurrects in glory
with Christ. But should there be this greatest of blessings, then we *can*
be certain—within the logic of the Pascalian wager—that the most beauteous of unions and bonds would permeate the mansions of paradise.
Fellowship in the resurrected state not only possesses a clear essentiality
but is also wholly opposed to the understandable but impossible need for
paradise to be a comfortable (but ultimately reductive) repetition of the
best of earth. We do not recover earth and earthly flesh, that is not the
way of salvation. While what is gained in Christ's self-emptying offers us
graces reflective of friendship and spousal love on earth, it is of another
and higher order altogether. Friendship, united in the resurrected Christ,
is the transcendent uncreated image to which all virtuous earthly unions
tend as likeness to that image. Viewing paradise as a mere continuation of
earth undermines the resurrection, just as conceiving it to be something
so far beyond the senses, alienated from all incarnational meaning. It is
one thing to recognize that earthly relationality provides an indication, a
genuine phenomenological trace of its source; it is quite another to view
that trace as the archetype. Friendship in the resurrection is not a likeness
to earthly friendship by way of derivation or mirroring, for that would
not quench our thirst, or satiate our desire for completion and fulfillment. Instead, friendship among the blessed is an immensity grounded
upon the infinite and intensifying discovery of Trinitarian Love. Such a
friendship would be the greatest adventure, the profoundest discovery,
the shimmering estuary of *caritas* where all *eros* and *agape* resolve themselves at the flesh, wounds, and feet of the bridegroom. It would radically
complete what Aquinas sets out as the higher ordered friendship, which
loves all connections to the other.

> Friendship extends to a person in two ways: first in respect of
> himself, and in this way friendship never extends but to one's
> friends: secondly, it extends to someone in respect of another,
> as, when a man has friendship for a certain person, for his sake
> he loves all belonging to him, be they children, servants, or con-
> nected with him in any way. Indeed, so much do we love our
> friends, that for their sake we love all who belong to them, even

9. ST Suppl. 92, 1 ad. 4.

if they hurt or hate us; so that, in this way, the friendship of charity extends even to our enemies, whom we love out of charity
in relation to God, to Whom the friendship of charity is chiefly
directed.[10]

In paradisal friendship we would be disposed radically to fulfill
Aquinas' second way of union and extension. We would be wholly disposed and gifted through Christ's *kenosis* and infixion to be entirely available to love what is discoverable *as lovable* in all the creatures, beings, and
persons in any way related to the other. This supreme disposition exudes
from our flesh, glorifying it in the uncreated light. And since the other,
our friend, acts on the body of Being—now unveiled as the supreme Love
who realizes all persons as inexhaustibly lovable—our friends in heaven
would become the *greatest* of friends. Each would unveil the endless joy
of discovering God's infinite love at the heart of the beatific vision as intentionally revelatory of our own hearts inflamed. Discovering old and
new unions, friendships, loves in paradise manifests the spiritual dowry
Christ gave to us,[11] clothing us in fine garments, adorning us with jewels,
which are synonymous with his flesh, blood, fellowship, brotherhood,
and friendship.

10. ST II-II, 23, 1, ad. 2.
11. Cf. ST Suppl. 95.

17

Is There Sex or a Union in Its Place in the Resurrected State?

> Let him kiss me with the kisses of his mouth: for thy love is bet-
> ter than wine. Because of the savour of thy good ointments thy
> name is as ointment poured forth, therefore do the virgins love
> thee. Draw me, we will run after thee: the king hath brought me
> into his chambers: we will be glad and rejoice in thee, we will
> remember thy love more than wine: the upright love thee.[1]

THE ISSUE OF THE manifestation of sexual tending in the afterlife is an admittedly curious question, but becomes an increasingly pressing one when we acknowledge seriously the promise of the resurrection. Because our final happiness is not the disembodied vision of God in heaven, but the overwhelmingly robust incarnated status of the resurrected life, then we are obligated, albeit in a limited manner, to approach the potential nature and *actus* of the body in such a state. What is emphasized from heaven to the resurrected state is the fecundity and fullness of identity and difference, of unity and of otherness, which holds them in the perennially supreme conversation of human and divine relationality. The two states are entirely united in the ecstatic vision and glory of God, yet they are and *must* be differentiated meaningfully, otherwise what then would be the point of this gratuitous addition of the flesh? Should our perfected embodiment be

---

1. Song 1:2–4.

inessential, a spiritual accoutrement to an already completed state, we end only in an anti-climax, a devalued incarnation, the bit of parsley to cleanse the palate at the end of the main course.

What then is the state of human experience in heaven, in our dis-embodied state? Certainly, it is not unconscious nor is it fully awake befitting the wakefulness that occurs with bodies refreshed in the morning. It is a dormitive-cognition, a sleep in which the will is at rest, the intellect is fully in the divine vision, and not the mere appearances, of the Beautiful. It is the beatific wisdom that was parceled to the prophets in their anticipatory slumber set against the nightmare "slouching towards Bethlehem."[2] But now this divine wisdom reaches past the veil completing all prophetic encounter and putting the matter to rest, where now the center can finally hold. Everything in this dormitive-cognition is identical with the True, Good, and Beautiful, which, as God himself, acts in the place of the body, making up the difference, dramatically overcoming the lack of embodiment. But this is the experience of perfection *via* the fully true dream, a heaven of ecstatic dormition and grace-filled rest. We grow up and we lose our ability to sleep, to enter into rest as children do. We are fitful and let the world of fallen forms separate us from the prophetic and from the sleep that prepares us to resurrect refreshed and indefatigable.

> Children don't even think about being tired.
> They run like little puppies. They make the trip twenty times.
> And, consequently, twenty times more than they needed to.
> What does it matter to them. They know well that at night
> (But they don't even think about it)
> They will fall asleep
> In their bed or even at the table
> And that sleep is the end of everything.
> This is their secret, that is the secret to being indefatigable.
> Indefatigable as children.
> Indefatigable like the child Hope.
> And always to start over again in the morning.
> . . .
> It's this same bottomless sleep
> As continuous as being itself
> . . .
> It's in this same sleep that children bury their whole being
> Which maintains, which creates for them every day new legs,
> Their brand new legs.

2. Yeats, "The Second Coming," *Collected Poems*, 187.

And also that which is in their new legs: new souls.
Their new souls, their fresh souls.
Fresh in the morning, fresh at noon, fresh in the evening.
Fresh like the roses of France.
Their souls with the undrooping collars. This is the secret to being
    indefatigable.
Just sleep. Why don't people make use of it.
I've given this secret to everyone, says God, I haven't sold it.
He who sleeps well, lives well. He who sleeps, prays.[3]

In heaven we recover the sleep that our waning and lost innocence forever craves up to the moment of death. In its disembodied state, we experience the great dormitive-cognition that children immemorially encounter, the rest that gives them the salvific appetite of infancy and newness to help them survive later on, the eroding littleness of a life where rest is increasingly replaced with resignation. It is this resignation that signs our death warrant, that confirms we have not the power to resurrect, that we have nothing within us to refresh ourselves, that should we be refreshed it comes from without, not from within, and that what is beyond us must fill us again with its rest.

Heaven is, again, meaningfully different from the resurrected state. Resurrection necessitates the refreshment of the mind, soul, and body to be risen from the dust, to be recovered, renewed, becoming transformed and indefatigable.[4] This does not occur to persons who do not have within them the sleep that is as bottomless and continuous as Being itself. The dormitive-cognition, the eternal light that gives us perpetual rest in heaven, refreshes us and prepares us to put on the flesh of the new man.[5] In God everything is timely: "there is a time for everything, and a season for every activity under the heavens."[6] The season of the resurrection is the time for perfection in wakefulness.

Awake, sleeper,
    And arise from the dead,
    And Christ will shine on you.[7]

---

3. Péguy, *The Portal of the Mystery of Hope*, 116–17.

4. Cf. Isa 26:19: "Your dead will live; their corpses will rise. You who lie in the dust, awake and shout for joy, for your dew is as the dew of the dawn, and the earth will give birth to the departed spirits."

5. Eph 4:22–24.

6. Eccl 3:1.

7. Eph 5:14.

Clothed in the flesh of Christ, we are to experience that beatific vision through the nuance and particularity of flesh and blood. We are to awake to our bodies, which walk and breathe, smell and touch, whose senses are given privileged participation within the eternal.

With such a vigorous accounting of fellowships, unions, and friendships in the resurrection, one that does not shirk the dignity of the body, we may surprisingly but rightly turn to the status of sexual intimacy in paradise. Or, more specifically, what becomes of that most intimate of carnal unions? Do our glorified bodies simply leave sexual intimacy behind since its earthly goal of procreation is no longer relevant in paradise? There is no longer death, and thus no need for generation to compensate for the deficit in life. Because mortality is wholly overcome and absent from the equation, there is no inner *dynamis* to preserve our lives through sustenance that staves off death, just as, again, there is no place for sexual intimacy to augment the population. Earth is complete, God's judgment is final, there are no new persons to be created. Both our generative and nutritive powers would be fruitless in paradise.[8] The Thomistic logic appears to be without flaw, and entirely aligned with a unified understanding of the two co-parts, soul and body, which together form the human person. In this existential metaphysics, these co-parts engage and realize themselves as co-naturally responsive to the world of Being that they inhabit. Paradise, as supreme world of Being, presents a radically different situatedness for the body. The body is transformed along with the soul, in order to be enjoined to the beatific vision.

The idea that paradise would include an abundance of sex that bears no fruit, brings no life, drastically undermines the union of flesh and blood both on earth and in the glorified body. Such a union is wholly

---

8. ST Suppl. 81, 4, *sed contra; resp*: It is written (Matt 22:30): "'In the Resurrection they shall neither marry nor be married.' Further, generation is directed to supply the defect resulting from death, and to the multiplication of the human race: and eating is directed to make up for waste, and to increase quantity. But in the state of the Resurrection the human race will already have the number of individuals preordained by God, since generation will continue up to that point. In like manner each man will rise again in due quantity; neither will death be any more, nor any waste affect the parts of man. Therefore, the acts of the generative and nutritive powers would be void of purpose. . . . [T]hose natural operations which are directed to cause or preserve the primary perfection of human nature will not be in the Resurrection: such are the actions of the animal life in man, the action of the elements on one another, and the movement of the Heavens; wherefore all these will cease at the Resurrection. And since to eat, drink, sleep, beget, pertain to the animal life, being directed to the primary perfection of nature, it follows that they will not be in the Resurrection."

unfitting, for it is something all too pedestrian, all too easily accomplished here on earth. It is more of the stuff of hell and its self-enclosed egos of whom each uses the body of the other for the advantage of the self to hide its own decomposition. This view of sex in the resurrected state is clearly opposed to the sacredness of love-*making* by denigrating its powerhouse purposiveness to bring new life. What pleasure could an unfulfilled act of sexuality have in relation the beatific vision?

Or, to play devil's advocate, does the Thomistic view smack of short-sightedness when unpacking the intensity of intimacy furiously sought to be attained in the act of sexual union? Or at least, is there *more* to be dwelt upon regarding how sexual intimacy is transformed and carried over into the resurrected state. If our glorified bodies mean we have eyes and ears and voices to praise God, and with such intensity, *because* they are infused and enriched with the blood of the Lamb which makes God exceedingly more visible to our senses,[9] then it appears wholly at odds that we would be resurrected as eunuchs, or more drastically void of sexual organs altogether. If every part of the glorified body is, through Christ's *kenosis* and infixion, incarnationally united to us, what becomes of our sexual organs? Every aspect of our flesh and blood is raised, transformed, so that each wound is no longer a defect, and each of the senses and every body part praises God; then again what must we genuinely understand of our sexual organs and of human intimacy? Are we simply to bypass them as inconvenient along the way to a neutralized, disembodied spirituality? But this seems to be unwise and inauthentic given how Christ beckons us with nuptial language, calling us into the intimacy of the bedchamber as bridegroom to his bride.

For Aquinas, there is no shame or lust in paradise, and each person is resurrected to his or her particular and individual stature.[10] Resurrection preserves and elevates the unique differences of our embodiments and

9. Cf. ST Suppl. 91, 3, *resp*: "The renewal of the world is directed to the end that, after this renewal has taken place, God may become visible to man by signs so manifest as to be perceived as it were by his senses."

10. St. Thomas goes so far to stress that the unborn who die in their mother's wombs will rise, each uncovering his or her uniqueness through conformity to Christ. See ST Suppl. 75, 2, ad. 5: "We are born again by the grace of Christ that is given to us, but we rise again by the grace of Christ whereby it came about that He took our nature, since it is by this that we are conformed to Him in natural things. Hence those who die in their mother's womb, although they are not born again by receiving grace, will nevertheless rise again on account of the conformity of their nature with Him, which conformity they acquired by attaining to the perfection of the human species."

spiritual appetites. What then could be an authentic and beautiful way to dwell on how sexual intimacy—where two persons conquer the divide and unify as one in joy and ecstasy—is meaningfully transformed and elevated in paradise? If the resurrected state is not a static end, but a dynamic embrace of God's infinite fountain of creativity and love, wouldn't it be strange not to possess an active intensifying union within that radiating vital force, one that is united to the image or source principle that drives earthly love-*making*? Shouldn't we act on that divine love-*making/ creating* experience in a way that befits not only our embodied but our resurrected state? We must be mindful not to express this intimacy as if identical to the angels, for while we possess a spiritual substance, we are not spiritual substances *per se*, it does not befit our natures. If we were, the resurrection would not be the state of our ultimate happiness, for the state of separated soul would be sufficient. What we seek in paradise is what is glimpsed in E. E. Cumming's "somewhere i have never travelled, gladly beyond":

> somewhere i have never travelled, gladly beyond
> any experience, your eyes have their silence:
> in your most frail gesture are things which enclose me,
> or which i cannot touch because they are too near
>
> your slightest look easily will unclose me
> though i have closed myself as fingers,
> you open always petal by petal myself as Spring opens
> (touching skillfully, mysteriously) her first rose
>
> or if your wish be to close me, i and
> my life will shut very beautifully, suddenly,
> as when the heart of this flower imagines
> the snow carefully everywhere descending;
>
> nothing which we are to perceive in this world equals
> the power of your intense fragility: whose texture
> compels me with the colour of its countries,
> rendering death and forever with each breathing
>
> (i do not know what it is about you that closes
> and opens; only something in me understands
> the voice of your eyes is deeper than all roses)
> nobody, not even the rain, has such small hands[11]

Much of the glory and the folly of earthly life and human decision revolve around this sexual, hierarchically nuptial, climax. Additionally, the

---

11. Cummings, "somewhere i have never travelled, gladly beyond," *100 Selected Poems*, 44.

pro-creative power to engender another has always been the core of human existence. The tension between sex and enduring union—between sex as the chief desire to push past death and into the *ecstasis* of immortality, and the little death in which it deterministically resolves itself each time, is grounded in the Edenic *mythos* of exile[12] and mystically rehabilitated in Christ as bridegroom, with human intimacy residing essentially, anxiously, uneasily in between.[13] In Miguel de Unamuno's *Treatise on the Love of God*, we know this tension as the most tragic act in all the world:

> Love is what is most terrible and tragic in the world. Love is the child of deceit and the parent of disenchantment, love is the consolation in disconsolateness. Love furiously seeks through its object something that lies beyond it and, not finding it, despairs. . . . In love we seek to perpetuate ourselves on Earth only on the condition that we die, that we surrender our lives to others. The humblest little animals, the lowest living beings, multiply by dividing, splitting in two, ceasing to be the singles they once were. And every act of engendering is a ceasing to be what once was, a splitting, a partial death. Perhaps the supreme delight of engendering is nothing but a taste of death in advance, the rending of one's own vital essence . . . because only in others can we become eternal. There is, without a doubt, something tragically corrosive in the depth of love in its primitive, animal form, in the unconquerable instinct that impels a man and a woman to mix their bodies in furious embrace.[14]

Sexual love is the most tragically corrosive act in the world, it draws all like moths to a flame precisely because it indiscriminately presents to those made of earth and clay the promise of *completed* incarnational intentionality. In sex, we dive into the other, we encircle briefly that transfixing and transposing of the soul, and then glimpse the transfigured redemption of flesh and blood through the rupture in temporality that places the united somewhere between time and eternity. Love-*making* gives us a moment in climax of becoming the other *as other* not only immaterially but in a way that would distinguish us from the angels, specifically reflecting human beings as soul *and body*. It gives us a foretaste of Christ's martyrological intentionality that accomplishes becoming the

12. Cf. Gen 3.

13. Cf Prov 5:18–19: "May your fountain be blessed, and may you rejoice in the wife of your youth. A loving doe, a graceful deer—may her breasts satisfy you always, may you ever be intoxicated with her love."

14. Unamuno, *Treatise on the Love of God*, 7.

other *as other* both immaterially and, crucially, physically. But no human sexual act completes what it promises: bodies die down, souls retire into themselves, the union separates because it cannot sustain itself. Love-*making* is furiously drawn out through history, engendering more life to try again and again to free itself from the little death. Only Christ, as bridegroom, completes this powerhouse tragic desire within sexual intimacy, fulfilling the making of love, or love-*making*, in the highest order. Our efficacious pro-creative power as participating in the eternal finds its image *only* in God's pro-creative *Actus* who formed us from the depths of the earth and created our inmost beings.[15] Thus, it seems that there must be a genuine role or place for the meaning of sexual intimacy within the resurrection. What we understand of love-*making* in paradise transcends what we understand of it as sex on earth, but not in a way that all identity to it is lost. Otherwise why, again, stress that we resurrect into full glorified bodies, if the sexual organs have no transcendent role to play? To deny the role of sex lends secretly but analogously to the rejection of any relevant role for the senses or any aspect of embodiment, from hands that touch Christ's wounds, to feet which carry us through the co-substantiated mansions of paradise. Put another way, why do we need any of the senses in the resurrection if God can already be experienced immaterially in heaven? But grace *perfects* nature: the whole soul is *for* the whole body and the whole body is *for* the whole soul, this wholeness transcendentally attaches itself to the relationship between the glorified soul and body. There is no genuine advocacy for our resurrected state unless the *whole* body is understood to be glorified in God's exceeding grace. On closer inspection, truly virtuous love-*making*, the relentlessly gentle and gently relentless coupling of one lover to the beloved, is perhaps the most primordial act on earth that points to the desire for resurrection. It enters transiently but unsustainably into the orbit of an enduring unity that alone overcomes death. What is always sought is the nuptial union of gentleness and firmness, of love being made and given, through the self-emptying of the bridegroom to his bride.

---

15. Cf. Ps 139:13–16: "For you created my inmost being; you knit me together in my mother's womb. I praise you because I am fearfully and wonderfully made; your works are wonderful, I know that full well. My frame was not hidden from you when I was made in the secret place, when I was woven together in the depths of the earth.

Your eyes saw my unformed body; all the days ordained for me were written in your book before one of them came to be."

What gentleness, my child, what firmness in gentleness, what
gentleness in firmness.
One and the other bound indissolubly, one forwarding the
other, one setting off the other, one upholding the other, one
nourishing the other.
Gentleness entirely armed with firmness, firmness entirely
armed with gentleness.
One enclosed in the other, the other enclosed in the one, like a
double stone in a double fruit
` Of firmness.
A gentleness all the better guaranteed by firmness, a firmness
all the better guaranteed by gentleness.
One bearing the other.
For there is no true gentleness except founded on firmness,
And there is no true firmness except clothed in gentleness.[16]

We could never claim comprehensively to understand how the role
of sexual intimacy is transformed in the resurrection. But we can reasonably recognize that love-*making*—as forming, creating, shaping love
with flesh into flesh—provides on earth the dearest and painfully sublime
instantiation of a true incarnational intentionality. This acknowledgment
must also cause us phenomenologically to pause on how our flesh and
relationality is experienced in the resurrected state. Perhaps paradise is
the true climax hinted at and yearned for within all love-*making*. In the
glorified state, we finally complete the task, making ourselves unending
vessels of love to fill into overflow the beloved, as the other fills us, as
Christ has filled us. This intimacy is not a mirror image or mere continued reflection of earthly union. Aquinas is right to reject generative and
nutritive powers as having any purpose in sustaining paradise. But this
does not negate their roles altogether. What is reflected in our glorified
bodies should actually be *our* bodies and souls glorified. Paradise, we can
imagine, has its own love-*creating*, love-*enshrining*, love-*permeating*, love-
exuding, love-*radiating* form of love-*making*. This again, is not a *reflection*
of earthly love-*making* ever in battle with death. Paradisal love-*creating* is
the image to which all likenesses tend, not by univocity but by analogy. Its
capital image is Christ, the bridegroom beckoning us with *every* summit
of *every* joy within *every* completed end to his bedchamber.

What we see in the resurrection is vision made manifest through
Christ. What we smell are the perfumes of Christ, what we hear is music

---

16. Péguy, *The Mystery of the Holy Innocents*, 114–15.

united to his word,[17] and we touch *through* his flesh and blood and taste *with* his flesh and blood, which are rivers, and oceans, estuaries, mountains, fruits, wine, undreamt landscapes all co-substantiated through our flesh and blood. In paradise, no part of the body is triggered because it lacks something. Thus, because there is no lack in paradise, there is no need for what embodiment offer us. Our senses are not needed because they do not *need* to point out and yearn for what we do not possess and desire for enjoyment, peace, and survival. We are in the complete possession of our beatitude. Yet, this lack of need does not indicate their lack of essential presence in the resurrection. It is essential that the earthly body, which for so long hungered and panted after what it lacked, be raised in its fullness, glorified in its completion, only achieved because we unite with our true other half, the truly complete person, Christ. Christ completes our striving open natures as relational beings. In him, we truly become what we always sought to be, the other *as other* as our own. In Plato's *Symposium*, humans were not created as we appear now, but comprised of four arms, four legs and a head with two faces. Zeus split these beings into two separate parts, fearing their power, thus condemning them to exist perpetually in search of their other halves. When one striving-half meets their other striving-half, the pair is subsumed and overwhelmed:

17. Cf. Chesterton, *A Miscellany of Men*, 18–24: "The wind awoke last night with so noble a violence that it was like the war in heaven; and I thought for a moment that the Thing had broken free. For wind never seems like empty air. Wind always sounds full and physical, like the big body of something; and I fancied that the Thing itself was walking gigantic along the great roads between the forests of beech. Let me explain. The vitality and recurrent victory of Christendom have been due to the power of the Thing to break out from time to time from its enveloping words and symbols. Without this power all civilisations tend to perish under a load of language and ritual. One instance of this we hear much in modern discussion: the separation of the form from the spirit of religion. But we hear too little of numberless other cases of the same stiffening and falsification; we are far too seldom reminded that just as church-going is not religion, so reading and writing are not knowledge, and voting is not self-government. It would be easy to find people in the big cities who can read and write quickly enough to be clerks, but who are actually ignorant of the daily movements of the sun and moon. . . . The wind sang and split the sky like thunder all the night through; in scraps of sleep it filled my dreams with the divine discordances of martyrdom and revolt; I heard the horn of Roland and the drums of Napoleon and all the tongues of terror with which the Thing has gone forth: the spirit of our race alive. But when I came down in the morning only a branch or two was broken off the tree in my garden; and none of the great country houses in the neighbourhood were blown down, as would have happened if the Thing had really been abroad."

> Now, since their natural form had been cut in two, each one longed for its own other half, and so they would throw their arms about each other, weaving themselves together, wanting to grow together. . . . Love is born into every human being; it calls back the halves of our original nature together; it tries to make one out of two and heal the wound of human nature.[18]

What becomes of sexual intimacy in paradise is glorious completion. Our glorified bodies possess sexual organs not because we *need* them to complete something lacking in us. Our whole bodies are glorified because each aspect is a critical indicator of our desire for our permanent home. Love-*making* emphatically distinguishes us from the angels. It confirms that our intentionality desires union that befits the soul and body. The resurrected state completes the glorious waitingness of the virginal[19] as it completes the relentless incompleteness of every earthly striving, every frenetic sexual union, every weaving of ourselves, in and towards the other, which could never outwit time, sin, weakness, and death.

> I'd like to weld you together and join you into something that is naturally whole, so that the two of you are made into one. Then the two of you would share one life, as long as you live, because you would be one being, and by the same token, when you died, you would be one but not two in Hades, having died a single death. Look at your love, and see if this is what you desire: wouldn't this be all the good fortune you would want?[20]

There would not be sex in paradise because such an action would not be paradisal. All union, intimacy, completion is accomplished and held in full *Actus* in the incarnational climax as beatific vision. In the resurrected state, one's entire body and soul would be bathed in union with the bridegroom. There would be no parting, no separation, no need to enter the other, to renegotiate a union, everything would be *ad fontes*.[21] This definitively contrasts to all earthly sexual intimacy, whether it be the virginal and chaste, erotic, or mystical. All earthly *eros*, no matter how transcendent, must find itself incomplete, unable incarnationally and entirely to self-empty into the beloved and be wholly infixed by the

18. Plato, *Symposium*, 191b-d.

19. Cf. 2 Cor 11:2: "For I am jealous for you with a godly jealousy; for I betrothed you to one husband, so that to Christ I might present you as a pure virgin."

20. Plato, *Symposium* 192 d-e.

21. Cf. Ps 42:1: "*Quemadmodum desiderat cervus ad fontes aquarum ita desiderat anima mea ad te Deus.*"

beloved. At its most sanctified, these earthly incomplete intimacies relish the sweet and throbbing wound from our bridegroom's absence.[22]

> I saw in his hand a long spear of gold, and at the iron's point there seemed to be a little fire. He appeared to me to be thrusting it at times into my heart, and to pierce my very entrails; when he drew it out, he seemed to draw them out also, and to leave me all on fire with a great love of God. The pain was so great, that it made me moan; and yet so surpassing was the sweetness of this excessive pain, that I could not wish to be rid of it. The soul is satisfied now with nothing less than God. The pain is not bodily, but spiritual; though the body has its share in it, even a large one. It is a caressing of love so sweet which now takes place between the soul and God, that I pray God of His goodness to make him experience it who may think that I am lying. During the days that this lasted, I went about as if beside myself. I wished to see, or speak with, no one, but only to cherish my pain, which was to me a greater bliss than all created things could give me.[23]

It is this absence as nearness and nearness as absence that compels prayer, surrender, love-making, and all the glory and folly of human intimacy. We seek to hold once again the sweetness and redolent rhythmic union of the divine arrow driven into the quick. We long for the resurrected state where every beginning of our own selves would have no end, for each aspect of who we are would be enveloped in the God-man. His *kenosis* is an infixion within us. He has permeated us with the Word and, like Doubting Thomas, we have placed our fingers and our bodies within him. This is why when the Pharisees are fasting, Christ as bridegroom with his attendants did not fast. He was *with* them, and because he is united to them, there is abundance, completion, apogee. Sex and every earthly intimacy are a reflection of fasting, the abstinence and hollowness

22. Cf. St. Teresa of Ávila, *Life of St. Teresa*, xxix, §13: "It is by no efforts of the soul that it sorrows over the wound which the absence of our Lord has inflicted on it; it is far otherwise; for an arrow is driven into the entrails to the very quick, and into the heart at times, so that the soul knows not what is the matter with it, nor what it wishes for. It understands clearly enough that it wishes for God, and that the arrow seems tempered with some herb which makes the soul hate itself for the love of our Lord, and willingly lose its life for Him. It is impossible to describe or explain the way in which God wounds the soul, nor the very grievous pain inflicted, which deprives it of all self-consciousness; yet this pain is so sweet, that there is no joy in the world which gives greater delight. As I have just said, the soul would wish to be always dying of this wound."

23. St. Teresa of Ávila, *Life of St. Teresa*, xxix, §17–18.

that forges through history and unveils centuries of longing since the bridegroom went away. Much of earthly intimacy cannot recognize itself as incarnational fasting and is confused like Plato's leaky jar, which thinks it can fill itself of its own power when doing so only extinguishes its vital substance in the process.[24] Craving the other *as other* is an act of spiritual fasting. And this is why there is such profundity of resonating truth to theology of the body and to enshrining and illuminating the proper dignity of sexual union, one that comes to terms with this spiritual fasting, rather than deludes itself into pseudo-fulfillment. True sexual enlightenment is the phenomenological and mystical realization that we are ever in need of the one sustenance who is fully Lover and Beloved and who in his flesh and blood completes us as his own.

> John's disciples and the Pharisees were fasting; and they came and said to Him, "Why do John's disciples and the disciples of the Pharisees fast, but Your disciples do not fast?" And Jesus said to them, "While the bridegroom is with them, the attendants of the bridegroom cannot fast, can they? So long as they have the bridegroom with them, they cannot fast. But the days will come when the bridegroom is taken away from them, and then they will fast in that day."[25]

24. Plato, *Gorgias* 488e-499e.

25. Mark 2:18–20.

18

Summary Remarks on Play, Laughter, and Pets as Paths of Intimacy with the Bridegroom

On Play . . . with a Little Laughter in the Midst

> Then our mouth was filled with laughter, and our tongue with shouts of joy; then they said among the nations, "The LORD has done great things for them."[1]

THAT FULLNESS OF INTIMATE union with bridegroom is best understood through earthly play. Play is the enactment of the sacred, it is a realm invested with meaning because it is lived in *unison* with the good as dappled in the divine joy. Rather than attempting to manufacture right and wrong from the often petty worldly ways in which vice is dressed up as virtue, and a mediocrity of kindness is seen as acceptable preservation, play needn't demand obedience, but overflows with filial bonds forged in the love that anticipates paradise. Play is thus virtue, not under the mode of a trying and difficult obedience, but virtue *as virtue-exemplar*, blushed with Beauty at the behest of our remnant innocence.[2] For we do have a

---

1. Ps 126:2.

2. Cf. Schlick, *Philosophical Papers, Vol. II*, 125: "We do not call him the best man, who is obliged unceasingly to resist his own impulses and is constantly at war with his

remnant innocence in us; if it were simply absent, the agonizing descent of our fallenness would no longer possess its sting. Play prepares us to recognize that sting, and then the penetration of the sword, for what they are, and to live virtuously even if we must remain within the dryness of an obediential speculative recognition of the Good.[3] It preserves us to endure that dryness; it is the secret companion to Grace and the interior logic of Christ's words: "Suffer the little children, and forbid them not to come unto Me, for of such is the Kingdom of Heaven."[4] For while none can make up an alternative path to what grace freely yet essentially bestows, this does not mean that we cannot and should not place ourselves within its pre-thematic transcendence.

The holiest appetite for transcendence is play-filled love, and through it we are the clay shaped only by the Beautiful, the Good, and the True, becoming the vessel most ready for grace. A play-filled heart merges its personhood so fully into the glory of the moment, where time is not merely paused or forgotten but rather finally lived in its wondrous fullness. We experience Christ's loving infixion, which fills us with new-ness, promise, and joy, and our senses are awakened to hear, see, smell, taste and touch with the reverence of a creator for its creation. In this merging of time into the finally-lived-present, we have a foretaste of how we co-substantiate the architecture of paradise with Christ. We are in play with Christ forming all things, apprentices to the master architect. And Christ is delighted with us every day, his mirth is his most secret wisdom yet so very radiant.[5] We play before him at all times, and in all times:

---

own desires; we say this, rather, of the man whose inclinations are kindly and benevo-lent from the start, so that he simply does not fall into doubt and self-conflict. The man who struggles with and conquers himself is perhaps the type of the great man but not of the good one. . . . There is the deepest wisdom in the biblical injunction: 'unless ye become as little children.'"

3. Cf. Luke 6:20–21: "Looking up at His disciples, Jesus said: 'Blessed are you who are poor, for yours is the kingdom of God. Blessed are you who hunger now, for you will be satisfied. Blessed are you who weep now, for you will laugh.'"

4. Matt 19:14; Cf. Mark 10:15–16: "I tell you the truth, 'Anyone who doesn't receive the Kingdom of God like a child will never enter it.' Then he took the children in his arms and placed his hands on their heads and blessed them."

5. Cf. Chesterton, *Orthodoxy*: "And as I close this chaotic volume, I open again the strange small book from which all Christianity came; and I am again haunted by a kind of confirmation. The tremendous figure which fills the Gospels towers in this respect, as in every other, above all the thinkers who ever thought themselves tall. His pathos was natural, almost casual. The Stoics, ancient and modern, were proud of

The LORD possessed me in the beginning of his ways, before he made anything from the beginning. I was set up from eternity, and of old before the earth was made. The depths were not as yet, and I was already conceived, neither had the fountains of waters as yet sprung out: the mountains with their huge bulk had not as yet been established: before the hills I was brought forth: He had not yet made the Earth, nor the rivers, nor the poles of the world. When he prepared the heavens, I was present: when with a certain law and compass he enclosed the depths: When he established the sky above, and poised the fountains of waters: When he compassed the sea with its bounds, and set a law to the waters that they should not pass their limits: when be balanced the foundations of the earth; I was with him forming all things: and was delighted every day, playing before him at all times; Playing in the world: and my delights were to be with the children of men. Now therefore, ye children, hear me: Blessed are they that keep my ways. Hear instruction and be wise, and refuse it not. Blessed is the man that heareth me, and that watcheth daily at my gates, and waiteth at the posts of my doors.[6]

In C. S. Lewis' *The Lion, the Witch and the Wardrobe* we witness the terrible betrayal and cruel death of our Christ-figure, Aslan. But after having just come back to life and knowing that much more strife and suffering is ahead of Aslan and the Pevensie children, Lewis presents the most audacious decision of Aslan to have a romp, a play with the children. Here Christ communicates his self-emptying not solely in the sheer seriousness of the passion, but in his abundant fecundity of joy. Play is entrance into the kingdom of heaven, to the infixion that fills us up and raises us into paradise. To fight the powers of hell, nothing other than the ecstasy of heaven can combat it. Our hearts must exude the perfume of Christ to overwhelm the stench of banal indifference and

---

concealing their tears. He never concealed His tears; He showed them plainly on His open face at any daily sight, such as the far sight of His native city. Yet He concealed something. Solemn supermen and imperial diplomatists are proud of restraining their anger. He never restrained His anger. He flung furniture down the front steps of the Temple, and asked men how they expected to escape the damnation of Hell. Yet He restrained something. I say it with reverence; there was in that shattering personality a thread that must be called shyness. There was something that He hid from all men when He went up a mountain to pray. There was something that He covered constantly by abrupt silence or impetuous isolation. There was some one thing that was too great for God to show us when He walked upon our Earth; and I have sometimes fancied that it was His mirth."

6. Prov 8:22–34.

cowardly vice. Play communicates more truly how life should be lived in the midst of the competing beauty and terror of existence. Its immediacy and exuberance rediscover wondrous creation, creative fidelity, and realize connaturally that God's goodness is infused into our bones, so much so that happiness becomes quite inseparable from the play-filled lover.[7] It is in this play that we are granted a preview of the magnificent union, the nuptial intimacy with our bridegroom. Lewis' Christ-figure regains his strength after having risen from the dead. Before anything else, he decides to play as no one has ever played before. The brides and bridegroom play chase running in the high grass, and around the table of terrible sacrifice they fall onto the warm and verdant ground panting, but they are neither tired nor hungry nor thirsty. And why should they be? They are filled with everything needful because filled with Christ. Let us never forget that Christ entered existence as the unborn child, and grew into his mission *through* childhood. His mother and father are the archetype of good and holy parents filled with love and joy. This is not a family without play—without gentleness wrapped in firmness and firmness wrapped in gentleness—this is the Holy Family, the most beautiful union of fidelity, redemptive suffering, love and victory. Each of those powers functions through play as thorough openness to the heart of creation.

> "Oh, children," said the Lion, "I feel my strength coming back to me. Oh, children, catch me if you can!" He stood for a second, his eyes very bright, his limbs quivering, lashing himself with his tail. Then he made a leap high over their heads and landed on the other side of the Table. Laughing, though she didn't know why, Lucy scrambled over it to reach him. Aslan leaped again. A mad chase began. Round and round the hill-top he led them, now hopelessly out of their reach, now letting them almost catch his tail, now diving between them, now tossing them in the air with his huge and beautifully velveted paws and catching them again, and now stopping unexpectedly so that all three of them rolled over together in a happy laughing heap of fur and arms

7. Cf. Dostoevsky, *Demons*, 237: "'Have you seen a leaf, a leaf from a tree?' 'I have.' 'I saw one recently, a yellow one, with some green, decayed on the edges. Blown about by the wind. When I was 10 years old, I'd close my eyes on purpose, in winter, and imagine a leaf—green, bright, with veins, and the sun shining. I'd open my eyes and not believe it, because it was so good, then I'd close them again.' 'What's that, an allegory?' 'N-no . . . Why? Not an allegory, simply a leaf, one leaf. A leaf is good. Everything is good.' 'Everything?' 'Everything. Man is unhappy because he doesn't know he's happy; only because of that. It's everything, everything! Whoever learns will at once immediately become happy, that same moment.'"

and legs. It was such a romp as no one ever had except in Narnia; and whether it was more like playing with a thunderstorm or playing with a kitten Lucy could never make up her mind. And the funny thing was that when all three finally lay together panting in the sun, the girls no longer felt in the least tired or hunger or thirsty.[8]

The Lion Lays Down with the Lamb: What about Our Pets?

The wolf will live with the lamb, the leopard will lie down with the goat, the calf and the lion and the yearling together; and a little child will lead them.[9]

We must always be mindful that paradise does not function as a repeat for earth, just as earth was no recycling of Eden. If the fallen were somehow granted access inside the gates of Eden and able to survey the wondrous landscape, we would almost be of a different species than the prelapsarian in terms of our epistemological engagement. The latter would raise their eyes, and as they walk there would be with each movement an ease of connatural communication with the divine. Each of the senses would experience only the purely given, unfettered, unending life, which surrounds them, exteriorizing and interiorizing its creative fecundity with each breath. We who have knowledge of good and evil and perfused with this deteriorating worldly wisdom within every affective action would be unable to experience our world as they do—fully liberated from death and disorder. Our faithful accounting of the inklings of the resurrected state, while guided by a rigorous hope for the Beautiful *beyond* imagining, must not be confused with the comfort *well within* imagining. In every exile we lose something, and even if we gain a gift of immeasurable excellence—as the *felix culpa* of original sin opens the door to the relentless blessing of the bridegroom—we cannot ignore that something has changed, has vanished, is no longer present as it was. Christ overcomes death not by returning us to the Garden but by making death the very vestment of eternal life. He wears that death, now overcome in his glorified body, rising with his scars. Let us keep this truth of exile and

---

8. Lewis, "The Lion," *The Chronicles of Narnia*, 185.
9. Isa 11:6.

redemption in mind when confronting Aquinas' powerful arguments against the return of our animals in the resurrected state.

> If plants and animals are to remain, either all of them will, or some of them. If all of them, then dumb animals, which had previously died, will have to rise again just as men will rise again. But this cannot be asserted for since their form comes to nothing, they cannot resume the same identical form. On the other hand, if not all but some of them remain, since there is no more reason for one of them remaining forever rather than another, it would seem that none of them will. But whatever remains after the world has been renewed will remain forever, generation and corruption being done away. Therefore, plants and animals will altogether cease after the renewal of the world.[10]

Aquinas' rationale falls well within the intelligible rejection of nutritive and generative powers in paradise. Should the highest actions within and defining these creatures be bound to such powers, then heaven is not their proper and finale abode. While we are embodied spiritual substances who act out our aeviternal status in time, the animal, including our beloved pets, are natural beings, each fulfilled and completed in a natural end. To put this into more dramatic perspective: we are far closer to the angels than to the animals. This is due to our participation in God's image and likeness. This *imago dei* is reserved only for man and angels, befitting our intellectual and open transcendent natures. And our likeness differs from creatures that *only* possess likeness to God. Rather than it being a more deterministic and static likeness, ours in dialogue with image becomes a transcendentally active power that relatively places us above the angels.

Perhaps Aquinas' stance is a needful reminder of the necessity to shed earthly attachments until we embrace the one thing needful, namely Christ's love. In doing so, we learn the painful, purgative lesson of redemption: we do not recover the home we lost when sin exiled us. Our exile is of such a sort that any return is impossible, because our excision has collapsed our former home into dust and rubble. We do not repeat the comforts of earth that are all too easy to be recreated on earth. Salvation, like history, never works by repetition. There has never been an exacting accomplished reclamation of the past, every political and theological version is a shadowland of its former self. God, who is perfect, would never in his wisdom commit this error of errors. He knows better than any of

10. ST Suppl. 91, 5, *sed contra*.

us the consequences and effects of our freedom. Thus, if there is a place for our pets in paradise, there must be a genuine transcendent meaning beyond fear that the "better place" is empty and uninviting, and outside the creature comforts that actually reduce paradise to irrelevance.

But in keeping with the tradition of the Thomistic *sed contra*, perhaps there is room for our own "on the contrary," which can demonstrate a potential path for our animals in the resurrected state. And here specifically is the issue, namely the *resurrected* state. It is one thing to view heaven, and its state of the separated soul, and try haphazardly to amalgamate some semblance of a place for the pets' participation and affective soul within that light. It is quite another to wonder about the architecture and scenery of the resurrection. Throughout this work, we have stressed the likeness and especially the *difference* between ourselves and angels in terms of what befits our state of perfection as properly reflective of the unity of our body and soul. When Christ resurrected on the third day, he was able to be heard, seen, and touched. His being was comprised of flesh and blood, and he walked, talked, and moved in a world of time and space. In its most basic and foundational sense, to have a body means to take up space, to be in contact with other things that take up space, which have length, breadth, texture, contour, are active and inert. To have a body means to be in a world. All bodies are in a world. But intellectual souls united to bodies, where each is *for* the transcendent benefit of the other, means that we are uniquely world-forming creatures. It seems that the resurrected state could not be a blank roomless room, a vacuum of nothingness, nor is it a mere ideational state of relation. Grace perfects nature: if we are world-forming on earth, how intensive is our co-substantiation of the architecture of paradise through Christ's flesh and blood as identical with heaven itself? We must press even further: if we are always taking-in the other *as other*, interiorizing and exteriorizing the self repeatedly throughout our lives, then a resurrection of an isolated person, really a shell of a person, appears to be the very antithesis of our incarnational intentionality. A world of beings co-exists with all our actions and to claim otherwise in the resurrected state appears to be contradictory.

While we only see through the glass darkly at present, we can phenomenologically wager that it makes far more sense that we resurrect with the memorial exigencies, the animals, plants, trees, places, things, that are intrinsically bound up in constituting our own incarnational intentionality than simply absent of them. The grandmother so very loved is housed in the memory of another, as the little girl in a petticoat watching the farm animals on the flickering train during the Great War. She is in every way and in every age in the other, unrecorded and unremarked—the brick red colored jacket, the gloves pulled off for Mass, a moving form of strength equaled only by an incarnate shyness. The house of Being is constructed by memory and it is only entered when forgetting is identical with recollection: "By loss of memory we are reborn, for memory is death."[11] For memory demands it be furnished a foundation beyond the image; it craves with excess and defect, the scent and sound and the sight that blinds and blushes. And it seeks to be liberated from the painful yoke of recollective estrangement, where the surprising otherness of the once unremarked calls to us and reminds the stranger within of what is lost or was never gained. In memory we are more often than not learning to forget under the guise of remembering what never was, for memory never lets us remember *as is*. It seems then that the age or ages we are in heaven cannot be simply answered with a single number, but conjures a whole world of meaning and nuance that demands humility and attention.

We cannot know how things that cannot make it on their own make it to paradise. But neither can we make it on our own. We cannot know how our pets, memories, and even the objects that illuminate our longer way are to be participants in the afterlife or how they would appear in themselves and to us for, again, the resurrection is not a repeated reductive reflection of earth. Still, because of the Love that overflows immemorially uniting these things to our beings as the exteriorization of our being in-and-to-the-world, it appears more likely that they are present in transformed vitality in paradise. Also, if we are to resurrect into a world, why would there be a world of things and beings unattached to our sanctity, unattached to our *longior via* which brought us to the Trinitarian fountain and promise of eternal life? In the first place, our own "on the contrary" points out three paths for our animals and even, potentially, for the things whose created goodness assisted in bringing us into the hearth of divinity:

1. Distinct from the state of the separated soul, the resurrected state means a body, and a body means a world, and a world means an abundance of creatures and things.

---

11. Auden, "Paid on Both Sides," *Collected Poems*, 12.

2. Our natures are world-forming, our incarnational intentionality means that who we are is always outside ourselves and alongside the world. How then does it do justice to our open natures, if that otherness is quashed in paradise? Such a state seems more akin to the disintegration in hell.

3. If we concede that the resurrection means a new world for the bride, a "new heaven and a new earth,"[12] filled with the waters of life, and the city we co-substantiate through Christ's flesh and blood can only be described poetically with the most precious of jewels,[13] why would this co-substantiation be wholly foreign to our memorial longer way or to Christ's who was born of man?

For C. S. Lewis, humans are able to impart onto their pets a certain imprint of their selfhood, and thus if the human person achieves salvific immortality, then in turn the animal companion who has taken on this *self* receives this gift as well:

> The theory I am suggesting . . . makes God the centre of the universe and man the subordinate centre of terrestrial nature: the beasts are not co-ordinate with man, but subordinate to him, and their destiny is through and through related to his. And the derivative immortality suggested for them is not a mere *amende* or compensation: It is part and parcel of the new Heaven and

12. Rev 21:1–7: "Then I saw 'a new Heaven and a new Earth,' for the first Heaven and the first Earth had passed away, and there was no longer any sea. I saw the Holy City, the new Jerusalem, coming down out of Heaven from God, prepared as a bride beautifully dressed for her husband. And I heard a loud voice from the throne saying, 'Look! God's dwelling place is now among the people, and he will dwell with them. They will be his people, and God himself will be with them and be their God. "He will wipe every tear from their eyes. There will be no more death" or mourning or crying or pain, for the old order of things has passed away.' He who was seated on the throne said, 'I am making everything new!' Then he said, 'Write this down, for these words are trustworthy and true.' He said to me: 'It is done. I am the Alpha and the Omega, the Beginning and the End. To the thirsty I will give water without cost from the spring of the water of life. Those who are victorious will inherit all this, and I will be their God and they will be my children.'"

13. Rev 21:17–21: "The angel measured the wall using human measurement, and it was 144 cubits thick. The wall was made of jasper, and the city of pure gold, as pure as glass. The foundations of the city walls were decorated with every kind of precious stone. The first foundation was jasper, the second sapphire, the third agate, the fourth emerald, the fifth onyx, the sixth ruby, the seventh chrysolite, the eighth beryl, the ninth topaz, the tenth turquoise, the eleventh jacinth, and the twelfth amethyst. The twelve gates were twelve pearls, each gate made of a single pearl. The great street of the city was of gold, as pure as transparent glass."

new Earth, organically related to the whole suffering process of the world's fall and redemption.[14]

Furthering this argument, we can say that such animals are worthy, in a way, of the resurrected life because they first invoked in us the gentle, playful otherness needed in order to achieve a holy, loving, and selfless personhood. If we know ourselves only in the face of otherness, can we appropriately envision a heaven without this animal-and-human relationality that bore for us the often gentler and kinder vision of our selfhood than the diminished versions we so often received and imparted through our corrupted states?[15] If earth began in the *mythos* of the garden filled with creatures foreshadowing the animals around the manger each longing for the new earth, how can this "new earth" of the resurrection be void of that life? St. Paul who speaks of heaven as home, states that "creation itself would be set free from slavery to corruption and share in the glorious freedom of the children of God."[16] This implies a new world, not Eliot's wasteland of fractured images resulting from our diminishing presences in and to each other.[17] What is sought is something else altogether, something sensed purely in play and in animal kinship, where love touches all things, even the most disfigured, and transfigures them with Beauty, untroubled peace working wholly within God's intent:

> Brothers, have no fear of men's sin. Love a man even in his sin, for that is the semblance of Divine Love and is the highest love on Earth. Love all God's creation, the whole and every grain of sand in it. Love every leaf, every ray of God's light. Love the

---

14. Lewis, *The Problem of Pain*, 145.

15. Cf. Job 12:7–10: "But ask the animals, and they will teach you, or the birds in the sky, and they will tell you; or speak to the Earth, and it will teach you, or let the fish in the sea inform you. Which of all these does not know that the hand of the LORD has done this? In his hand is the life of every creature and the breath of all mankind."

16. Rom 8:21.

17. Cf. Eliot, "The Wasteland," *Collected Poems*:
   "A heap of broken images, where the sun beats,
   And the dead tree gives no shelter, the cricket no relief,
   And the dry stone no sound of water. Only
   There is shadow under this red rock,
   (Come in under the shadow of this red rock),
   And I will show you something different from either
   Your shadow at morning striding behind you
   Or your shadow at evening rising to meet you;
   I will show you fear in a handful of dust."

animals, love the plants, love everything. If you love everything, you will perceive the divine mystery in things. Once you perceive it, you will begin to comprehend it better every day. And you will come at last to love the whole world with an all-embracing love. Love the animals: God has given them the rudiments of thought and joy untroubled. Do not trouble it, don't harass them, don't deprive them of their happiness, don't work against God's intent. Man, do not pride yourself on superiority to the animals; they are without sin, and you, with your greatness, defile the Earth by your appearance on it, and leave the traces of your foulness after you—alas, it is true of almost every one of us! Love children especially, for they too are sinless like the angels; they live to soften and purify our hearts and, as it were, to guide us. Woe to him who offends a child! Father Anfim taught me to love children. The kind, silent man used often on our wanderings to spend the farthings given us on sweets and cakes for the children. He could not pass by a child without emotion. That's the nature of the man.[18]

18. Father Zosima in Dostoevsky, *The Brothers Karamazov*, 361.

19

The Mystery in Brief

Recovering friendships and intimacies from their worldly forms

FELLOWSHIP IS THE MOST visible manifestation of this longer way, which is fulfilled only in paradise. God is Love, and virtuous union enables us to see "with the eyes of Christ." [1] True intimacy and friendliness are the spiritual dowries[2] predisposing us to our union with the beatific vision. They are a central facet of the heavenly city, and are, through Christ, at root in its very architecture. Friendship in Christ, as fellowship with the blessed, enables us to co-substantiate heaven's rooms, valleys, corridors, and waters. Paradise would never be a diversity of peoples alone.[3] How can

---

1. Pope Benedict XVI, *Deus Caritas Est* §18.

2. Cf. ST Suppl. 95, 2, ad 2: "Beatitude is not directed to the union but is the union itself of the soul with Christ. This union is by an operation, whereas the dowries are gifts disposing to this same union."

3. See Chesterton, *Illustrated London News*, Sept. 8, 1917, *Collected Works Vol. XXXI*, 155: "A queer and almost mad notion seems to have got into the modern head that, if you mix up everybody and everything more or less anyhow, the mixture may be called unity, and the unity may be called peace. It is supposed that, if you break down all doors and walls so that there is no domesticity, there will then be nothing but friendship. Surely somebody must have noticed by this time that the men living in a hotel quarrel at least as often as the men living in a street."

praise of God and of the ardent joy of the beatific vision be inexhaustibly rich if the community is not truly in communion? How can the blessed be enjoined in praise if they do not love the divine in the other, discover *all* there is to love in the other, which is the very essence of friendship,[4] fulfilled in being a friend of God?[5] And "without friends, no one would want to live, even if he had all other goods."[6] Paradise without intimacy is an oxymoron, a contradiction in terms.

Now, to be sure, we recognize that intimacies must take on a dramatically excelling and different experience than many, if not most, friendships and bonds on earth. Like all worldly human actions, no friendship ever fully emancipates itself from the deadening grip of original sin. Vice has infected and wounded all things. Our sinfulness malforms intentionality with its sophistic, parasitical, un-examined, and failed loves, which separate what cannot be separated: intimacy and virtue. To gain a closer approximation of friendships in paradise, we extracted the substance of friendship as the desire for the divine in the other with equal and even greater zeal than one desires Christ for himself. But such an understanding of intimacies and bonds within the fallen world disposes us to discovering so many substitutes and surrogates for genuine fellowship. As we saw in O'Neill, this prompts us to wonder what happens to those partial forms where there is a tending towards authentic friendship but which fails to exercise its virtue? What becomes of the person who stubbornly refuses God and who by his actions, or even in spite of them, has nevertheless helped another along the way to salvation? A good life lived must always sense the trembling mystery of our only true home. To experience the glimmer of heaven on earth and in us, it is essential that, like everything else, it is won through the longer way of suffering, compassion, and

4. Cf. Aristotle, *Nicomachean Ethics*, XIII. See also Plato, *Laws*, IV, 716c-d.

5. See Diotima to Socrates in Plato, *Symposium*, 211e–212b: "But if it were given to man to gaze on beauty's very self unsullied, unalloyed, and freed from the moral taint that haunts the frailer loveliness of flesh and blood—if, I say, it were given to man to see the heavenly beauty face to face, would you call his an unenviable life, whose eyes had been opened to the vision, and who had gazed upon it in true contemplation until it had become his own forever? . . . And remember that it is only when he discerns beauty itself through what makes it visible that a man will be quickened with the true, and not the seeming virtue—for it is virtue's self that quickens him, not virtue's semblance. And when he has brought forth and reared this perfect virtue, he shall be called the friend of God, and if ever it is given to man to put on immortality, it shall be given to him."

6. Aristotle, *Nicomachean Ethics*, 1155a.

kenotic love. We must live with this mystery, and love with a furiousness enlightened by the virtuous.

To clarify the agony of this mystery once more let us turn once again to the Angelic Doctor. Aquinas sets out a very difficult scenario for us to digest: the blessed know the suffering of the damned, they do not pity them, and even rejoice in their sufferings.[7] This scenario would extend to the blessed who knows the suffering of the other who had helped him along the way of salvation but could not help himself. How are we to reconcile the summit of joy with the sight of the eternally diminishing, alienated soul? If so many of our earthly friendships involve a range of allegiances and relationalities that distract us from salvation, what remains of those original friendships in the resurrected state? Are they simply unrecognizable, do we start over? Again, each of these questions reveals the most serious of mysteries: the potential total loss of kenotic love itself within another human being, which we cannot know to exist or not to exist through our own power. We can *only* know that this painful mystery beckons us here and now to love truly and intensively, with all the zeal of the virtues formed through the compassion Christ offers us relentlessly. And it is through this endlessly relentless love alone that we tremble glimpsing that sight of heaven incarnated within each of us. We are always straddling that delicate line that must never envision heaven as a reductive extension of earth—and so we must practice through to our death the act of letting go all that is dear—while somewhere, somehow, recognizing that paradise must deeply befit and exceed all our human conceptions of what it is to be flesh and blood, to be of earth and clay, to be world-forming like our dear Christ.

> Her heart felt as if it were breaking in her breast, bleeding and bleeding, young and fierce. From grief over the warm and ardent love which she had lost and still secretly mourned; from anguished joy over the pale, luminous love which drew her to the farthest boundaries of life on this Earth. Through the great darkness that would come, she saw the gleam of another, gentler sun, and she sensed the fragrance of the herbs in the garden at world's end.[8]

7. Cf. ST Suppl. 94.

8. Undset, *Kristin Lavransdatter II: The Wife*, 253.

Bibliography

Aeschylus, Sophocles, and Euripides. *The Greek Plays: Sixteen Plays by Aeschylus, Sophocles, and Euripides*. Translated by Mary Lefkowitz and James Romm. New York: Modern Library, 2017.

———. *Tragedies and Fragments of Aeschylus*, Volumes 1–2. Translated by Edward Hayes Plumptre. Boston: Heath, 1909.

Alighieri, Dante. *The Divine Comedy* (The Inferno, The Purgatorio, The Paradiso). Translated by John Ciardi. New York: NAL Trade, 2003.

———. *La Vita Nuova*. Translated by David Slavitt. Cambridge: Harvard University Press, 2010.

St. Ambrose. *The Letters of St. Ambrose, Bishop of Milan*. Translated by Henry Walford. Oxford: James Parker, 1881.

St. Anselm. *The Devotions of St. Anselm*, edited by C. C. J. Webb. London: Methuen, 1903.

———. *Proslogium, Monologium, Cur Deus Homo, Guanilo's In Behalf of the Fool*. Translated by Sidney Norton Deane. Lasalle, IL: Open Court, 1962.

Ante-Nicene Fathers, Volume 9. Edited by A. Cleveland Cloxe and Allan Menzies. Buffalo: Christian Literature, 1896.

Arendt, Hannah. *Eichmann in Jerusalem: A Report on the Banality of Evil*. New York: Penguin, 1994.

———. *The Human Condition*. Garden City, NY: Doubleday, 1959.

———. "Martin Heidegger at Eighty." *The New York Review of Books* 17.6 (1971) 41–55.

———. *The Origins of Totalitarianism*. New York: Harcourt, 1973.

Aristotle. *The Basic Works of Aristotle*. Edited by R. McKeon. New York: Random House, 1941.

Auden, Wystan Hugh. *W. H. Auden: Collected Poems*. Edited by Edward Mendelson. New York: Modern Library, 2007.

St. Augustine. *Against the Academicians and The Teacher*. Translated by Peter King. Indianapolis: Hackett, 1994.

———. *Augustine Day by Day*. Edited by John Rotelle. Totowa, NJ: Catholic Book, 1986.

———. *Augustine: On the Free Choice of the Will, On Grace and Free Choice, and Other Writings*. Edited by Peter King. Cambridge: Cambridge University Press, 2010.

———. *City of God*. Edited by Vernon Bourke. New York: Image, 1958.

———. *Confessions*. Translated by Henry Chadwick. New York: Oxford University Press, 1998.

————. *Day by Day with Augustine*. Edited by Donald X. Burt. Collegeville, MN: Liturgical, 2006.

————. *On Free Choice of the Will*. Translated by Thomas Williams. Indianapolis: Hackett, 1993.

————. *Of the Morals of the Catholic Church and On the Morals of the Manicheans*. Translated by Richard Stothert. London: Aeterna, 2014.

————. *St. Augustine: On the Holy Trinity, Doctrinal Treatises, Moral Treatises. Nicene and Post-Nicene Fathers: First Series, Volume III*. Edited by P. Schaff. New York: Cosimo Classics, 2007.

————. *The Works of Saint Augustine: A Translation for the 21st Century*. New York: New City, 2004.

Bachelard, Gaston. *Intuition of the Instant*. Translated by Eileen Rizo-Patron. Evanston, IL: Northwestern University Press, 2013.

Baker, Kenneth. *Fundamentals of Catholicism, Volume 2*. San Francisco: Ignatius, 1983.

Bakhtin, Mikhail. *Problems of Dostoevsky's Poetics*. Translated by Caryl Emerson. Minneapolis, MN: University of Minnesota Press, 1984.

Balthasar, Hans Urs von. *The Christian and Anxiety*. San Francisco: Ignatius, 2000.

————. *The Christian State of Life*. San Francisco: Ignatius, 2002.

————. *Dare We Hope That All Men Be Saved? With a Short Discourse on Hell*. San Francisco: Ignatius, 2014.

————. *Explorations in Theology I: Word Made Flesh*. Translated by A. V. Littledale and Alexander Dru. San Francisco: Ignatius, 1989.

————. "The Fathers, The Scholastics, and Ourselves." *Communio* 24.2 (1997) 347–96.

————. *A First Glance at Adrienne Von Speyr*. San Francisco: Ignatius, 1981.

————. *Church and World*. Translated by A. V. Littledale. Montreal: Palm, 1967.

————. *The Glory of the Lord: A Theological Aesthetics, Volume 4: The Realm of Metaphysics in Antiquity*. San Francisco: Ignatius, 1989.

————. *The Glory of the Lord: A Theological Aesthetics, Volume 5: The Realm of Metaphysics in the Modern Age*. San Francisco: Ignatius, 1991.

————. *Love Alone Is Credible*. Translated by D. C. Schindler. San Francisco: Ignatius, 2004.

————. *The Moment of Christian Witness*. Translated by Richard Beckley. San Francisco: Ignatius, 1994.

————. *Our Task: A Report and a Plan*. San Francisco: Ignatius, 1994.

————. *A Theology of History*. San Francisco: Ignatius, 1994.

————. *Theo-Logic II: Truth of God*. San Francisco: Ignatius, 1994.

————. *Two Sisters in the Spirit: Therese of Lisieux and Elizabeth of the Trinity*. San Francisco: Ignatius, 1992.

————. *Who Is a Christian?* Translated by Frank Davidson. San Francisco: Ignatius, 1993.

Barnhart, Joe E., ed. *Dostoevsky's Polyphonic Talent*. Lanham, MD: University Press of America, 2005.

Bartlett, John. *Bartlett's Familiar Quotations: A Collection of Passages, Phrases, and Proverbs Traced to Their Sources in Ancient and Modern Literature*. Cambridge: John Wilson and Son, 1903.

Beckett, Samuel. *Malone Dies*. New York: Grove, 1956.

————. *Oh les Beaux Jours*. Paris: Minuit, 1963.

————. *Samuel Beckett's Waiting for Godot*. Edited by Harold Bloom. New York: Blooms Literary Criticism, 2008.

Belloc, Hilaire. *A Conversation with an Angel: And Other Essays*. New York: Harper, 1929.

————. *The Path to Rome*. London: George Allen and Unwin, 1916.

————. *The Silence of the Sea*. London: Cassell, 1941.

————. *Sonnets and Verse*. New York: Mcbridge, 1924.

————. *Verses*. London: Duckworth, 1910.

Bentham, Jeremy. *An Introduction to the Principles of Morals and Legislation*. Oxford: Clarendon, 1879.

————. *The Works of Jeremy Bentham, Vol II*. Edinburgh: William Tait, 1838.

Bergson, Henri. *An Introduction to Metaphysics*. Translated by T. E. Hulme. New York: Putnam's Sons, 1912.

————. *Matter and Memory*. Translated by Nancy M. Paul and W. Scott Palmer. London: George Allen and Unwin, 1970.

————. *The Two Sources of Morality and Religion*. Translated by R. Ashley Audra and Cloudsley Brereton. South Bend, IN: University of Notre Dame Press, 1991.

Bernanos, Georges. *Les Grands Cimitiers Sous La Lune*. Paris: Librairie Pion, 1938.

St. Bernard of Clairvaux. *Bernard of Clairvaux: Selected Works*. Translated by Gillian Rosemary Evans. New York: Paulist, 1987.

————. *On Grace and Free Choice*. Translated by Daniel O'Donovan. Kalamazoo, MI: Cistercian, 1988.

————. "On the Love of God." In *Late Medieval Mysticism*, edited by Ray C. Petry, 54–65. London: SCM, 1957.

————. *Some Letters of Saint Bernard*. Translated by Samuel J. Eales. London: Ballantyne, 1904.

Berry, John Anthony. "Tested in Fire: Hans Urs von Balthasar on the Moment of Christian Witness." *Melita Theologica* 62 (2012) 145–70.

Blot, François René. *In Heaven We'll Meet Again: The Saints and Scriptures on Our Heavenly Reunion*. Manchester: Sophia Institute, 2016.

Boethius. *Consolatio Philosophiae*. Edited by James J. O'Donnell. Bryn Mawr, PA: Bryn Mawr College, 1990.

Breton, Stanislas. *The Word and the Cross*. Translated by Jacquelyn Porter. New York: Fordham University Press, 2002.

Brown, Montague. "St. Thomas Aquinas on Human and Divine Forgiveness." *The Saint Anselm Journal* 6.2 (2009) 1–8.

Buddha. *The Dhammapada: A Collection of Verses Being One of the Canonical Books of the Buddhists*. Translated by Friedrich Max Muller. London: Watkins, 2006.

Callard, Agnes. "The Philosophy of Anger." *Boston Review: A Political and Literary Forum*, April 22, 2020.

Camus, Albert. *Caligula and Three Other Plays*. Translated by Stuart Gilbert. New York: Vintage, 1962.

————. *The First Man*. Translated by David Hapgood. New York: Vintage, 1996.

————. *The Myth of Sisyphus and Other Essays*. New York: Vintage, 1991.

————. *Notebooks: 1951–1959*. Translated by Ryan Bloom. Chicago: Dee, 2008.

Caputo, John D. *Heidegger and Aquinas*. New York: Fordham University Press, 1982.

————. *The Mystical Element in Heidegger's Thought*. New York: Fordham University Press, 1986.

――――. *The Weakness of God: A Theology of the Event*. Bloomington, IN: Indiana University Press, 2006.

Catholic Church. *Catechism of the Catholic Church*. Vatican City: Libreria Editrice Vaticana, 2000.

――――. *The Office for the Dead: According to the Roman Breviary, Missal and Ritual*. Toronto: Gale, 2010.

Ckekhov, Anton. *The Lady with the Little Dog and Other Stories, 1896–1904*. Translated by Ronald Wilks. London: Penguin, 2002.

――――. *Selected Stories of Anton Chekhov*. Translated by Rchard Pevar and Larissa Volokhonsky. New York: Modern Library, 2000.

Chenu, Marie-Dominque. *Introduction a L'Etude de S. Thomas d' Aquinas*. Paris: Vrin, 1993.

――――. "Le Plan de la Somme Theologique de S. Thomas." *Revue Thomiste* 45 (1939) 93–107.

Chesterton, Gilbert Keith. *All Things Considered*. New York: John Lane, 1916.

――――. *The Catholic Church and Conversion*. San Francisco: Ignatius, 2006.

――――. *The Collected Works of G. K. Chesterton, Volume 1: Heretics, Orthodoxy, the Blatchford Controversies*. San Francisco: Ignatius, 1986.

――――. *The Everlasting Man*. San Francisco: Ignatius, 1993.

――――. "Jesus or Christ." *The Hibbert Journal* (1909) 746–58.

――――. *A Miscellany of Men*. New York: Dodd, Mead and Company, 1912.

――――. *Saint Francis of Assisi*. New York: Doubleday, 2001.

――――. *St. Thomas Aquinas: The Dumb Ox*. New York: Doubleday, 1956.

――――. *William Blake*. Looe, UK: House of Stratus, 2000.

Clarke, William. Norris. *Explorations in Metaphysics: Being, God, Person*. South Bend, IN: University of Notre Dame Press, 1995.

――――. "The Limitation of Act by Potency: Aristotelianism or Neoplatonism." *The New Scholasticism* 26 (1952) 167–94.

――――. *The One and the Many: A Contemporary Thomistic Metaphysics*. Notre Dame, IN: University of Notre Dame Press, 2001.

Chrétien, Jean-Louis. *The Ark of Speech*. Translated by Andrew Brown. London: Routledge, 2004.

St. Chrysostom. *Saint Chrysostom's Homilies on the Gospel of Saint Matthew: Nicene and Post-Nicene Fathers of the Christian Church Volume 10*. Edited by Philip. Schaff. Whitefish, MT: Kessinger Publishing, 2010.

Cummings, Edward Estlin. *100 Selected Poems*. New York: Grove, 1994.

Davie, Donald, ed. *The New Oxford Book of Christian Verse*. Oxford: Oxford University Press, 1981.

Debout, Jacques. *My Sins of Omission*. Translated by J. F. Scanlan. London: Sands, 1930.

De Lubac, Henri. *Catholicism: Christ and the Common Destiny of Man*. Translated by Lancelot C. Sheppard and Elizabeth Englund. San Francisco: Ignatius, 1988.

――――. *The Drama of Atheistic Humanism*. Translated by Mark Sebanc. San Francisco: Ignatius, 1995.

――――. *Theology in History*. Translated by Anne Englund Nash. San Francisco: Ignatius, 1996.

De Maistre, Joseph. *St Petersburg Dialogues: Or Conversations on the Temporal Government of Providence*. Translated by Richard A. Lebrun. Montreal: McGill University Press, 1993.

Derrida, Jacques. *The Gift of Death*. Translated by David Wills. Chicago: University of Chicago Press, 1995.

Desmond, William. *Ethics and the Between*. Albany, NY: State University of New York Press, 2001.

———. *The Gift and the Passion of Beauty: On the Threshold between the Aesthetic and the Religious*. Veritas. Eugene, OR: Cascade, 2018.

———. *Hegel's God: A Counterfeit Double?* Aldershot, UK: Ashgate, 2003.

———. *The Intimate Strangeness of Being: Metaphysics after Dialectic*. Washington, DC: Catholic University of America Press, 2012.

Dostoevsky, Fyodor. *The Brothers Karamazov*. Translated by Constance Garnett. New York: MacMillan, 1922.

———. *The Brothers Karamazov*. Translated by Richard Pevear and Larissa Volokhonsky: New York: Farrar, Straus and Giroux. 1990.

———. *The Demons: A Novel in Three Parts*. Translated by Richard Pevear and Larissa Volokhonsky. New York: Vintage, 1995.

———. *The Karamazov Brothers*. Translated by Ignat Avsey: Oxford: Oxford University Press, 1994.

———. *The Idiot*. Translated by *The Idiot*. Translated by Frederick Whishaw. London: Vizetelly, 1887.

———. *The Idiot*. Translated by David Magarshack. London: Penguin, 1955.

———. *The Idiot*. Translated by Richard Pevear and Larissa Volokhonsky. New York: Vintage, 2003.

———. *The Idiot*. Translated by Henry Carlisle and Olga Carlisle. New York: Signet, 2010.

The Douay-Rheims New Testament of Our Lord and Savior Jesus Christ. Compiled by Rev. George Leo Haydock. Monrovia, Liberia: Catholic Treasures, 1991.

The Douay-Rheims Old Testament of the Holy Catholic Bible. Compiled by Rev. George Leo Haydock. Monrovia, Liberia: Catholic Treasures, 1992.

Eliade, Mircea. *The Myth of the Eternal Return: Cosmos and History*. Princeton: Princeton University Press, 2005.

———. *The Sacred and the Profane: The Nature of Religion*. Translated Willard R. Trask. New York: Harcourt, 1959.

Eliot, T. S. *Christianity and Culture*. London: Harvest, 1967.

———. *Four Quartets*. New York: Mariner, 1968.

———. *Thoughts After Lambeth*. London: Faber and Faber, 1931.

———. *T. S. Eliot: Collected Poems, 1909–1962*. Orlando: Harcourt, 1991.

Engelland, Chad. *Phenomenology*. Cambridge, MIT, 2020.

Fulkerson, Matthew. *The First Sense: A Philosophical Study of Human Touch*. Cambridge: MIT, 2013.

Gilson, Caitlin Smith. *Immediacy and Meaning: J. K. Huysmans and the Immemorial Origin of Metaphysics*. London: Bloomsbury, 2018.

———. *Metaphysical Presuppositions of Being-in-the-World: A Confrontation between St. Thomas Aquinas and Martin Heidegger*. New York: Continuum, 2010.

———. *The Philosophical Question of Christ*. London: Bloomsbury, 2014.

———. *The Political Dialogue of Nature and Grace: Toward a Phenomenology of Chaste Anarchism*. London: Bloomsbury, 2015.

———. *Subordinated Ethics: Natural Law and Moral Miscellany in Aquinas and Dostoyevsky*. Eugene, OR: Cascade, 2020.

Gilson, Étienne. *The Art of Misunderstanding Thomism*. West Hartford, CT: St. Joseph's College, 1966.

———. "Autour de Pompanazzi." *Archives d'Histoire Doctrinale et Litteraire du Moyen Age* xxviii (1961) 163–278.

———. *Being and Some Philosophers*. Toronto: Pontifical Institute of Mediaeval Studies, 1952.

———. *The Christian Philosophy of St. Thomas*. New York: Random House, 1956.

———. *The Elements of Christian Philosophy*. New York: Mentor Omega, 1963.

———. *God and Philosophy*. New Haven, CT: Yale University Press, 1941.

———. *History of Christian Philosophy in the Middle Ages*. London: Sheed and Ward, 1965.

———. *Intelligence in the Service of Christ the King*. New York: Scepter, 1978.

———. *Jean Dun Scot: Introduction a ses positions fondamentales*. Librairie Philosophique J. Vrin. Paris: Vrin, 1952.

———. *Linguistics and Philosophy: An Essay on the Philosophical Constants of Language*. Notre Dame, IN: University of Notre Dame Press, 1988.

———. *Methodical Realism*. Translated by Philip Trower. Poulsbo, WA: Christendom University Press, 1990.

———. *The Philosopher and Theology*. Translated by Cecile Gilson. New York: Random House, 1962.

———. *Reason and Revelation in the Middle Ages*. New York: Scribner, 1966.

———. "Regio dissimilitudinis de Plato à Saint Bernard de Clairvaux." *Mediaeval Studies* 9 (1947) 108–30.

———. *The Spirit of Mediaeval Philosophy*. Translated by A. H. C. Downes. New York: Scribner, 1940.

———. *The Spirit of Thomism*. New York: Harper, 1964.

———. *The Terrors of the Year Two-Thousand*. Toronto: St. Michael's College, 1984.

———. "Les Terreurs de l'an Deux Mille." *Revue de l'Universite d'Ottawa* 19 (1949) 67–81.

———. *The Unity of Philosophical Experience*. San Francisco: Ignatius, 1999.

Gilson, Frederick. "And Dwelt among Us." Unpublished, 1994.

Girard, René. *The One by Whom Scandal Comes*. Translated by M. B. DeBevoise. East Lansing, MI: Michigan State University Press, 2014.

———. *The Scapegoat*. Translated by Yvonne Freccero. Baltimore: Johns Hopkins University, 1986.

———. *Things Hidden since the Foundation of the World*. Translated by Stephen Bann and Michael Metteer. Stanford, CA: Stanford University Press, 1987.

———. *Violence and the Sacred*. Translated by Patrick Gregory. Baltimore: Johns Hopkins University, 1979.

Gonzales, Philip. *Reimagining the Analogia Entis: The Future of Erich Przywara's Christian Vision*. Grand Rapids: Eerdmans, 2019.

Gray, Thomas. *Elegy Written in a Country Churchyard*. New York: Limited Editions Club, 1938.

Grippe, Ed. "The Hell of Our Choosing: Sartre's Ethics and the Impossibility of Interpersonal Conversion." In *Ethics and Phenomenology*, edited by Mark Sanders and J. Jeremy Wisnewski, 117–44. Lanham, MD: Lexington, 2012.

Guardini, R. *Meditations before Mass*. Translated by Elinor Castendyk Briefs. Bedford, UK: Sophia, 2013.

———. *Pascal for Our Time*. Translated by Brian Thompson. New York: Herder, 1966.

———. *Prayers from Theology*. Translated by R. Newnham. New York: Herder, 1959.

———. *Sacred Signs*. Translated by Grace Branham. Wilmington, DE: Glazier, 1979.

Hackett, W. Chris. "The Soul and 'All Things': Contribution to a Postmodern Account of the Soul." In *The Resounding Soul: Reflections on the Metaphysics and Vivacity of the Human Person*, edited by Eric Austin Lee and Samuel Kimbriel, 307–29. Veritas. Eugene, OR: Cascade, 2015.

Hart, David Bentley. *The Beauty of the Infinite: The Aesthetics of Christian Truth*. Grand Rapids: Eerdmans, 2003.

———. *The Hidden and the Manifest: Essays in Theology and Metaphysics*. Grand Rapids: Eerdmans, 2017.

Hartmann, Herbert. "St. Thomas and Prudence." PhD diss., University of Toronto, 1979.

Hegel, Georg Wilhelm Friedrich. *Faith and Knowledge*. Translated by Walter Cerf and H. S. Harris. New York: State University of New York Press, 1988.

———. *The Logic of Hegel*. Translated by William Wallace. Oxford: Oxford University Press, 1904.

———. *The Natural Law*. Translated by T. M. Knox. Philadelphia: University of Pennsylvania Press, 1975.

———. *Phenomenology of Spirit*. Translated by A. V. Miller. Oxford: Oxford University Press, 1977.

Heidegger, Martin. "Art and Space." Translated by Charles H. Seibert. *Man and World* 6 (1973) 3–8.

———. *Basic Problems of Phenomenology*. Translated by Albert Hofstadter. Bloomington, IN: Indiana University Press, 1982.

———. *Basic Writings*. Edited by David Farrell Krell. San Francisco: Harper, 1993.

———. *Being and Time*. Translated by John Macquarrie and Edward Robinson. New York: Harper and Row, 1962.

———. *Discourse on Thinking*. Translated by J. M. Anderson and E. H. Freund. New York: Harper and Row, 1966.

———. *Early Greek Thinking*. Translated by David Farrell. Krell and Frank A. Capuzzi. New York: Harper and Row, 1975.

———. *The End of Philosophy*. Translated by Joan Stambaugh. New York: Harper and Row, 1973.

———. *The Essence of Reasons*. Translated by Terrence Malick. Evanston, IL: Northwestern University Press, 1969.

———. *The Essence of Truth*. Translated by Ted Sadler. New York: Continuum, 2002.

———. *The Fundamental Concepts of Metaphysics: World, Finitude, Solitude*. Translated by William McNeill and Nicholas Walker. Bloomington, IN: Indiana University Press, 1995.

———. *Hegel's Concept of Experience*. Translated by J. Glenn Gray and Fred D. Wieck. New York: Harper and Row, 1970.

———. *Hegel's Phenomenology of Spirit*. Translated by Parvis Emad and Kenneth Maly. Bloomington, IN: Indiana University Press, 1988.

———. *Heraclitus Seminar, 1966–1967*. With Eugen Fink. Translated by Charles H. Seibert. Tuscaloosa, AL: University of Alabama Press, 1979.

———. *History of the Concept of Time: Prologomena*. Translated by Theodore Kisiel. Bloomington, IN: Indiana University Press, 1985.

———. *Identity and Difference*. Translated by Joan Stambaugh. New York: Harper and Row, 1969.

———. *An Introduction to Metaphysics*. Translated by Ralph Manheim. New York: Doubleday, 1961.

———. *Kant and the Problem of Metaphysics*. Translated by James S. Churchill. Bloomington, IN: Indiana University Press, 1963.

———. *The Metaphysical Foundations of Logic*. Translated by Michael R. Heim. Bloomington, IN: Indiana University Press, 1984.

———. *Nietzsche*. Translated by Joan Stambaugh, David Farrell Krell and Frank Capuzzi. San Francisco: Harper and Row,1991.

———. *On the Way to Language*. Translated by Peter Donald Hertz and Joan Stambaugh. New York: Harper and Row, 1971.

———. *On Time and Being*. Translated by Joan Stambaugh. New York: Harper and Row, 1972.

———. "Only a God can Save us Now": An interview with Martin Heidegger." Translated by David Schlender. *Graduate Faculty Philosophy Journal* 6 (1977): 5–27.

———. *Parmenides*. Translated by Andre Schuwer and Richard Rojcewicz. Bloomington, IN: Indiana University Press, 1992.

———. *The Phenomenology of Religious Life*. Translated by Matthias Fritsch and Jennifer Anna Gosetti-Ferenci. Bloomington, IN: Indiana University Press, 2010.

———. *The Piety of Thinking*. Translated by J. G. Hart and J. C. Maraldo. Bloomington, IN: Indiana University Press, 1976.

———. *Plato's Doctrine of Truth in Philosophy in the Twentieth Century*. Edited by Henry D. Aiken and William Barrett. New York: Random House, 1962.

———. *Plato's Sophist*. Translated by Andre Schuwer and Richard Rojcewicz. Bloomington, IN: Indiana University Press, 1997.

———. *Poetry, Language, Thought*. Translated by Albert Hofstadter. New York: Harper and Row, 1971.

———. *Ponderings II-VI: The Black Notebooks 1931–1938*. Translated by Richard Rojcewicz. Bloomington, IN: Indiana University Press, 2016.

———. *The Principle of Reason*. Translated by Reginald Lilly. Bloomington, IN: Indiana University Press, 1991.

———. *Phenomenological Interpretations of Aristotle*. Translated by Richard Rojcewicz. Bloomington, IN: Indiana University Press, 2001.

———. *The Question Concerning Technology and Other Essays*. Translated by William Lovitt. New York: Harper and Row, 1977.

———. *The Question of Being*. Translated by William Kluback and Jean. T. Wilde. New Haven, CT: Yale University Press, 1958.

———. *Schelling's Treatise on the Essence of Human Reason*. Translated by Joan Stambaugh. Athens, OH: Ohio University Press, 1985.

———. *What Is a Thing?* Translated by W. B. Barton, Jr. and Vera Deutsch. Chicago: Henry Regnery, 1967.

———. *What Is Called Thinking?* Translated by J. Glenn Gray and Fred D. Wieck. New York: Harper and Row, 1968.

———. *What Is Philosophy?* Translated by William Kluback and Jean. T. Wilde. New Haven, CT: Yale University Press, 1958.

Heraclitus. *Heraclitus: The Cosmic Fragments*. Translated by G. S. Kirk. Cambridge: Cambridge University Press, 1954.

Hopkins, Gerard Manley. *The Gospel in Gerard Manley Hopkins*. Edited by Margaret R. Ellsberg. Walden, NY: Plough, 2017.

Huey, F. B. "Obedience—A Neglected Doctrine." *Christianity Today* 12.8, 1968, 6–11.

Hugo, Victor. "La Conscience." *La Légende des Siècles*. Translated by Dublin University Magazine. https://www.gutenberg.org/files/8775/8775-h/8775-h.htm

Huizinga, Johan. *The Waning of the Middle Ages*. Mineola, NY: Dover, 2013.

Hume, David. *An Enquiry Concerning Human Understanding*. London: J. B. Debbington, 1861.

———. *An Enquiry Concerning the Principles of Morals*. Chicago: Open Court, 1907.

Husserl, Edmund. *Cartesian Meditations: An Introduction to Phenomenology*. Translated by Dorian Cairns. Hague: Nijhoff, 1977.

———. *The Idea of Phenomenology*. Translated by William P. Alston and George Nakhnikian. The Hague: Nijhoff, 1974.

Hütter, Reinhard. *Aquinas on Transubstantiation: The Real Presence of Christ in the Eucharist*. Washington, DC: Catholic University Press, 2019.

Huysmans, Joris Karl. *The Oblate*. Translated by Edward Perceval. London: Kegan Paul, 1918.

Jacobse, Johannes. "Eugene Ionesco and the Elder on Mount Athos." (05/31/2011). https://www.aoiusa.org/eugene-ionesco-and-the-elder-on-mount-athos/.

Jaeger, Werner. *Theology of the Early Greek Philosophers*. New York: Oxford University Press, 1947.

Jaspers, Karl. *The Perennial Scope of Philosophy*. Translated by Ralph Manheim. New York: Philosophical Library, 1949.

———. *Philosophical Faith and Revelation*. Translated by E. B. Ashton. New York: Harper and Row, 1967.

———. *Way to Wisdom: An Introduction to Philosophy*. Translated by Ralph Manheim. New Haven CT: Yale University Press, 1954.

———. "The Tragic: Awareness, Characteristics, Interpretations." In *Tragedy: Modern Essays in Criticism*, edited by Laurence Michel and Richard B. Sewall, 6–26. Englewood Cliffs, NJ: Prentice-Hall, 1963.

Jaffa, Harry Victor. *Thomism and Aristotelianism*. Chicago: University of Chicago Press, 1952.

St. Jerome. *The Faith of the Early Fathers Volume Two*. Translated by William A. Jurgens. Collegeville, MN: Liturgical, 1979.

St. John of the Cross. *The Collected Works of St. John of the Cross*. Translated by Kieran Kavanaugh and Otilio. Rodriguez. Washington, DC: ICS, 1991.

———. *The Collected Works of St. John of the Cross, Volume 2*. Translated by David Lewis. New York: Cosimo, 2007.

———. *A Spiritual Canticle of the Soul and the Bride Christ*. Translated by David Lewis. Grand Rapids: Christian Classics Ethereal Library, 2000.

Jonas, Hans. "The Nobility of Sight." *Philosophy and Phenomenological Research* 14.4 (1954) 507–19.

Journet, Cardinal, Charles. *Aquinas*. Edited by Anthony Kenny. New York: Doubleday, 1969.

———. *The Meaning of Grace*. Glen Rock, NJ: Paulist, 1962.

Julian of Norwich. *Revelations of Divine Love: Short Text and Long Text.* Translated by Elizabeth Spearing. London: Penguin, 1988.

Kant, Immanuel. *Critique of Pure Reason.* New York: Hackett, 1996.

———. *The Philosophy of Law: An Exposition of the Fundamental Principles of Jurisprudence as the Science of Right.* Translated by William Hastie. Edinburgh: T. & T. Clark, 1887.

Kazantzakis, Nikos. *God's Pauper: Saint Francis of Assisi.* Translated by Peter A. Bien. Oxford: Cassirer, 1975.

———. *Journeying: Travels in Italy, Egypt, Sinai, Jerusalem and Cyprus.* Translated by Themi Vasils and Theodora Vasils. Boston: Little Brown, 1975.

Kenner, Hugh. *Paradox in Chesterton.* New York: Sheed and Ward, 1947.

Kenny, Anthony. *The Five Ways. St. Thomas Aquinas' Proofs of God's Existence.* Notre Dame, IN: University of Notre Dame Press, 1980.

Kierkegaard, Søren. *The Concept of Anxiety: A Simple Psychologically Orienting Deliberation on the Dogmatic Issue of Hereditary Sin.* Translated by Reidar Thomte. Princeton, NJ: Princeton University Press, 1980.

———. *Concluding Unscientific Postscript.* Translated by Alastair Hannay. Cambridge: Cambridge University Press, 2009.

———. *The Essential Kierkegaard.* Edited by Howard V. Hong and Edna. H. Hong. Princeton, NJ: Princeton University Press, 2000.

———. *Fear and Trembling and Sickness unto Death.* Translated by Walter Lowrie. Princeton, NJ: Princeton University Press, 1954.

———. *The Moment and Late Writings.* Translated by Howard V. Hong and Edna H. Hong. Princeton, NJ: Princeton University Press, 1998.

———. *The Parables of Kierkegaard.* Edited by Thomas Oden. Princeton, NJ: Princeton University Press, 1989.

———. *Philosophical Fragments, Johannes Climacus.* Translated by Howard V. Hong and Edna H. Hong. Princeton, NJ: Princeton University Press, 1985.

———. *The Sickness unto Death: A Christian Psychological Exposition for Upbuilding and Awakening.* Translated by Howard V. Hong and Edna H. Hong. Princeton, NJ: Princeton University Press, 1983.

———. *The Soul of Kierkegaard: Selections from His Journals.* Edited by Alexander Dru. Mineola, NY: Dover, 2003.

———. *Works of Love.* Translated by Howard V. Hong and Edna H. Hong. New York: Harper, 2009.

Kirk, G. S., J. E. Raven, and M. Schofield, eds. *The Presocratic Philosophers.* New York: Cambridge University Press, 1983.

Kreeft, Peter. *Everything You Wanted to Know about Heaven but Never Dreamed of Asking.* San Francisco: Ignatius, 1990.

Kretzmann, Norman, and Eleanore Stump, eds. *The Cambridge Companion to Aquinas.* New York: Cambridge University Press, 1993.

Leahy, David G. *Faith and Philosophy.* New York: Ashgate, 2003.

———. *Novitas Mundi.* New York: New York University Press, 1980.

Leigh, David. "Forgiveness, Pity, and Ultimacy in Ancient Greek Culture." *Ultimate Reality and Meaning* 27.2 (2004) 154–61.

Lepicier, Alexis Henri Marie, *The Unseen World: An Exposition of Catholic Theology in Reference to Modern Spiritism.* New York: Benzinger Brothers, 1929.

Leslie, Shane. *The End of a Chapter.* New York: Scribner, 1916.

Levinas, Emmanuel. *Emmanuel Levinas: Basic Philosophical Writings*. Edited by Adriaan T. Peperzak, Simon Critchley, and Robert Bernasconi. Bloomington, IN: Indiana University Press, 1996.

———. *Is It Righteous to Be? Interviews with Emmanuel Levinas*. Edited by Jill Robins. Stanford, CA: Stanford University Press, 2001.

———. *The Levinas Reader*. Edited by Sean Hand. Oxford: Blackwell, 1989.

———. *Totality and Infinity: An Essay on Exteriority*. Translated by Alphonso Lingis. Dordrecht: Kluwer, 1991.

Lewis, C. S. *The Abolition of Man*. New York: Harper, 2001.

———. *The Chronicles of Narnia*. New York: Harper, 2004.

———. *C. S. Lewis Signature Classics: Mere Christianity, The Screwtape Letters, A Grief Observed, The Problem of Pain, Miracles, and The Great Divorce*. New York: Harper, 2001.

———. *The Four Loves*. New York: Harper, 2001.

———. *A Grief Observed*. New York: Harper, 2001.

———. *Till We Have Faces: A Myth Retold*. New York: Harper, 1984.

———. *The Weight of Glory and Other Addresses*. New York: Harper, 2001.

Lonergan, Bernard. *Collected Works of Bernard Lonergan. Grace and Freedom: Operative Grace in the Thought of St. Thomas Aquinas*. Edited by Frederick E. Crowe and Robert M. Doran. Toronto: University of Toronto Press, 2000.

———. *Verbum: Word and Idea in Aquinas*. Notre Dame, IN: University of Notre Dame Press, 1967.

Lönnrot, Elias. "Kalevala." In *Poems for the Millennium, Volume Three*, edited by Jerome Rothenberg and Jeffrey C. Robinson, 451–59. Berkeley: University of California Press, 2009.

Lovejoy, Arthur. *The Great Chain of Being: A Study of the History of an Idea*. Cambridge: Harvard University Press, 1976.

Lowry, Rich. "The Humiliating Art of the Woke Apology." *National Review* (02/08/2021). https://www.nationalreview.com/2021/02/the-humiliating-art-of-the-woke-apology/.

Lynch, John W. *A Woman Wrapped in Silence*. New York: Paulist, 1968.

Marcel, Gabriel. *Creative Fidelity*. Translated by Robert Rosthal. New York: Fordham University Press, 2002.

Marion, Jean Luc. *God without Being*. Chicago: University of Chicago Press, 1995.

Maritain, Jacques. *Approaches to God*. Translated by Peter O'Reilly. New York: Harper, 1954.

———. *Art and Scholasticism and the Frontiers of Poetry*. Translated by Joseph W. Evans. South Bend, IN: University of Notre Dame Press, 1974.

———. *Degrees of Knowledge*. Translated by Gerald Phelan. New York: Scribner, 1959.

———. *Existence and the Existent*. Translated by Gerald Phelan. New York: Vintage, 1996.

———. *Freedom and the Modern World*. Translated by Richard O'Sullivan. London: Sheed and Ward, 1935.

———. *God and the Permission of Evil*. Translated by Joseph W. Evans. Milwaukee: Bruce, 1966.

———. *The Grace and Humanity of Jesus Christ*. Translated by Joseph W. Evans. New York: Herder and Herder, 1969.

———. *Moral Philosophy: An Historical Survey of the Great Systems.* New York: Scribner, 1964.

———. *The Peasant of the Garonne: An Old Layman Questions Himself about the Present Time.* Translated by Michael Cuddihy and Elizabeth Hughes. Eugene, OR: Wipf and Stock, 2013.

———. *The Preface to Metaphysics: Seven Lectures on Being.* London: Sheed and Ward, 1945.

———. *The Range of Reason.* Translated by Geoffrey Bles. New York: Scribner, 1952.

———. *Ransoming the Time.* New York: Scribner, 1941.

———. *St. Thomas and the Problem of Evil.* Milwaukee: Marquette University Press, 2009.

Mauriac, Francois. *The Inner Presence: Recollection of My Spiritual Life.* Indianapolis: Bobbs-Merrill, 1968.

McInerny, Ralph Matthew. *Aquinas and Analogy.* Washington, DC: Catholic University Press, 1996.

Meister Eckhart. *Breakthrough: Meister Eckhart's Creation Spirituality in New Translation.* Translated by Matthew Fox. Garden City, NY: Image, 1980.

Merleau-Ponty, Maurice. *The Phenomenology of Perception.* Translated by Donald A. Landes. London: Routledge: 2013.

———. *The Primacy of Perception: And Other Essays on Phenomenological Psychology, the Philosophy of Art, History, and Politics.* Edited by James M. Edie. Evanston, IL: Northwestern University Press, 1964.

Mill, John Stuart. *Utilitarianism.* London: Longmans, 1879.

Milton, John. *Paradise Lost.* Edited by Roy C. Flannagan. New York: Dover, 2005.

Moltmann, Jürgen. *Theology of Play.* Translated by Reinhard Ulrich. New York: Harper, 1972.

Moss, David. "Friendship: St. Anselm, *Theoria* and the Convolution of Sense." In *Radical Orthodoxy*, edited by John Milbank, Catherine Pickstock, et al., ?–?. London: Routledge, 1998.

St. Mother Teresa of Calcutta. "Whatever You Did unto One of the Least, You Did unto Me." An address at the National Prayer Breakfast, Sponsored by the U.S. Senate and House of Representatives, February 1994.

Neruda, Pablo. *On the Blue Shore of Silence.* Translated by Alastair Reid. New York: Harper, 2003.

Newman, John. Henry. *The Apologia Pro Vita Sua.* New York: Norton, 1968.

———. *An Essay in Aid of a Grammar of Assent.* New York: Doubleday, 1955.

———. *The Idea of a University.* London: Longmans, 1893.

———. *Meditations and Devotions.* London: Longmans, 1933.

———. *Parochial and Plain Sermons, Volume VIII.* London: Longmans, 1908.

Newsome Martin, Jennifer. "The Christian Future of Metaphysics: The Carnal Turn in Catholic Theology." Unpublished lecture given at The Future of Christian Metaphysics Conference, Maynooth, April 2021.

———. *Hans Urs von Balthasar and the Critical Appropriation of Russian Religious Thought.* Notre Dame, IN: University of Notre Dame Press, 2015.

———. "Memory Matters: *Ressourcement* Theology's Debt to Henri Bergson." *International Journal of Systematic Theology* 23.2 (2021) 177–97.

Nichols, Aidan. *The Word Has Been Abroad: A Guide through Balthasar's Aesthetics.* Edinburgh: T. & T. Clark, 1998.

Nietzsche, Friedrich. *The Antichrist*. Translated by H. L. Mencken. New York: Knopf, 1918.

———. *Aphorisms on Love and Hate*. Translated by Marion Faber and Stephen Lehmann. New York: Penguin, 2015.

———. *Basic Writings*. Translated by Walter Kaufmann. New York: Modern Library, 2000.

———. *Beyond Good and Evil: Prelude to a Philosophy of the Future*. Translated by Helen Zimmern. New York: Macmillan, 1907.

———. *The Birth of Tragedy: Or Hellenism and Pessimism*. Translated by William A. Haussmann. Edinburgh: Foulis, 1910.

———. *The Essential Nietzsche: Beyond Good and Evil and The Genealogy of Morals*. New York: Quarto, 2017.

———. *Human, All Too Human*. Translated by R. J. Hollingdale. Cambridge: Cambridge University Press, 1986.

———. *Philosophy in the Tragic Age of the Greeks*. Translated by Marianne Cowan. Washington, DC: Regnery, 1998.

———. *Thus Spoke Zarathustra*. Translated by Walter Kaufmann. New York: Random House, 1995.

———. *Twilight of the Idols and the Anti-Christ: or How to Philosophize with a Hammer*. Translated by Reginald John Hollingdale. New York: Penguin, 1990.

———. *The Will to Power*. Translated by Walter Kaufmann and Reginald John Hollingdale. New York: Random House, 1967.

Nussbaum, Martha. *Anger and Forgiveness: Resentment, Generosity, Justice*. Oxford: Oxford University Press, 2016.

Nussbaum, Martha, and Richard Rorty, eds. *Essays on Aristotle's De Anima*. Oxford: Clarendon, 1992.

O'Connor, Flannery. *The Habit of Being*. New York: Farrar, Straus and Giroux, 1988.

———. *Mystery and Manners: Occasional Prose*. New York: Farrar, Straus and Giroux, 1969.

———. *A Prayer Journal*. Edited by W. A. Sessions. New York: Farrar, Straus and Giroux, 2013.

O'Regan, Cyril. *The Anatomy of Misremembering*. New York: Herder, 2014.

———. *Theology and the Spaces Apocalyptic*. Milwaukee: Marquette University Press, 2009.

O'Rourke, Fran. *Pseudo-Dionysius and the Metaphysics of Aquinas*. South Bend, IN: University of Notre Dame Press, 2005.

Ortega y Gasset, Jose. *Meditations on Quixote*. Translated by Evelyn Rugg and Diego Marin. New York, Norton, 1963.

Owens, Joseph. "Aquinas on Infinite Regress." *Mind* 71 (1962) 244–46.

———. *The Doctrine of Being in the Aristotelian Metaphysics*. Toronto: Pontifical Institute of Mediaeval Studies, 1951.

———. "A Note on Aristotle, De Anima 3.4, 429b9." *Phoenix* 30.2 (1976) 107–18.

———. *St. Thomas Aquinas on the Existence of God*. Albany, NY: State University of New York Press, 1980.

———. *St. Thomas and the Future of Metaphysics*. Milwaukee: Marquette University Press, 1957.

Parmenides. *Parmenides of Elea: A Text and Translation*. Edited by David Gallop. Toronto: University of Toronto Press, 1984.

Pascal, Blaise. *Pensees*. Translated by William Finlayson Trotter. New York: Dutton, 1958.

———. *The Provincial Letters; Pensees; Scientific Treatises—Volume 33 of the Great Books of the Western World Series*. Translated by William Finlayson Trotter et al. London: Encyclopaedia Britannica, 1952.

St. Patrick. *The Life and Prayers of Saint Patrick*. Boston: Wyatt North, 2013.

Pearce, Joseph. *Wisdom and Innocence: A Life of G. K. Chesterton*. San Francisco: Ignatius, 1997.

Pegis, Anton Charles. "Aquinas and the Natural Law: Some Notes toward a Reappraisal." Unpublished Lecture at Wellesley College, 1965.

———. *At the Origins of the Thomistic Notion of Man*. New York: Macmillan, 1963.

———. *Introduction to St. Thomas Aquinas*. New York: Modern Library, 1948.

———. "Man as Nature and Spirit." *Doctor Communis* 4 (1951) 52–63.

———. "Necessity and Liberty: An Historical Note on St. Thomas Aquinas." *The New Scholasticism* 15 (1941) 18–45.

———. *The Problem of the Soul in the 13th Century*. Toronto: Pontifical Institute of Mediaeval Studies, 1934.

———. "Some Reflections on Summa Contra Gentiles II, 56." *An Etienne Gilson Tribute*, edited by C. O'Neil, Milwaukee: Marquette University Press, 1959.

———. "St. Anselm and the Argument in the Proslogion." *Mediaeval Studies* 28 (1966) 228–67.

———. *St. Thomas and the Greeks*. Milwaukee: Marquette University Press, 1939.

———. "St. Thomas and the Meaning of Human Existence." In *Calgary Aquinas Studies*, edited by A. Parel, 49–64. Toronto: Pontifical Institute of Mediaeval Studies, 1978.

———. "St. Thomas and the Origin of Creation." In *Philosophy and the Modern Mind*, edited by F. X. Canfield, 49–65. Detroit: Sacred Heart Seminary 1961.

———. *St. Thomas and Philosophy*. Milwaukee, MI: Marquette University Press, 1964.

———. "St. Thomas and the Unity of Man." In *Progress in Philosophy*, edited by J. McWilliams, 153–73. Milwaukee: Marquette University Press, 1955.

Péguy, Charles. *Basic Verities*. Translated by Ann Green and Julian Green. New York: Pantheon, 1943.

———. *God Speaks: Religious Poetry*. Translated by Julian Green. New York: Pantheon, 1945.

———. *Man and Saints*. Translated by Julian Green. New York: Pantheon, 1944.

———. *The Mystery of the Holy Innocents and Other Poems*. Translated by Pansy Pakenham. Eugene, OR: Wipf and Stock, 2018.

———. *Notre Patrie*. Paris: Payen, 1905.

———. *The Portal of the Mystery of Hope*. Translated by David L. Schindler, Jr. Grand Rapids: Eerdmans, 1996.

———. *Temporal and Eternal*. Translated by Alexandre Dru. Indianapolis: Liberty Fund, 2001.

Peters, Francis. E. *Greek Philosophical Terms, A Historical Lexicon*. New York: New York University Press, 1967.

Pieper, Josef. *Death and Immortality*. Translated by Richard Winston and Clara Winston. South Bend, IN: St. Augustine, 2000.

———. *The Four Cardinal Virtues: Human Agency, Intellectual Traditions, and Responsible Knowledge*. South Bend, IN: University of Notre Dame Press, 1990.

———. *Happiness and Contemplation*. South Bend, IN: St. Augustine, 1998.

————. *Leisure: The Basis of Culture.* Translated by Alexander Dru. San Francisco: Ignatius, 2009.

Plato. *The Collected Dialogues of Plato Including the Letters.* Edited by Edith Hamilton and Huntington Cairns. New York: Pantheon, 1961.

————. *Plato: Complete Works.* Edited by John M. Cooper. Indianapolis: Hackett, 1997.

Pope Benedict XVI. *Deus Caritas Est.* Vatican City: Libreria Editrice Vaticana, 2005.

————. "General Audience: Wednesday 31 August 2011." Vatican City: Libreria Editrice Vaticana, 2011.

————. "General Audience: Wednesday 28 December 2011." Vatican City: Libreria Editrice Vaticana, 2011.

————. *Jesus of Nazareth, Part Two: Holy Week.* San Francisco: Ignatius, 2010.

————. "Meeting with Artists." Vatican City: Libreria Editrice Vaticana, 2009.

————. "Verbum Domini." Vatican City: Libreria Editrice Vaticana, 2009.

Pope Francis. "Gaudete et Exsultate." Vatican City: Libreria Editrice Vaticana, 2018.

————. "Incontro del Santo Padre Francesco con la Delegazione del Forum delle Associazioni Familiari." Vatican City: Libreria Editrice Vaticana, 2018.

————. "Laudato Si." Vatican City: Libreria Editrice Vaticana, 2015.

Pope Saint John Paul II. *Apostolic Letter Salvifici Doloris.* Vatican City: Libreria Editrice Vaticana, 1984.

————. *Encyclical Letter Fides et Ratio.* Vatican City: Libreria Editrice Vaticana, 1998.

————. "General Audience: Wednesday 21 July 1999." Vatican City: Libreria Editrice Vaticana, 1999.

Possenti, Vittorio. *Nihilism and Metaphysics: The Third Voyage.* Translated by Daniel B. Gallagher. Albany, NY: State University of New York Press, 2014.

Pseudo-Dionysius. *Pseudo-Dionysius: The Complete Works.* Translated by Paul Rorem. Glen Rock, NJ: Paulist, 1987.

Rahner, Hugo. *Man at Play.* New York: Herder, 1967.

Rand, Ayn. *Atlas Shrugged.* Translated by Leonard Peikoff. New York: Penguin, 2005.

Ratzinger, Joseph. *On Conscience.* San Francisco: Ignatius, 2007.

Ratzinger, Joseph, Heinz Schurmann, and Hans Urs von Balthasar. *Principles of Christian Morality.* San Francisco: Ignatius, 1986.

Renard, Henri. *The Philosophy of God.* Milwaukee: Bruce, 1951.

Rieff, Philip. *The Triumph of the Therapeutic: Uses of Faith after Freud.* Chicago: University of Chicago Press, 1987.

Rilke, Rainier Maria. *The Book of Hours: Prayers to a Lowly God.* Translated by Annemarie Kidder. Evanston, IL: Northwestern University Press, 2001.

————. *The Complete French Poems.* Translated by A. Poulin, Jr. Saint Paul, MN: Graywolf, 2002.

————. *The Dark Interval: Letters on Loss, Grief, and Transformation.* Translated by Ulrich Baer. New York: Modern Library, 2018.

————. *The Duino Elegies.* Translated by Stephen Cohn. Evanston, IL: Northwestern University Press, 1989.

————. *Sonnets to Orpheus.* Translated by David Young. Hanover: University Press of New England, 1987.

Robichaud, Denis. *Plato's Persona: Marsilio Ficino, Renaissance Humanism, and Platonic Traditions.* Philadelphia: University of Pennsylvania Press, 2018.

Rosen, Stanley. *Plato's Symposium.* New Haven, CT: Yale University Press, 1997.

Rousselot, Pierre. *The Intellectualism of St. Thomas*. Translated by James E. O'Mahoney New York: Sheed and Ward, 1935.

Russell, Bertrand. *Ethical Theory 1: The Question of Objectivity*. Edited by James Rachels. Oxford: Oxford University Press, 1998.

Santayana, George. *Egotism in German Philosophy*. London: Dent, 1916.

———. *The Essential Santayana, Selected Writings*. Edited by Martin A. Coleman. Bloomington, IN: Indiana University Press, 2009.

———. *The Idea of Christ in the Gospels: Or God in Man, A Critical Essay*. New York: Scribner, 1946.

———. *The Life of Reason, Volume 2: Reason in Society*. Mineola, NY: Dover, 1983.

———. *Platonism and the Spiritual Life*. Gloucester, MA: Peter Smith, 1971.

———. *Realms of Being*. New York: Scribner, 1942.

———. *Soliloquies in England and Later Soliloquies*. Ann Arbor, MI: University of Michigan, 1967.

Sartre, Jean Paul. *Being and Nothingness*. Translated by Hazel E. Barnes. New York: Washington Square, 1993.

———. *Critique of Dialectical Reason Volume 1: Theory of Practical Ensembles*. Translated by Alan Sheridan-Smith. London: Verso, 2004.

———. *Nausea*. Translated by Lloyd Alexander. New York: New Directions, 2007.

———. *No Exit and Three Other Plays*. Translated by Stuart Gilbert. New York: Vintage, 1989.

———. *Transcendence of the Ego*. Translated by Forrest Williams and Robert Kirkpatrick. New York: Noonday, 1962.

Savorana, Alberto. *The Life of Luigi Giussani*. Translated by Mariangela C. Sullivan and Christopher Bacich. Montreal & Kingston: McGill-Queen's University Press, 2018.

Schindler, D. C. "Love and Beauty, the 'Forgotten Transcendental,' in Thomas Aquinas." *Communio* 44.2 (2017). https://www.communio-icr.com/articles/view/love-and-beauty-the-forgotten-transcendental-in-thomas-aquinas

———. *Plato's Critique of Impure Reason: On Goodness and Truth in the Republic*. Washington, DC: The Catholic University of America Press, 2008.

Schindler, David L. "The Embodied Person as Gift and the Cultural Task in America: Status Quaestionis." *Communio* 35 (2008) 397–431.

———. *Ordering Love: Liberal Societies and the Memory of God*. Grand Rapids: Eerdmans, 2011.

Schlick, Moritz. "On the Meaning of Life." In *Life and Meaning*, edited by Oswald Hanfling, 60–73. Oxford: The Open University, 1987.

———. *Philosophical Papers, Volume II*. Edited by Henk. L. Mulder et al. Dordrecht: Reidel, 1979.

Searle, John. *Intentionality: An Essay in the Philosophy of Mind*. Cambridge: Cambridge University Press, 1983.

Sertillanges, Antonin Gilbert. *Les Sources de Lay Croyance de Dieu*. Paris: Perrin, 1920.

Shakespeare, William. *The Complete Works of William Shakespeare*. Ware, UK: Wordsworth, 1996.

Shestov, Lev. *All Things Are Possible (Apotheosis of Groundlessness)*. Translated by Samuel Solomonovitch Kotelianksy. New York: McBride, 1920.

———. *Athens and Jerusalem*. Translated by Bernard Martin. Athens, OH: Ohio University Press, 1966.

————. *Dostoevsky, Tolstoy, and Nietzsche*. Translated by Spencer Roberts. Athens, OH: Ohio University Press, 1969.

————. *Kierkegaard and the Existential Philosophy*. Translated by Elinor Hewitt. Athens, OH: Ohio University Press, 1969.

————. *In Job's Balances: On the Sources of the Eternal Truth*. Translated by Camilla Coventry and C. A. Macartney. London: Dent, 1932.

Simon, Julian. *The Ultimate Resource 2*. Princeton, NJ: Princeton University Press, 1996.

Simpson, Christopher Ben. "An Interview with William Desmond." *Radical Orthodoxy: Theology, Philosophy, Politics* 1 (2012) 357–73.

Solovyov, Vladimir. *Divine Sophia: The Wisdom Writings of Vladimir Solovyov*. Translated by Boris Jakim, Judith Deutsch Kornblatt and Laury Magnus. Ithaca, NY: Cornell University Press, 2009.

————. *The Meaning of Love*. Translated by Thomas R. Beyer. Hudson, NY: Lindisfarne, 1985.

Solzhenitsyn, Aleksandr. *The Gulag Archipelago: An Experiment in Literary Investigation*. Translated by Thomas P. Whitney. New York: Harper Collins, 1974.

Sophocles. *The Complete Greek Tragedies, Volume 2: Sophocles*. Edited by David Grene and Richmond Lattimore. Chicago: University of Chicago Press, 1992.

————. *The Three Theban Plays*. Translated by Robert Fagles. New York: Penguin, 1984.

St. Edith Stein. *Essays on Woman*. Translated by Freda Mary Oben. Washington, DC: ICS, 1996.

————. *Essential Writings*. Edited by John Sullivan. Maryknoll, NY: Orbis, 2002.

————. *The Science of the Cross*. Translated by Josephine Koeppel. Washington, DC: ICS, 2002.

Steptoe, Andrew. *The Mozart-Da Ponte Operas: The Cultural and Musical Background to Le Nozze di Figaro, Don Giovanni, and Così fan Tutte*. Oxford: Oxford University Press, 1988.

Sterba, James. "Retributive Justice." *Political Theory* 5.3 (1977) 349–62.

Strauss, Leo. *The City and Man*. Chicago: University of Chicago Press, 1978.

————. "Introduction to Political Philosophy: Aristotle. Sessions 10–16." Edited by Catherine Zuckert. Chicago: Estate of Leo Strauss, 1973.

————. *On Tyranny: Corrected and Expanded Edition, Including the Strauss-Kojève Correspondence*. Edited by Victor Gourevitch and Michael S. Roth. Chicago: University of Chicago Press, 2013.

Taylor, Alfred Edward. *The Faith of a Moralist Series I and II*. London: Macmillan, 1931.

————. *Plato: The Man and His Works*. London: Methuen, 1927.

————. *The "Parmenides" of Plato*. New York: Oxford University Press, 1934.

————. *Plato*. New York: New York University Press, 1926.

————. *The Problem of Conduct: A Study in the Phenomenology of Ethics*. Toronto: University of Toronto Press, 1901.

Tennyson, Alfred. *In Memoriam*. London: Macmillan, 1906.

St. Teresa of Avila. *The Collected Works of St. Teresa of Avila, Volume 1*. Translated by Kieran Kavanaugh and Otilio Rodriguez. Washington, DC: ICS, 1976.

————. *The Collected Works of St. Teresa of Avila, Volume 2*. Translated by Kieran Kavanaugh and Otilio Rodriguez. Washington, DC: ICS 1980.

————. *The Life of St. Teresa of Avila*. Translated by David Lewis. New York: Cosimo, 2006.

Tertullian. "The Apocalypse of Saint Peter." In *Ante-Nicene Fathers, Volume 9*, translated by A. Rutherfurd and edited by A. Menzies. Buffalo, NY: Christian Literature, 1896.

———. "Apology." In *Ante-Nicene Fathers, Volume 3*, edited by A. Cleveland Coxe, Alexander Roberts, and James Donaldson. Buffalo, NY: Christian Literature, 1885.

———. *Tertullian's Treatise on the Incarnation De Carne Christi*. Edited by Ernest Evans. London: SPCK, 1956.

Te Velde, Rudi. *Aquinas on God: The 'Divine Science' of the Summa Theologiae*. Aldershot, UK: Ashgate, 2006.

St. Thomas Aquinas. *On Being and Essence (De Ente et Essentia)*. Translated by Armand Maurer. Toronto: Pontifical Institute of Mediaeval Studies, 1949.

———. *Commentary on Aristotle's Politics*. Translated by Richard J. Regan. Indianapolis: Hackett, 2007.

———. *Commentary on the De Anima*. Translated by Kenelm Foster and Silvester Humphries. New Haven, CT: Yale University Press, 1951.

———. *Commentary on the Gospel of St. John*. Translated by James A. Weisheipl and Fabian R. Larcher. Albany, NY: Magi, 1998.

———. *Commentary on the Metaphysics*. Translated by John P. Rowen. South Bend, IN: Dumb Ox, 1995.

———. *Commentary on the Sentences*. Translated by Beth Mortensen. Steubenville, OH: Emmaus, 2017

———. *In Librum Beati Dionysii de Divinis Nominibus Expositio*. Edited by C. Pera and C. Mazzantini. Turin: Marietti, 1950.

———. *Meditations for Lent*. Translated by Rev. Philip Hughes. London: Sheed and Ward, 1937.

———. *Opera Omnia. Leonine Edition, Volume 3: Commentaria in Libros Aristoteles de Caelo et Mundo, de Generatione et Corruptione*. Rome: Ex Typographia Polyglotta, 1886.

———. *Quaestiones Disputatae de Potentia*. Translated by the English Dominican Fathers. Westminster, UK: Newman, 1952.

———. *Scriptum Super Libros Sententiarum*. Paris: Lethielleux, 1929.

———. *De Spiritualibus Creaturis*. Edited by L. W. Keeler. Rome: Gregoriana University Press, 1938.

———. *A Summa of the Summa*. Edited by Peter Kreeft. San Francisco: Ignatius, 1990.

———. *Summa Theologiae*. Edited by Thomas Gilby. New York: Cambridge University Press, 1967.

———. *Summa Theologiae: A Concise Edition*. Edited by Timothy McDermott. Notre Dame, IN: Ave Maria, 1989.

———. *Summa Contra Gentiles*. Translated by James F Anderson. South Bend, IN: University of Notre Dame Press, 1992.

———. *De Veritate*. Translated by Robert W. Mulligan. Chicago: Regnery, 1952.

Tolstoy, Leo. *Father Sergius*. Translated by Aylmer Maude and Louise Shanks Maude. Auckland: Floating, 2011

———. "The State Memorial and Natural Preserve: Museum-estate of Leo Tolstoy Yasnaya Polyana." No date. http://ypmuseum.ru/en/musey-detyam/-q-q/78-2011-08-21-19-31-00.html

Torrell, Jean-Pierre. "Collationes in Decem Preceptis." *Revue des Sciences Philosophiques et Théologiques* 69 (1985) 227–63.

Traherne, Thomas. *Centuries of Meditations*. Edited by Bertram Dobell. London: Dobell, 1908.

Tolkien, J. R. R. *The Letters of J. R. R. Tolkien*. Edited by Christopher Humphries. New York: Houghton Mifflin Harcourt, 2000.

Ulrich, Ferdinand. *Homo Abyssus: The Drama of the Question of Being*. Translated by D. C. Schindler. Washington, DC: Humanum, 2018.

Unamuno, Miguel. *Our Lord Don Quixote: The Life of Don Quixote and Sancho with Related Essays*. Translated by Anthony Kerrigan. Princeton, NJ: Princeton University Press, 1967.

———. *Tragic Sense of Life*. Translated by J. E. Crawford Flitch. Mineola, NY: Dover, 1952.

Undset, Sigrid. *Kristin Lavransdatter II: The Wife*. Translated by Tiina Nunnally. New York: Penguin, 1999.

Vattimo, Gianni, and Pier Aldo Rovatti, eds. *Weak Thought*. Albany, NY: State University of New York Press, 2012.

———. *Treatise on the Love of God*. Translated by Nelson R. Orringer. Champaign, IL: University of Illinois Press, 2011.

Vianney, St. John. *Little Catechism of the Cure of Ars*. Gastonia, NC: Tan, 1994.

Voegelin, Eric. *Autobiographical Reflections*. Edited by Ellis Sandoz. The Collected Works of Eric Voegelin, Volume 34. Baton Rouge, LA: Louisiana State University Press, 1989.

———. "Deformations of Faith." Lecture given at the seminar "Between Nothingness and Paradise: Faith." Center for Constructive Alternatives, Hillsdale College, MI, 1977.

———. "The Gospel and Culture." In *Jesus and Man's Hope*, edited by D. G. Miller and D. Hadidian, 59–101. Pittsburg: Pittsburg Theological Seminary Press, 1971.

———. *Hitler and the Germans*. Translated by Detlev Clemens and Brendan Purcell. The Collected Works of Eric Voegelin, Volume 31. Columbia: University of Missouri Press, 1999.

———. *Modernity without Restraint: The Political Religions; The New Science of Politics; and Science, Politics, and Gnosticism*. Edited by M. Henningsen. The Collected Works of Eric Voegelin, Volume 5. Columbia: University of Missouri Press, 1999.

———. *Order and History, Volume 1: Israel and Revelation*. Edited by M. P. Hogan. The Collected Works of Eric Voegelin, Volume 14. Columbia: University of Missouri Press, 2001.

———. *Order and History, Volume 2: The World of the Polis*. Edited by Athanasios Moulakis. The Collected Works of Eric Voegelin, Volume 15. Columbia: University of Missouri Press, 2000.

———. *Order and History, Volume 3: Plato and Aristotle*. Edited By Dante Germino. The Collected Works of Eric Voegelin, Volume 16. Columbia: University of Missouri Press, 1999.

———. *Order and History, Volume 4: The Ecumenic Age*. Baton Rouge, LA: Louisiana State University Press, 1974.

———. *Published Essays, 1953–1965*. Edited by Ellis Sandoz. The Collected Works of Eric Voegelin, Volume 11. Columbia: University of Missouri Press, 1990

———. *Published Essays, 1966–1985*. Edited by Ellis Sandoz. The Collected Works of Eric Voegelin, Volume 12. Baton Rouge, LA: Louisiana State University Press, 1990.

———. *Science, Politics, Gnosticism*. Chicago: Regnery, 1968.

———. *What Is History? And Other Late Unpublished Writings*. Edited by Thomas A. Hollweck and Paul Caringella. The Collected Works of Eric Voegelin, Volume 28. Columbia: University of Missouri Press, 1990.

Von Hildebrand, Dietrich. *Man, Woman and the Meaning of Love: God's Plan for Love, Marriage, Intimacy, and the Family*. Bedford, UK: Sophia Institute, 2002.

Von Speyr, Adrienne. *Confession*. San Francisco: Ignatius, 1985.

———. *The Cross: Word and Sacrament*. Translated by Graham Harrison. San Francisco: Ignatius, 2018.

Walsh, David. *After Ideology: Recovering the Spiritual Foundations of Freedom*. Washington, DC: Catholic University of America Press, 1995.

———. *Guarded by Mystery Meaning in a Postmodern Age*. Washington, DC: Catholic University of America Press, 1999.

———. *The Modern Philosophical Revolution: The Luminosity of Existence*. Cambridge: Cambridge University Press, 2008.

Watkin, Edward Ingram *The Catholic Centre*. London: Sheed and Ward, 1945.

Waugh, Evelyn. *Brideshead Revisited*. New York: Back Bay, 2008.

Webb, Eugene. *Eric Voegelin: The Philosopher of History*. Seattle: University of Washington Press, 1981.

Whitehead, Alfred North. *The Dialogues of Alfred North Whitehead*. Edited by Lucien Price. Boston: Godine, 2001.

Wilhelmsen, Frederick. *Christianity and Political Philosophy*. London: Routledge, 2017.

———. "The Natural Law, Religion and the Crisis of the Twentieth Century." *Modern Age* 10.2 (1966) 145–48.

Wilhelmsen, Frederick, and Willmoore Kendall. "Cicero and the Politics of the Public Orthodoxy." In *Christianity and Political Philosophy*, 25–59. London: Routledge, 2017.

———. *Citizen of Rome: Reflections from the Life of a Roman Catholic*. Peru, IL: Sherwood and Sugden, 1978.

Williams, William Carlos. *The Collected Poems of William Carlos Williams, Vol. 1: 1909–1939*. New York: New Directions, 1991.

Williams, Charles. *The Figure of Beatrice*. Berkeley: Apocryphile, 2005.

Wippel, John F. *The Metaphysical Thought of Thomas Aquinas: From Finite Being to Uncreated Being*. Washington, DC: Catholic University of America Press, 2000.

———. "Truth in Thomas Aquinas (Part I-II)." *Review of Metaphysics* 43 (1990) 295–326.

Wittgenstein, Ludwig. *Culture and Value*. Translated by Peter Winch. Chicago: University of Chicago Press, 1980.

———. *Lectures on Ethics*. Edited by Edoardo Zamuner, Ermelina Valentina Di Lascio and D. K. Levy. Chichester, UK: Wiley, 2014.

———. *Philosophical Grammar*. Translated by Anthony Kenny. Oxford: Blackwell, 1974.

Wood, Ralph C. "Dostoevsky on Evil as a Perversion of Personhood." In *Dostoevsky's Polyphonic Talent*, edited by Joe E. Barnhart, 1–24. Lanham, MD: University Press of America, 2005.

———. "Ivan Karamazov's Mistake." *First Things*, December 2002. https://www.firstthings.com/article/2002/12/ivan-karamazovs-mistake.

Wyers, Frances. *Miguel de Unamuno, the Contrary Self*. London: Tamesis, 1976.

Yeats, William Buttler. *The Collected Poems of W. B. Yeats.* Edited by Richard J. Finnernan. New York: Scribner, 1996.

Young, Sarah. *Dostoevsky's The Idiot and the Ethical Foundations of Narrative.* London: Anthem, 2004.

Yu, Anthony. "The New Gods and Old Order: Tragic Theology in Prometheus Bound." *Journal of the American Academy of Religion* 29.1 (1971) 19–42.

Zubiri, Xavier. *On Essence.* Translated by A. Robert Caponigri. Washington, DC: Catholic University Press, 1980.

Index